Media Studies: Ethnomethodological Approaches

editor

Paul L. Jalbert

University of Connecticut

University Press of America ® Inc.
Lanham • New York • Oxford

International Institute
for Ethnomethodology
& Conversation Analysis

Copyright © 1999 by
International Institute for Ethnomethodology
& Conversation Analysis

University Press of America,® Inc.
4720 Boston Way
Lanham, Maryland 20706

12 Hid's Copse Rd.
Cumnor Hill, Oxford OX2 9JJ

Library of Congress Cataloging-in-Publication Data

Media studies : ethnomethodological approaches / editor Paul L.
Jalbert.
p.   cm. (Studies in ethnomethodology and conversation
analysis ; 5)
Includes bibliographical references and index.
1. Mass media—Methodology. I. Jalbert, Paul L. II. Series :
Studies in ethnomethodology and conversation analysis ; no. 5.
pg1.3.M389   1998   302.23'01—dc21   98-45628 CIP

ISBN 0-7618-1286-5 (cloth: alk. ppr.)
ISBN 0-7618-1287-3 (pbk: alk. ppr.)

⊖™ The paper used in this publication meets the minimum
requirements of American National Standard for Information
Sciences—Permanence of Paper for Printed Library Materials,
ANSI Z39.48—1984

Volumes in the Series
1. George Psathas (Ed.) *Interaction Competence* (1990)
2. E. C. Cuff *Problems of Versions
in Everyday Situations* (1994)
3. Paul ten Have and George Psathas (Eds.) *Situated Order:
Studies in the Social Organization of Talk
and Embodied Activities* (1995)
4. Stephen Hester and Peter Eglin (Eds.)
Culture in Action (1997)
5. Paul L. Jalbert (Ed.) *Media Studies: Ethnomethodological
Approaches* (1998)

for Nicole and Anna

Table of Contents

Acknowledgments

With few exceptions, no one really accomplishes anything alone. It is with great pleasure that I take this opportunity to thank and express my gratitude to the many people who have made this project possible. While, for quite some time, it seemed that we would never get this collection "off the ground," we now witness, in our hands in the form of "the book," the fruit of our labor.

First off, to all of the contributors, I want to tell you how much I value the expertise you demonstrated in your respective areas of analytical application and the extraordinary care you all took in the preparation of your chapters, adhering to the highest standards of rigor in our craft.

This anthology would not have been possible without the confidence and trust that my two long time mentors have had in me. They are George Psathas and Jeff Coulter. Thanks to both of you, respectively Senior Editor and Associate Editor of this series, for your enthusiastic support of this project. Your continued critical appraisal of my work and that of several of the contributors has always made our work better.

While all contributors are responsible for the final versions of our chapters, the way they got to be so tidy and crisp was largely due to the impeccable attention to detail of Bja Fehr, who organized this collection. Her task was to compile and typeset this work; but she did much more than that. Her persistent commitment to excellence, from syntax and grammar to spelling and punctuation to analytical insights suggested to several of the authors, is found on every page of this book. Words cannot express my gratitude to you for your selfless contribution.

Acknowledgments

Many thanks also to Bill Husson and Dave Bates for their assistance in copy editing the volume, and in general lending support to this project; to Doug Macbeth, Dave Bates, Alan Zemel, and Bob Kerr for their help in sorting out the technical details required to produce the images in chapters 6 and 9; and to Ken Swain who lent his creative powers to the project by creating a cover befitting the analytical power of the pages in this volume.

Thanks to Helen Hudson and Peter Cooper of University Press of America for their help with the details of production.

I thank the Research Foundation of the University of Connecticut, which supported this project through a grant.

Finally, I thank Mary Anne DeVeau, my life-long partner and best friend, for her untiring love and sustenance. Thank you for being my first and last critic.

Paul L. Jalbert
Fairfield, CT

Contributors

Dušan Bjelić is a professor of Criminology at the University of Southern Maine, Portland, Maine. He received his PhD in sociology from Boston University. His research interests are in science and in the practical culture of media. His book *Galileo's Pendulum and the Quest for Methodological Ascesis* is forthcoming from SUNY Press.

David Bogen is Assistant Professor of Sociology at Emerson College in Boston, MA. He received his MA and PhD from Boston University. He is the author (with Mike Lynch) of *The Spectacle of History: Speech, Text, and Memory at the Iran-Contra Hearings* (1996), and *Order without Rules: Critical Theory and the Logic of Conversation* (forthcoming). His current research focuses on the relationship between ethnomethodology and technology design.

Wil Coleman has taught at the University of Manchester and Manchester Metropolitan University. His central research interests lie in the philosophy of social science and social theory, with particular focus on the topic of language.

Peter Eglin received his BA from University College London and PhD from the University of British Columbia. Since 1976, he has taught at Wilfrid Laurier University where he is currently Associate Professor in Sociology. His ethnomethodological research concerns membership categorization in deviance construction. He also conducts critical inquiry into

xi

intellectual responsibility and human rights. His publications include *Talk and Taxonomy* (1980) and, with Stephen Hester, *A Sociology of Crime* (1992) and *Culture in Action* (1997).

Richard Fitzgerald received his BA from the University of Wales, Bangor where he is currently a PhD candidate. His research interests are in ethnomethodology, conversation analysis, and membership categorization analysis, particularly in the area of media discourse.

Dave Francis is a Senior Lecturer in the Department of Sociology at Manchester Metropolitan University. He received his BEd and PhD from the University of Manchester. His current research interests are in ethnomethodological studies of work, organizational decision making and philosophical issues in qualitative inquiry. He has published articles dealing with negotiation talk, business gaming, sociological interviewing, classroom storytelling, membership categorization, and is currently collaborating (with Stephen Hester) on a book, *Language, Society and Social Interaction*.

Stephen Hester received his BA and PhD in Sociology from the University of Kent, Canterbury. Formerly Associate Professor at Wilfrid Laurier University, he is currently Senior Lecturer in Sociology at the University of Wales, Bangor. His research interests are in Ethnomethodology and Conversation Analysis, deviance and education. His publications include *Deviance in Classrooms* (1975, with David Hargreaves and Frank Mellor), *A Sociology of Crime* (1992, with Peter Eglin), and *Culture in Action: Studies in Membership Categorization Analysis* (1997, co-edited with Peter Eglin).

Paul L. Jalbert is Associate Professor of Communication Sciences at the Stamford Regional Campus of the University of Connecticut. He received his BA from Boston College and his MA and PhD from Boston University, all in Sociology. His research investigates the ideological manifestations in the reportage of international events and issues. He has published work in the areas of Africa, the Caribbean, and the Middle East. His work is informed by insights developed in ethnomethodology, ordinary language philosophy, speech act theory, and pragmatics. He is currently planning work on a book and/or film about the war in the former Yugoslavia.

Contributors

Michael Lynch is Professor of Sociology in the Department of Human Sciences at Brunel University, West London, UK. His research investigates the discursive and textual production of organizational activities. His first book, *Art and Artifact in Laboratory Science* (1985) is an ethnomethodological study of day-to-day work in a neuroscience laboratory. His second book, *Scientific Practice and Ordinary Action* (1993) examines and criticizes ethnomethodological and constructivist studies of scientific and everyday practices. In other studies he investigated activities in medical and legal settings. His book with David Bogen (see above) describes the intersection of testimony and history at the Iran-contra hearings. His current research explores the intersection of scientific, technological, and legal aspects of the use of DNA "fingerprinting" in criminal investigations.

Douglas Macbeth is an Associate Professor at the School of Educational Policy and Leadership of the Ohio State University. His teaching and research address the interactional order of classroom discourse and instruction, and the analysis of "situated" activity. He is developing a research program in the sociology of classroom order as structures of practical action and installation. Relying on the analysis of videotape, he has been producing classroom research footage, presentational videotapes and classroom documentaries in multicultural settings for several years. He has published and presented his work to disciplinary and interdisciplinary associations in education, anthropology and sociology.

Liz Marr is a Senior Lecturer in the Department of Sociology at Manchester Metropolitan University. Her research interests center around Information and Communication Technologies (ICTs), the media and organizational work. She is currently engaged in a study of the impact of on-line technologies on the working practices of journalists, and is collaborating with Dave Francis and Dave Randall on studies of the virtual museum.

Dave Randall is a Senior Lecturer in the Department of Sociology at Manchester Metropolitan University. His research interests center on Computer Supported Cooperative Work (CSCW), and in particular the use of ethnomethodologically informed ethnography to support design work. He has published articles in these areas, including studies of air traffic control, banking services and the virtual museum.

xiii

Wes Sharrock is a Professor of Sociology at the University of Manchester, where he has been since 1965. His research interests are the philosophy of social science and the study of work. His publications include *The Ethnomethodologists* (with R. J. Anderson), *Perspectives in Sociology* (with E. C. Cuff and D. W. Francis), *Classic Disputes in Sociology* (with R. J. Anderson and J. A. Hughes), *The Sociology Game* (with R. J. Anderson and J. A. Hughes), *Working for Profits* (with R. J. Anderson and J. A. Hughes), *Philosophy and the Human Sciences* (with R. J. Anderson and J. A. Hughes), and *Computers, Minds and Conduct* (with Graham Button, Jeff Coulter and J. R. E. Lee). He is currently completing a textbook in social theory and a book on Thomas Kuhn.

Jeff Stetson received his PhD from Boston University in 1992. The focus of his research is the ethnomethodologically based analysis of media and social change. Since graduate school, he has spent most of his time teaching at two universities in Japan where he lives with his wife Mikako, and their two daughters, Mia and Kai. He is currently working on a text about social change in that region. His working title is: "Pieces of a Puzzle: Footnotes to a Future History."

Preface

This anthology represents the first collection of studies of mass media texts of various genres from an ethnomethodological point of view. The distinctiveness of this point of view resides in its analytical attention to the ways in which sense may be made of these cultural products. Although ethnomethodology is not alone in paying attention to issues of meaning, we would argue that its analytical focus on the *logic* of textual production and reception enables its practitioners to avoid the stipulative classifications of traditional content analysis, the sterility of hermeneutical debates, and the ethical quagmires of the critique of ideologies.

Although the studies collected herein all manifest a commitment to the theoretical attitude, it will be clear that *theorizing* is not the objective of ethnomethodological analysis, as such theorizing is classically construed in media studies. On the contrary, the aim is not to produce explanations but, rather, analytical elucidations of how media texts actually work. The authors of these studies seek to reveal the operational structures, practices, and devices informing the empirical materials under scrutiny. The central argument which animates this field of inquiry is that these properties of texts (discursive, imagistic, and both) are profoundly informative of (sometimes *constitutive* of) the sense which they can make. Moreover, the explicated structures, practices, and devices at work in the texts are normally unavailable within the commonsense attitude of daily life. In several of the contributions which ensue, their authors derive a variety of theoretical and methodological arguments about competing and/or alternative ways of working with materials drawn from the domain of mass communication media on the basis of their analyses.

It is not the purpose of this Preface to attempt a summary characterization or precis of the chapters. So many of the analytical points being made are embedded in the detail of the materials under examination such that only distortion or oversimplification would result from such an attempt. I shall, instead, try to characterize the intellectual sensibility upon which all of these contributions draw and which all of them, in diverse ways, nurture and seek to promote. I have already alluded to the deliberate suspension of the impulse toward generic theorizing. In its place, ethnomethodology insists upon analysis, but of a very specific sort. Insofar as generalizing theories tend to encourage such practices as coding, operationalizing, statistical inference, and model building, they base themselves upon idealized or "worked-up" versions of the data they purport to account for and explain. By contrast, it is a characteristic of ethnomethodological work that it refrain from all forms of decontextualization of its materials in order to derive generalizable analyses of the *endogenous* methods of their production by the agents who produce them. This enterprise, then, seeks to specify the conventional procedures which people employ, rely upon, and take for granted in engaging in the practices in which they engage: Here, the practices of interest are those involved in broadcast media, newspaper reportage, non-fiction film, and talk radio.

Sociological perspectives such as ethnography and symbolic interactionism have shared this emphasis upon describing the social world *from within*, so to speak. Another way of expressing this shared programmatic ambition is to speak of "studying social reality from the actors' point of view." Treated as a technical challenge, such an ambition amounts to much more than engaging in participant-observational inquiries, in attempting to "take the role of the other" or in "seeing the world in the way in which others see it." From the standpoint of ethnomethodology, the challenge involved in implementing such ambitions is much deeper; it requires paying very close attention to the details of human conduct in real-time and to the articulation of descriptive vocabularies which accurately characterize the concepts, reasoning, knowledge, and competencies more broadly, upon which such conduct depends *and* exhibits.

Many of the contributors whose work is represented in this anthology, including myself, began to appreciate what ethnomethodology had to offer in the study of media materials when we encountered the remarkable work of the late Harvey Sacks on the logic of categorization practices in everyday life. Subsequent work by Lee, Schenkein, Greatbatch, Anderson and Sharrock, and others, extended and developed Sacks' many insights and applied them to mass media texts. Along with Sacks' and Schegloff's pioneering work on the sequential organization of communicative activities, further analytical resources were discovered in the writings of Wittgenstein and Austin on the rule-governed nature of language, meaning, and human practices.

My own interest in the analysis of media productions originated in the idea that such productions are vehicles for the transmission of ideologies in society. In particular, the work of Vološinov had alerted me to the political dimension of the use of language. Subsequently, when studying at Boston University, I was introduced to ethnomethodology, phenomenology, and the sociology of knowledge. The focus in my program was intensely empirical, analytical, and influenced by Schutz, Garfinkel, and Sacks. The insights I gained from these perspectives led me to develop a more rigorous practice in the inquiries I pursued. While I had achieved some political-economic understanding of ideological phenomena in general, the study of particular manifestations, such as Mannheim had attempted, remained elusive. With the precision tools of ethnomethodology, I believe that I became equipped to make the study of such manifestations more grounded in empirical materials than I had accomplished before. I am not proposing here that all elucidations, even of *political* reportage, must contribute to discussions of ideologies. This, however, was my own entré into this fascinating field.[1]

The present collection is offered as an advancement of the analytical ambitions mentioned above; that is, simultaneously, a furthering of both the work of media studies and ethnomethodology. Each chapter is not only an example of the best intellectual rigor which is sought after by practitioners of ethnomethodology, but also an exemplary extension of this kind of inquiry to the heartland of mass media research.

Paul L. Jalbert
Spring, 1998

Note

1. For citations of the works by these authors, consult the References at the end of this anthology.

Chapter 1

Seeking and Finding Society in the Text

Wes Sharrock and Wil Coleman

In many ways taking their cue from the work of the Frankfurt School (Adorno and Horkheimer, 1972), sociologists of the mass media have typically been concerned with the actual or potential power of the media to mold public opinion and attitudes. In particular, sociologists have sought to argue that the media have a key role in sustaining false images of social reality. Significantly, many studies have focused on the content of television output (for example, Glasgow Media Group, 1976, 1980, 1985), with news programs figuring prominently, the sociologist seeking to bring to light those features of society – for example, its inequalities of power, status and reward – which are allegedly hidden or repressed in television's "texts." As we discuss in what follows, one of the problems with such studies is that they assume the viewer to be ignorant of and blind to the very things so plainly visible to the sociologist. In partial recognition, at least, of this fact, a good deal of contemporary media theory attempts to bring the viewer back into the picture (Cobley, 1994; Corner, 1997; Morley, 1992). In place of what, after Garfinkel (1984[1967]), can be dubbed the "media dope," we have instead a picture of an active and intelligent consumer (Fiske, 1987; 1991). Yet "bringing the viewer back in" is never done unproblematically: The sociological impulse to explain viewers' "decodings" of media output in social and causal terms is never entirely absent. In this respect the study we discuss below (Morley, 1992) can be treated as exemplary. We begin our discussion, however, by addressing some more general similarities and differences between sociological and ethnomethodological inquiries.

I

Both sociological and ethnomethodological inquiries begin when the practical attitude of everyday life is suspended and practical concerns are bracketed out. Such inquiries take as topics for theoretical reflection what in the ordinary way are taken-for-granted features of everyday life, treating them as *social phenomena*. There is more than one way of theorizing – or we could as well say representing – social phenomena as the different genres of sociology make abundantly clear: Typically, sociology adopts one mode of theorizing, ethnomethodology another. Yet sociology and ethnomethodology are alike in this respect: Both are founded in the theoretic attitude.

Moreover, sociological and ethnomethodological inquiries share a common interest in the orderliness intrinsic to social phenomena, or, in other words, in the way such phenomena are structured. Instead, therefore, of social phenomena we might justifiably speak of social structures, going on to note how sociological and ethnomethodological modes of inquiry are both concerned, in whole or part, with representing social structures theoretically, that is, via a process of analytical abstraction.[1] This point should not be construed as implying that either sociological or ethnomethodological inquiries are concerned with conceptual matters at the expense of substance, or that for inquiries of either sort, substantive matters are matters of no significance; rather, it is to say that from the point of view of theoretical inquiries, substantive matters figure only insofar as they can be treated in formal (conceptual) terms. The same point can be made differently: Whatever the social structures theorized, and whatever practical, ethical or political bearing they may have upon society's members, such concerns are suspended for the purposes and the duration of theoretical inquiries.

There is an important difference between sociological and ethnomethodological inquiries, however. Ethnomethodology treats its inquiries as licensed solely by its interest in social structures formally construed, that is, in terms of their internal logics. Sociology, on the other hand, typically conflates formal and substantive matters (and, as we shall demonstrate, media sociology is by no means innocent of this charge). For ethnomethodology, the inquirer is governed by her theoretical interests. This is not to deny that her inquiries might turn out to have a bearing upon the practical concerns of society's members. But whatever practical benefits may issue from her inquiries, they are extrinsic to them. What is more, insofar as her inquiries lead her to seek explanations, both the problems occasioning them and the explanations she provides are internal to her inquiries, qua theoretical inquiries. The sociological inquirer, however, typically treats her inquiries as providing explanations for problems of a substantive sort, namely, of the sort raised by society's members in the course of their practical dealings with the world and one another. The explanations she proffers, therefore, are also substantive in kind. To this, the ethnomethodological inquirer objects that substantive explanations, like the substantive problems and issues that occasion them, belong to the domain to be investigated and are therefore, from the point of view of the theoretic attitude, in themselves putative objects of inquiry.

The conflation of theoretical and substantive concerns is clearly evidenced in sociology's treatment of what it calls "the social actor." The category social actor, as it figures within sociology, amounts to formalization and abstraction, a theoretical reconstruction, of the category "person." As such, it is made to exhibit many (if not all) of the qualities properly attributed to persons, in particular, that of possessing intentions and motives, and being able to formulate goals. Yet by transforming "persons" into "social actors" by theoretical reduction, these selfsame qualities and attributes become problematic insofar as they too must be theorized. We shall return to this theme subsequently.

We have already noted a shared interest in social structures on the part of both sociological and ethnomethodological inquirers. We made the point that a theoretical, as opposed to a practical, interest in social structures is one that shows itself in attention to their formal features. The point can be made more precisely. The term social structure stands as a gloss. As such, it can serve to bring to focused (and so, incipiently, theoretical) attention the overwhelming fact that everyday life and experience is structured. Ordinarily, this fact is of little interest in itself; there is no reason why it should be. Yet at the same time, of course, it is the case that – again, perfectly ordinarily and unremarkably – society's members have frequent cause and occasion to focus upon the various different structures (as they construe them) that impinge upon, provide the context to, render possible, constrain, etc., various aspects of their everyday life and experience. Among the many structures that, relevant to context and occasion, can become topics of their attention are the structures of institutions, including media institutions and the hierarchical structures of status and prestige, of authority and control, they exhibit; the temporal structures of media output and programming; and the structures of deference evident in social custom and morés and displayed in untold ways in, say, television news, drama, and entertainment. Suppose, for present purposes, we continue to gloss these various structures collectively as "social structures." If we do so, we shall invariably go on to notice the similarities between – even the identity of – the sociologist's and what, for want of a better term, we may call the layperson's mode of attention to such putative "social structures"; the issue is one, with good reason, raised by ethnomethodologists. Yet this way of making the point can obscure important differences, less often, perhaps, addressed.

It is not insignificant that in the ordinary way, it is not what might be termed social structures as such, or in themselves, that interests anyone. On the contrary, in the ordinary way, our and anyone else's interests (what Schutz (1962b) calls our "context of relevancies") are much more specific. What concerns us is, for example, the way the mass media are structured in terms of ownership and control. This kind of interest often, but not always, has a practical need behind it: a school-leaver wanting to become a reporter will need to find out something about the structure of media institutions; a television viewer wanting to complain about a program will have to know to whom and how to complain, and so will need to have some knowledge of the relevant structures of authority in the broadcasting company. But practical needs are not the only ones. Consider, for example, the music buff whose love for the music leads him to find out all about the structure of the recording industry. To repeat our point: In the ordinary way, none of us expresses any interest in social structures generically conceived. What, then, are we to make of the fact that the sociologist will gloss all (or perhaps only some) of the above as social structures?

In trying to answer that question we can begin by noting the very considerable degree of overlap between the sociologist's and the non-sociologist's range of interests (and here, the following remarks are to be heard as excluding ethnomethodology). The media sociologist, for example, is interested in precisely the same sorts of things that frequently concern the ordinary viewer of television programs: issues of bias and misrepresentation, issues of politics and power, issues to do both with the content of programs and their presentation. But there is another area of overlap, too. Sociologists and non-sociologists alike can possess expertise in, for instance, media production or journalism. The sociologist can be someone knowledgeable in the ways of media institutions, and a good deal of media sociology is of this order, with the sociologist as someone equipped with knowledge that (in the ordinary way) the average viewer lacks. This knowledge and expertise is not, of course, in itself sociological, and what "sociological knowledge" might amount to is a question we leave open for the present.

It will be useful for the moment to keep in mind the person possessing knowledge concerning, say, the structure and organization of media institutions. Imagine her in a teaching role. Imagine her seeking to give her students a clear picture of how a typical, privately-owned, television company is organized. One thing she will do will be to focus on how such a company is structured. Because she is talking about a typical company, a degree of abstraction from concrete particulars will be necessary. She'll remind her students that there's the typical structure of such a company which is relatively invariant, and there are the people who make up that structure. She'll remind them that, on the one hand, there's the structure, and, on the other, there are all the things that go on on a daily basis: reporters going about their business, editors theirs, for example, plus the work of technical staffs of all sorts, and the general run of office work of all kinds. She'll probably emphasise the role played by communication, both formal and informal, in that structure. She may also go on to remind her students of the jobs of cleaning and maintenance that have to get done. Tied up, of course, with the idea of structure is the notion of role, for a generic feature of such abstractions is the use of typifications of persons, by which we mean they are represented as persons-of-a-sort, be they news personnel or canteen workers. So our sociologist-cum-teacher will talk about the typical television executive, the typical news reporter, the typical arts reporter, the typical television cameraperson, and so on. (On "typifications" see Schutz, 1962a: 283.) She will also assume that along with each role and typically associated with it, is a more or less discrete and more or less stable set of what can be called social goods including knowledge, skills, tasks, tastes, opinions, wealth, power, status, and so on.

At this juncture we want to make two points. First, sociologists and non-sociologists alike engage in abstraction; they do so when they talk, for example, of the structure and organization of a typical media institution. Secondly, the sociologist uses notions of structure and role in just the same way as any other member of the society. For example, anyone (sociologist and non-sociologist alike) wanting to account for what she perceives as media bias will typically, in her explanation, make reference to such things as the structures of ownership and control of media institutions, to the financial role of shareholders, the agenda-setting role of advertisers, to the decision-making roles of editors and others. Sociologist and non-sociologist stand on the same ground; unless the sociologist possesses this particular knowledge of media institutions she will be no less ignorant as any other member of society.

We have said that both sociology and ethnomethodology have as their topic social structures, and that the term is a gloss. Further, we have said that both sociology and ethnomethodology focus upon social structures as such, or in and of themselves. But for each the term social structure might be said to stand for something very different. For ethnomethodology, it serves to remind us of the structuredness of life and experience in toto, social in kind because shared and sharedly intelligible. For ethnomethodology, the term social structure does not serve to delimit a restricted subject matter, a distinct set of structures (of some kind) that demand their own exclusive methods of investigation. All this is very different for sociology, for by social structures the sociologist understands some specific structures akin to a discrete object, or set of objects, that is or are to be distinguished from others (and, as we know, sociologists differ over the question of what kind of structures they are, their ontological status, and so on). Our second point, therefore, is that the sociologist (we are still excluding ethnomethodology) treats social structure (and the same goes for "role") as a theoretical term. It has to be said, of course, that in distinguishing social structures in this way, the sociologist is following ordinary usage, in that anyone can speak, for example, of the structure of the BBC, or the structure of the newspaper industry in the UK, at the same time distinguishing "structure," as we noted above, from all that is not structure. Moreover, in the ordinary way, appeal to the notion of "structure" (as in the structure of the music business) can serve to explain a person's behavior or an event, as when explaining, say, a television executive's decision in the light of institutional structures and constraints. The same is true of sociology's treatment of "structure"; there, too, the notion of "structure" is used to explain behavior or the outcome of events.

This brings us to a further point we wish to make, and it pertains to the sociologist's use of the notion of "theory." In the ordinary way, we can all entertain various theories about the organization and structure of institutions etc. with which we are to a degree unfamiliar. Some of these theories may be true, others false. The sociologist employs the same notion of theory. She supposes that what we have labeled social-structures-as-such are similarly open to having theories entertained about them, theories that can be found true or false, accurate or inaccurate. There are no theories of this sort in ethnomethodology. It is in this sense that it is true to say that ethnomethodology is not a theoretical enterprise, and it is essential to carefully distinguish the theoretical attitude or stance, a way of looking, from the construction of discrete theories. Failure to make this distinction can lead to the conflation of the formal and the substantive we constantly have occasion to refer to.

To sum up: The sociological (and ethnomethodological) inquirer's attitude is a theoretical one. By "theoretical" attitude we mean one that demands an attention to the formal features of their topic – what we have called social structures as such, or in themselves – as abstractions from out of the concrete. So it is that for this inquirer, practical concerns have ceased to be relevant; for this inquirer (and we include here the ethnomethodological inquirer), social structures are to be inspected for their most general features, qua social phenomena. Her theoretical interests are revealed by how she proceeds to represent them, that is, how she renders them visible. Hence we find, both in sociology and ethnomethodology, the use of specifically "sociological" vocabularies whose terms possess sociological, theoretical uses and whose extensions are to be found within the theoretical domain. Our point is that ethnomethodology is true to this logic, but sociology is not. Sociology, as we have already stated, confounds inquires of a theoretical or "formal" sort with those dealing with matters of substance.

II

Sociology (again, we are at pains to distinguish it from ethnomethodology) makes a move which can be analyzed as consisting of two steps. First, it takes (as does ethnomethodology) what we have called social structures as such as its topic of inquiry. Yet (and this is the second step), it construes social structures narrowly and as a theoretical term. To say that it treats social structure as a theoretical term is to say that it advances an idea of social structure (a representation of social structures as such) and goes on to seek to elucidate social structures' generic features, finding examples of such structures exemplified in ordinary occasions and events, seeking, what is more, to theorize the relationship of structure and structural elements to non-structure and non-structural elements in order to explain the latter in terms of the former.

This brings us back, once more, to the notion of the social actor. We have already said that within sociology, the category social actor features as a theoretical reconstruction of the category "person." We now want to develop this point for the issues it raises are very pertinent to media sociology.

Sociology treats of social structures "as such." But at the same time, it also seeks to demarcate social structures from that which is extrinsic to structure. Now, social structures are relationships between social structural positions, or roles. Roles are not persons but places for persons to occupy. They are idealizations. In the ordinary way, this presents no problems: The fact that biographical particulars of persons are ignored when looking, for example, at the structure of media institutions, in no way counts against the utility of such abstractions. For we must remember that, in the ordinary way, these abstractions have their uses: They no more pose "epistemological" problems for their users than does that abstraction of the actual city, the "map", pose "epistemological" problems for the person using one to find her way around it. But the sociologist has cut her abstractions off from any conceivable real-world use: for the idea of social structures in themselves has no real-worldly use; its use, if it has one, is solely within the domain of theory. Cut adrift from any conceivable quotidian use, her abstractions, her representations of social structures pose – or seem to pose – a host of what we may call "philosophical" difficulties.

The sociologist's problem therefore hinges on social structures generically conceived. We have already indicated how this gives rise to debates over their limits, extent, and ontology. The fact is that in the ordinary way "structure" can serve to explain behavior, so, too, it does so for the sociologist. Yet now, operating with an idealization of social structures as such, "structure" takes on a privileged status. We have said that in the ordinary way, appeals to institutional and other "structures" can be used to explain behavior. But now consider the sociological use of this technique. A gamut of behaviors are treated by the sociologist as instances of social behavior (that is, they are understood generically); now they are to be explained, and explained exhaustively, by appeal to social structures. In this light, consider, once again, "roles." In talking about a "role," sociologists and lay-persons will both assume, *inter alia*, typical beliefs, attitudes, responses, etc., that go along with it, plus the typical sorts of motives, intentions and purposes anyone occupying it may be expected to have. Moreover, a role is performed, and central to any performance that is intelligibly role-relevant are these selfsame intentions, motives and purposes. But the question this poses the sociologist is: Are intentions, motives and purposes part of any role or extrinsic to it? If the sociologist concludes that they are internal to role (and hence to structure), then she has recuperated them to structure and they have no independent effectivity. If, alternatively, she treats them as extrinsic to role, then the concept of "role" at once becomes empty.

Insofar as sociology remains blind to the distinction we drew concerning the differences between formal and substantive inquiries, sociology is led insensibly to assume that attention to structures implies a failure to attend to the persons who animate them.[2] It can then only proceed to argue either that persons (along with their intentions, motives and purposes) must also be theorized, together with their relation to social structures, or it must argue that persons (together with their intentions etc.) are, at best, epiphenomena of social structures. Yet either alternative leads to much the same conclusion, namely, the collapse of persons, intentions, motives and purposes into social structure. But this only serves to reopen the question of what it is that animates these structures. It is this that leads to the sociological problem of "agency" and the social actor. The sociologist is led either to deny agency in the manner of Althusser (see, for example, Althusser, 1971), or to reattempt (albeit vainly) to retheorize it.[3] We shall have cause to note how these dilemmas continue to figure within sociology as we go on to consider the work of David Morley and his colleagues in the field of media sociology (Morley, 1992), noting *inter alia* how the failure to distinguish formal from substantive inquiries serves to vitiate any findings such a sociology may seek to advance.

III

We shall now elaborate some of the points made above. We have drawn attention to the fact that the "bracketing" of intention, motive and purpose in the pursuit of theoretical inquiries can readily lead to it being assumed that they possess, at best, an uncertain ontological status. Thus, for example, the bracketing of social structures, qua formal structures, leads to a distinction being made between what is objective and what is subjective, the former term being applied to social structures, the latter to those bracketed-out intentions, etc. Construing the theoretical divorce of formal structures from intention, motive and purpose as a substantive opposition between what is veridical (and hence "objective") and that which (it is supposed) must be intuited, or, at best, can be known only inferentially (and is hence "subjective") privileges the former at the expense of the latter. But it also misconstrues both terms of the putative opposition. For suppose the sociologist construes intentions, motives and purposes as subjective; as such, they might just conceivably be thought of as constituting the "inner" aspect, as it were, of roles. Yet even, *ex hypothesi*, if such an account were to be sustained (and we would argue that it cannot be for it cannot be rendered coherent), it would have as its conclusion the denial of all effectivity to those intentions, etc. Either they must be granted an effectivity independent of social structures (in which case the sociological account will be seen as deficient and inadequately theorized), or they must be recuperated to social structure, in which case the notion of the social actor is rendered empty of all content, becoming seeable only as that which is determined by always-already-in-place social structures.

The consequences of these muddles are everywhere to be seen. They allow the sociologist to advance the specious argument that while the attitude of everyday life – now to be labeled as commonsense – may privilege individual autonomy, intentionality and consciousness (identified, in the manner outlined above, with what is subjective), sociology knows better. Sociology, it is argued, explains subjectivity as the effect of structures. Steven Lukes, as cited by John Eldridge (1993) in a recent collection of essays on the mass media, can be taken as advancing a typical version of this view. Eldridge applauds Lukes for identifying "a disjunction between social consciousness or collective representations on the one hand, and social realities on the other" (p. 335). Yet we repeat: What the sociologist calls social realities (or objective structures) are no more than the analytically-derived formal structures of social phenomena divested of their relation to human intentionality and motive. Intention and motive therefore come to be imagined as possessing an external relation to objective social structures. The internal (in the logical sense) relation of intention and motive to social structure is therefore missed. Morley's (1992) work nicely exemplifies the point. Indeed, anyone surveying the range of media sociology will note how the agency-structure problematic is its abiding theme. By divesting the output of the mass media of authorial intention, and concerning itself exclusively with that output as text (namely, in terms of formal structures), media sociology presumes itself to have delineated its appropriate subject-matter. Yet because it conflates formal and substantive inquiries, media sociology finds itself faced with the problem of meaning in relation to such "texts." This is not surprising, for the so-called problem of meaning figures within what is but a variant of the structure- agency problematic. That is to say, questions of whether the meaning of a text lies within the text itself or is imported to it from outside (from the reader or from "society"), and so whether it is "objective" and veridical or "subjective," is a replication of the problem of whether the social actor possesses intentions etc. in and of herself, or whether they are the product of external social structures.

Semiotics (the putative "science of signs" initiated by Saussure (1983)) is often recruited into these debates. It suggests that we think of "texts" as relatively autonomous, both of authorial intention and of their would-be referents (the "reality" they might be assumed to "reflect"). In this view, "texts" are in some fashion (either with or without the qualified support of authors and readers) productive of their own meaning. Stuart Hall (1980), for instance, writes of how semiotics "was correct in its attempts to identify signification as a practice for the production of meaning, as against earlier theories which assumed that 'reality' was somehow transparently reflected in language" (p. 132). A second example makes the same point with rather different emphasis: "Meaning production is a process which is contextualized and inextricably integrated with wider social and cultural practices" (Jensen and Jankowski, 1991: 41). The "problem of meaning" also figures in debates over how any particular media (or any other) text should be read and how interpreted. The question frequently arises of whether textual studies (and, a fortiori, media studies) implicitly (and illegitimately) construct an "ideal reader" of media texts, and whether, in rejection of that model, the aim should be to reconstruct the gamut of possible readings of any one text. Such debates are invariably concerned with questions as to the degree of active "decoding" (a frequently preferred term) required to read any text, and thence (and again, this is true of much media sociology) with the question of the extent to which meaning is "objectively" present in any, some, or all texts, or whether all meanings are entirely "subjective" in kind.

Within the space opened up by "the problem of meaning," one move that at first sight might appear to resolve it would be to treat meaning as emergent from the formal features of texts themselves. This is not the place to debate structuralist linguistics; nevertheless, we point once more to the conflation of formal and substantive matters that such a move would entail. Our objection is as follows: The theorization of "text" entails an abstraction, an idealization, in which the idea of "texts in general" comes to predominate. Over and above the examination of any actual texts, abstraction requires (or so it seems) that the inquirer attend solely to what is essential to texts, namely, to what feature or features distinguishes them from other e.g. material objects in the world. It is this that leads to "the problem of meaning" we have previously mentioned, for the inevitable answer is that what "texts" really and essentially are is structures of meaning, and that meaning is what is essential to texts. "Meaning" then becomes a curious something-or-other; its sources mysterious, its objectivity in doubt, its ontological status obscure.[4]

So it is that the very notion of "text" as it figures within theoretical discourse is an abstraction. It is this "text" as the product of theorization, that then allows the theorist to include within the scope of "text" not just written materials, but film, video, photographs, paintings, architecture, bodily gestures, speech – all, in short, that can be said to "signify" anything whatever to anybody. But what may seem to the theorist as an advance, a gain in theoretical perspicuity and acuity is, we argue, a loss, and what is lost is any sense of how any actual written material, or any actual film or television program, say, might function in any real context. (As we note, below, Morley is often seen, and saw himself, as rejecting much of the theoretical apparatus outlined here; nevertheless he remains, as we shall demonstrate, firmly enmeshed within many of its governing assumptions.)

Our objection is that the theoretical object, "text" as theorized, is a very different animal from texts (let alone other kinds of mass media output) as they figure within contexts of everyday life. There, any "problem of meaning" is a particular one, and one exhausted by questions about the meanings of words, about the implications of images, or the intentions of speakers and authors. Only the adoption of the theoretic attitude might lead anyone to suppose that above and beyond these mundane issues there exists a "problem of meaning." "The problem" is, of course, chimerical. Suppose we remain within the orbit of "text" as conventionally understood, as written material: Our point is not simply one that is exhausted by reiterating that in the ordinary way this is not a problem faced by writers or readers. Though the point is an important one, we are saying more than that "the problem" is not one faced, for example, by persons learning to read, whether they be children or adults. The point is important, of course, for the illiterate person is quite aware that there are texts, that texts are meaningful, and so on; it is simply that she is unable to read them. No, our point is, rather, that the so-called "problem" cannot be rendered in any coherent fashion: That is what we mean when we dub it "chimerical." There simply is no way of formulating "a (global) problem of meaning" above and beyond that of particular, local problems, problems for particular persons on particular occasions of writing and reading – problems to do, say, with failures to remember or understand particular words, or problems concerned with sentence-construction or grammar. The sociological inquirer, qua theoretician, seems to espy "the problem" looming when she adopts the stance of one who would temporarily, and for the purposes of theoretical inquiry, suspend her quotidian and taken-for-granted membership of what thence comes to be seen as "the social world." She would do so in order to obtain the privileges and advantages of membership in the class of theoreticians, who would see the selfsame world under the auspices of what Thomas Nagel (1986) has called "the view from nowhere". Yet the locution, "the view from nowhere," is profoundly misleading, for what Nagel advances does not amount to "a view" at all, and to call it such only serves to generate confusion. Why we find "the problem of meaning" incoherent is for this reason: The theorist seeks to absent herself from her picture of the world. She wishes to see the world not as any biographically particular individual might see it, someone, that is, with a point of view, but as someone unencumbered by a personal history, by language, or by a culture. So, she hopes, she will see it as it really is, as if "from nowhere in particular." The incoherence we point to comes to this: For such a would-be individual the society, the culture, she seeks to understand would be utterly unintelligible. There could be no "problem of meaning" for her, in that the very notion of "meaning" would also be unintelligible. And to the response that our remarks are question-begging (in that they assume what should be open to question, namely, that "meanings" are only intelligible to putative members of society), we can only say that the alternative would treat "meanings" as just other sorts of things-in-the-world. But if the theorist's "problem" is one of distinguishing non-meaningful from meaningful things, then that distinction is itself based on the knowledge that there are "meaningful things." This is why we say the whole issue is incoherent.

We repeat our point: The supposed "problem" faces neither persons who are members of the society, nor the stranger (who is, it hardly needs to be said, in the position somewhat akin to that of the child in the home society, learning to find her way about). The absenting of the person of the theorist from quotidian interests in texts for the purposes of theoretical inquiry is in no manner comparable to a suspension of her membership. In saying this, we are simply repeating the point, often made from within ethnomethodology, and as often misunderstood, that the sociological inquirer is a member. It is a logical point we are making, and, as such, has nothing to do with the sociologist seeking to rid herself of prejudice and bias; to think that it has is precisely to make that conflation of formal and substantive matters to which we have previously adverted.

We have referred to semiotics and to structural linguistics, for the reason that they form the background of much of the work in media sociology. It must be remembered that many of the issues pursued in media sociology (like sociology as a whole) are theory-driven. They can, and in large part do, remain at the level of "high theory." Yet inevitably "the world as theorized" must be related back to "the world of everyday experience and practice." It is then that we find what are by now familiar attempts to make the world as experienced fit the world as theorized, with the latter being granted authority over the former in the shape of the distinction between "appearance" and "reality." (We need hardly repeat our point concerning the confusions endemic in that formulation: Not only does it display a misunderstanding over the nature of theorizing, but the relationship of the-world-as-theorized to the world as experienced from "within" is misconstrued as well. It is what we have described as the confounding of formal and substantive inquiries.) Yet if "high theory" can afford to be scornful of "commonsense" (now assumed coextensive with "appearance") the practical demands of media studies and the perceived need to come up with a sociology able to grapple with the exigencies of the real world – questions of "bias" and "misrepresentation," for example – requires a degree of vulgarization of high theory. To that extent, sociology must respect commonsense and allow it its place (that sociology typically puts commonsense in the wrong place is partly our point). To be blunt: Sociology (including that branch of it called "media studies") can only operate insofar as the relationship of theory to lived realities is fudged.

High theory's disdain of practical consequences is particularly evident in its treatment of the social actor. We have already noted one consequence of theoretical formalism: Intentions, motives and the like come to be treated as epiphenomena of social structure, standing in a contingent relation to it. Here, by way of example, is Morley (1992) referring to Laclau and Mouffe in support of his chosen methodology of inquiry into the effects of mass media output. He comments that Laclau and Mouffe "maintain that human subjectivity, far from being the source of people's actions and social relations, is the effect of the latter. They [Laclau and Mouffe] argue that it is only in our social relations that we assume 'subject positions' and that, moreover, our subjective identity is multifaceted and 'overdetermined'" (p. 134). Our point is that it is hard to sustain such a position as Laclau and Mouffe's when the practical tasks of media analysis are pressing; in order to deal with these tasks the media sociologist is often forced (again, we have Morley in mind) to grant, at the very least, so-called relative autonomy to the social actor. That is, the social actor is allowed a certain residue of intentionality, independent of structures. We have already indicated the theoretical defeat such a move signals; our present point is that such accommodations are inevitable the moment high theory must be reconciled to everyday practical realities. If, for instance, media sociologists are committed to the practical and political tasks of liberating television viewers from what is claimed to be their bondage to prepackaged mass media "messages," it is obvious that space must be found for viewers to "resist" the blandishments of television output and to adopt a critical attitude toward it. The tension between the desire to celebrate the autonomy of the social actor and the demands posed by high theory is to be seen throughout media sociology. Before we turn to a closer examination of Morley's study, we return briefly to Stuart Hall and to a paper often granted the epithet "seminal" by media sociologists. We refer to his paper "Encoding/decoding" (Hall, 1980). It provides a nice example of how the pronouncements of high theory have to be compromised if they are to be made to serve practical ends. Consider Hall's depiction of the process whereby media messages are produced and consumed.[5] He speaks of the "encoding" of media texts as they are mediated via the apparatus of what he calls, in order, "technical infrastructure," "relations of production," "frameworks of knowledge," and "meaning structures" (p. 130). The process of "decoding," as he calls it, works with the same terms, but this time in reverse order. What Hall offers is a highly technicist ("theoretical") redescription of the communication process. At no point within it do we find any space for talk of persons, yet Hall is perfectly happy to speak of "broadcasters" and "audiences" (p. 131) as if they were unproblematically identical to his theoretical abstractions. Such slippages are the ubiquitous features of the practical work of sociological theorizing, Hall providing just one example.

IV

If the problem of "social determination" and "agency" is a besetting one in sociology (including, as we have seen, media sociology), it is clearly related to another central question for media sociology concerning the effects of media output on viewers and listeners. This is then bound up with questions concerning the scope for various different "readings" made by viewers and listeners of media output. Further, these questions are then to be asked against the background of the fact – which the media sociologist seeks to explain – that the "interpretations" made by viewers of what they see and hear fall into certain patterns. In general, women will "read" television "texts" – or at least, particular sorts of "texts" – differently from men; working class men will "read" them differently from middle class men. Is this (the media sociologist wonders) due to their being determined by their gender or their class position? Do viewers have no choice in what readings they make? Or are perhaps, for example, the interpretations made by working class men the result – in part or whole – of their conscious resistance to what they see and hear?

Many of these problems seem difficult, even intractable. What makes things so difficult for the student of media sociology is that it tends to be forgotten that in many ways these "problems" are not peculiar to the topic, viz. the mass media, but are endemic throughout sociology. They are sociological problems. But by sociological "problems" we understand "confusions," largely confusions of the sort that follow when conceptual issues are misconstrued as empirical. Morley's study provides a nice example: Although it is presented, and is usually taken as being, a piece of empirical research, on closer examination it reveals itself to be a curiously hybrid animal, the product of conceptual miscegenation.

At this juncture, some remarks are in order concerning the *Nationwide* project (Morley, 1980 - in Morley, 1992, pp. 84-118. All subsequent citations are of this latter). *Nationwide* was a UK television news review program of the early to mid 1970s. Morley sought to apply the theoretical materials of the "encoding/decoding" sort advanced by Hall to the analysis of television "texts" and their audiences. It was an attempt to remedy a perceived lacuna in the existing body of materials that sought to analyze, in particular, news programs, in order to uncover the ideological "messages" they were alleged to contain. By the time that Morley was doing his research, it had become apparent to many researchers that there was at the very least a danger that the analyst of television "texts" would read into those "texts" what she expected to find, rather than, as it were, allowing them to speak for themselves. In short, it was the very problem that we discussed earlier, the "problem of meaning," that concerned these researchers, raising issues to do with the validity and objectivity of research findings. Since it was clear that television "texts" could be read in more than one way, and that even contrary conclusions could be derived from one and the same text, it became exceedingly unclear as to what might be the "right" way to read them, if, indeed, such a notion made any sense. Some researchers had come to the conclusion that texts contained a multitude of meanings, but the nagging question remained: Were these meanings already there in the text, waiting to be discovered, or were they brought to it by the reader? The conclusion reached by many (and still, we would maintain, the dominant view in media studies) is that texts both contain real objective meanings, and yet leave scope for different (more or less "subjective") readings or interpretations.

We need to remind ourselves of the reason why the media sociologist finds herself in this position. It concerns the notion of "ideology."[6] That is, insofar as media sociology seeks to show the ways the mass media purvey false images of social reality, the sociologist will necessarily require both an independent account of how reality is, and an independent account of mass media "texts" and the way they picture it. The gap between the two goes then towards constituting the notion of "ideology." Morley's work continues to figure in the sociological and media literature as an exemplary model for sociologists seeking to cut the Gordian knot of "subjective" versus "objective" meanings by his turning to audiences, and so opening up the whole field of "audience studies" (for example: Corner, 1997; Graddol and Boyd-Barrett, 1994; Moores, 1990; Richardson and Corner, 1992). This is one reason we attend to it here. Yet, as already noted, what we do not find in Morley's research is anything simply resembling an empirical inquiry into what different audiences might make of any particular program. Instead, the main body of his research is devoted to categorizing the "readings" made by his different groups of subjects. The categories are derived in the first instance from Parkin (1972) who, writes Morley (1992):

> elaborated his model as a way of understanding the typical position of members of different classes in relation to the dominant ideology of a society. We are more directly concerned with the question of the range of possible positions in which different sections of the audience may stand in relation to a given message. Parkin's schema, as adapted ... allows us to account for the three logical possibilities: that the decoder will either share, partly share, or reject the code in which a given message has been encoded. (p. 89)

On the basis of the above "logical possibilities," Morley goes on to identify three "codes": "dominant," "negotiated," and "oppositional." Members of the different groups have "differential access" to the use of the codes which "determine" their readings (the uncertainty as to whether subjects "employ" codes or are "determined" by them is not unexpected).

It is not our intention to devote the remaining pages of this paper to an exhaustive critique of Morley's research and findings. In many ways it would be quite reasonable to suggest that in terms of their substance, at least, both his research and findings have been superseded. What interests us are the theoretical aspects and implications of Morley's study. For we argue that there is in media sociology nothing that is not found in sociology as a whole, and, moreover, that media sociology can show, in a way very exactly, the problems endemic in sociology more broadly considered.

So while in matters of detail and execution, Morley's study might well be regarded by his fellow sociologists as inadequate (and the remarks and discussion we note, below, bear this point out), yet his conception of the nature of the problem motivating the research remains predominant.

The theoretical issues at the heart of debates in media sociology turn around matters connected with social structure and how to construe it; and the relationship, in particular, of media output and differential "readings" of it to social structural positions. At the time of Morley's research the structures of interest were deemed to be class structures. Subsequently, those structures have been studied in terms of gender divisions (see e.g. Morley, 1992: 11-13). But these differences aside, and leaving aside, too, differences in the exact details of methodology, the ruling ideas remain much the same.

In brief, what we shall show (largely by means of examples drawn from Morley's study) is that what Morley (and, indeed, as our examples indicate, his critics, too) construes as uniquely sociological knowledge – viz., knowledge of "social structures" – is in fact knowledge which is commonplace, routine and shared. Relatedly, we demonstrate that it is this knowledge which enables the production of "theory" rather than the converse being the case. That people speak from certain positions, that they speak as incumbents of roles, and that this can and should be taken note of when attending to what they do and what they say (e.g. as to how seriously we should take them, how informed they are, and so on) – these things are clearly and evidently (and unsurprisingly) known to Morley's subjects, as Morley evidently knows them too, and expects his readers to know them also. We observe Morley worrying over the question of whether persons are free to "read" television "texts" as they wish, or if their readings are determined by their class, gender and race positionings. Similarly, Morley's subjects can be observed subscribing to the same view to the effect that a person's class position can be determinate of how she interprets what she sees and hears.

What is curious is how the sociologist (Morley in this case) so radically fails to see, or misconstrues that which in so many ways must be obvious. This remark is not to be understood in an ad hominem fashion; on the contrary, we see Morley's research as testament to the prime facie intelligibility of the picture the sociologist constructs of "social structures," and, this notwithstanding, the fact that Morley and his subjects use exactly the same know-how, the same "methods" to make sense of what they see and hear.

Morley (1992), subsequent to his *Nationwide* study, has written that "the reason bourgeois political science makes any kind of sense at all, even to itself, is precisely because it is exploring a structured field in which class determinations do, simply on the level of statistical probability, produce correlations and patterns" (p. 56). We agree, of course there are correlations and patterns. But we cannot agree that "statistical probabilities" are what is at stake; that is to misconstrue the nature of the "correlations" he observes. We also find absurd the idea that these "correlations and patterns" can be explored in their relation to social structures, with the former construed as signs or symptoms of the latter, and having a contingent (and discoverable) relation to them. It is not at all surprising to find Morley equivocating over whether to allow an independent role for "agency" or whether to recuperate it to "structure." Consider, by way of example, the following discussion in which Morley responds to the critics of his *Nationwide* study (in Morley, 1992). First, we discover Fiske (1987) applauding Morley for realizing "that Hall (1980) ... had overemphasized the role of class in producing different readings and had underestimated the variety of determinants of reading" (Morley, 1992: 11). (It must be remembered Hall's work in the 1960s was a significant inspiration for Morley's study.) Morley then goes on to cite Turner's (1990) critique of the *Nationwide* study. Turner writes as follows: "Morley has to concede that social position 'in no way correlates' with the readings he had collected." Turner goes on to point out that "Morley admits ... that the attempt to tie his differential readings to gross social and class determinants, such as the audience's occupation group, was a failure ... the victim of crude assumptions" (Turner, 1990: 135-6; cited in Morley 1992: 11). What is of interest in this brief exchange is that while there is agreement that "class position" in no way directly determines "reading(s)", none of the participants is willing to give up on the idea that readings are to be mapped onto determinants of some sort. What is more, it is unclear from the exchange whether "determinant" is to be understood in a logical or a causal sense: The latter view tends to predominate, however, as we note below. That is not to say that the participants to this particular debate don't worry over the matter: they do, but in terms that effectively deny the possibility of it being resolved. The nearest we get to a "non-mechanistic theory of determination" [sic] is in Morley (1992) where he argues that "Had Hall or I been attempting to demonstrate some utterly mechanistic form of social determination, in which decodings were rigidly determined by class, then lack of correspondence [between readings and class positions] would, clearly, have been damning to the whole enterprise" (p. 12). But Morley goes on to argue that Hall and himself were proposing "a much more complex process, through which structural position might set parameters to the acquisition of cultural codes" and that the research indicated "a quite significant degree of patterning" which could be accounted for by "a non-mechanistic theory of social determination" (p. 12).

Having split "agency" from "structure," Morley has now to find a "theory" to reconnect them. Yet, as should now be clear, any such "theory" will necessarily treat any putative links in structural terms. In this manner, "agency" will once more disappear. The only scope left for an independent notion of "agency" is to treat it as external to structure, with all the problems that entails. The theoretical links that Morley suggests display all the characteristic confusions endemic in all such efforts. "[T]he point precisely is," he writes, "that the general micro-processes can only operate through micro-performances of power, none of which can be guaranteed in advance, even if the general pattern of events is subject to the logic of probabilities" (Morley, 1992: 19). He goes on, in the same passage, to signify his approval of the notion of "habitus" "as a way of grasping the articulations of the two dimensions of structure and action – as a matrix of competencies capable of generating and underwriting a wider variety of specific practices, rather [and here Morley cites Murdoch, 1989: 243] as 'jazz musicians improvise around a ... theme'" (Morley, 1992: 19). Yet it is hard to see how the improvisations of jazz musicians relates to the supposed "determination" of persons by their class positions. Indeed, a proper appreciation of the notion of "improvisation" would explode most of the pretensions of this analogy (see Sudnow, 1978).

These contradictions cannot be resolved within the sociological framework. In practice, as we noted earlier, the contradictions are fudged. Yet they come to the surface, nonetheless, as Morley's study nicely exemplifies. It is a study that needs to be read against the grain of its author's expressed intentions. Our case against it is that what it makes evident cannot license its conclusions. Indeed, we argue that its conclusions run counter to what it itself so clearly demonstrates.

V

We have spoken a good deal about the sociologist's construal of "social structure" and her construal of it as a theoretical term. Our concern in this last part of the chapter is to point to the fact that, contrary to sociological presumptions, knowledge of social structures is a thoroughly commonsense knowledge. What we call "commonsense knowledge of social structures" is shared by the media personnel who figure in Morley's research, by Morley himself, by his research associates, by his critics, and by his readers. What do we mean by commonsense knowledge of social structures? Much we have already adverted to: the fact that society's members can be expected to know the fact that social institutions of all kinds are structured; the fact that persons can be treated as "persons of a sort," namely, as incumbents of roles, and that, as such, a very great deal is predictable and orderly in their behavior, their attitudes, what they can be expected to know and so forth. Further, society's members can be relied upon to know that they themselves, like other people in the society, can be thought of as occupying certain "positions" within it, and that the position they (like the others) occupy gives them a particular "point of view" upon it. We spoke earlier of "social goods" (knowledge, skills, tastes, opinions, power, status, etc.) as differentially distributed. Such distribution is nonrandom. Ethnomethodology points to the fact that social goods are differentially distributed among categories of person (the term "category" being preferred over "role"), and that a more or less stable and discrete set of such goods is, for members, associable with each role (see, for example, Sacks, 1972b). In saying so, the ethnomethodologist is doing no more than explicating in some detail what any of society's members can be expected to know.

We have said that such knowledge is shared among society's members. But it must be remembered that knowledge of the distribution of social goods is itself knowledge which is socially distributed. (As is knowledge of the differential distribution of knowledge, and knowledge of the differential distribution of social goods. There is scope here for a multitude of epistemic positions each entailing a greater degree of epistemic "distance." We might think of this latter position as the one occupied by the ethnomethodological inquirer.) How this cashes out in relation to Morley's study is evident in the ways that Morley himself assumes that some people are going to have a "better," and others a "worse," understanding of how society is structured, and how, for example, power and its rewards are distributed. It is implicit, too, in much of the content and mode of address of the television program under consideration. It is clearly evident in the responses of Morley's subjects, as we shall see.

Members of society use socially available categories to locate themselves and others in social space. They do so in order to determine the sense of, to assess and judge, to verify and to criticize what (other) members of society say and do. Another way of making the same point is to say that persons, qua persons-of-a-sort, can always be construed as speaking and acting from a point of view. Construals of the nature of social reality are irremediably perspectival and "any" member of society will use her commonsense knowledge of social structures (and her knowledge of the distribution of social goods) in determining, for example, whether what some other member of society treats as "knowledge" is, "in fact," mere prejudice.

We have already pointed to the circularity of Morley's research project. We can summarize "the problem" for which he seeks a solution: How do television viewers find the society in "the (television) text?" He supposes the skills for finding it to be differentially distributed. This is (partly) be-cause the society he finds (and supposes all others should find in that it is "really there") is a class society. But what is clear from his research find-ings (if we did not know it already) is that any television viewer can find and can be expected routinely to find the society in "the text." For far from being something hidden, it is available in all the shared apparatus of social typing and role-attribution that we have glossed as "commonsense knowledge of social structure." What is not the case, however, is that all viewers will countenance finding the "class society" that Morley finds there. But that viewers are perfectly capable of determining for them-selves the social positioning of those appearing on television programs is hardly "news." We should suppose anyone lacking these skills to be remarkably socially inept. And, in any case, should we doubt it, the responses of Morley's subjects make it abundantly clear.

Morley, as we say, finds class society in media output. He is perfectly willing to acknowledge that others equally as perspicuous and scrupulous as himself might find something different. And, indeed, he is more than willing to agonize over the question of whether class structures, as distinct from structures of gender or race, are the most significant in contemporary British society. But what we suppose he cannot admit is that he might find class society there because he puts it there in the first place. This may seem a sweeping claim. Let us flesh it out in more detail.

Everything depends upon the initial categorizing and collecting of his subjects. The choice is crucial, for it sets the agenda for all that follows. He collects and groups his subjects on the basis of occupation. Now the relationship between "occupation" and "social class" is not a contingent one. Far from it, the very meaning of the term "social class" is bound up with notions of persons's positioning in the occupational structure. We note, then, how Morley categorizes his subjects. Morley expects, on the basis of the category alone, that his subjects will speak, think and act from a certain point of view. He expects his readers to share the assumption, for it is unsurprising and uncontentious. He then uses these categories to collect his subject-groups. Further, the elected categories are used (as we shall see) to interpret what his subjects tell his researchers in discussion groups. Given his assumptions concerning the salience of social class his election of the category "occupation" is commonsensically seeable as rel-evant. But the overriding salience (as he sees it) of social class enters into the choice of "occupations." So, for example, it is not the categories "shopkeeper," "clerical assistant," "teacher," "fine artist," "housewife," "doctor," "laboratory assistant" that we find in his study. The reason is that his categories can be commonsensically taken as collectively con-stituting a contrastive set appropriately linked to notions of "social class differences."

Consider, then, Morley's "four main types" of categories of subjects. These four main types were: managers, students, apprentices, and trade unionists. Morley then divides each of these types into two further subtypes. We shall not list all of them: Our interest at present is in Morley's election of these types, and in the way he presents those features of them he considers salient. Using his pretheoretical knowledge, he knows these groups to be representative of class society. For example, he expects his readers to see that, when considering the category "students," that "university arts students," "teacher training college students," and "further education students" may be usefully contrasted in that they are likely to have different responses to the same current affairs issues. Furthermore, they are such as to allow him to interpret their responses as ones differentially positioned in the class structure. Morley expects his readers to see the salience of the categories referred to. He expects (and we have no quarrel with that expectation) that "print management trainees; middle class" would make sense of the program differently from "further education students; mainly women; mainly black; mainly age 18-25; working class." It would be surprising if (middle class) "bank managers" didn't express different responses to those of "apprentices" ("working class").

What we now want to do is to contrast Morley's election of categories with those elected by his research subjects. Morley's subjects use occupational, class and other categories in order to assess what they see and hear in the television broadcast. They use, and display their skilled use of, what can be seen as relevant categories. It is these categories and these alone that capture the saliency of the subject matter addressed. Categories include, among others, mothers, housewives, women, businessmen, lower-middle-class [people], upper-working-class [people], the middle class, the rich, the poor, one-parent families, the average family in a council estate, husbands, wives, the average viewer, the consumer, the entrepreneur. These and other categories are seeably elected for their saliency, intelligibly related in orientation to an already organized world, a structured world, a world structured typically in terms of contrasts. But where Morley would treat these contrasts exclusively in terms of class contrasts, his research subjects can be observed employing others, such as contrasts between "rich" and "poor," or between "them" and "us".

By way of showing what we mean, consider the following example, taken from the transcripts of interviews with his subjects. Consider the use of the category "occupation." We have said that "occupation" can be understood in class terms. But we have also suggested that it need not. A "television presenter" can be seen as middle class. But s/he can also be seen as "someone doing a job." If we see them in class terms we shall be looking for examples of class bias for instance. But if we see them as people doing a job, questions of (class) bias might be seen to be going "a bit deep" – as we see from the following exchange between interviewer and interviewee from the *Nationwide* study:

> Q: Do you think that the presenters put a slant on the items they introduce?
> A: They're just doing a job, like everyone else ... I suppose now and then they might slip in the odd comment ... change it a bit ... but that's all going a bit deep really, isn't it? (Morley, 1992: 108)

Our point is that Morley's subjects use their commonsense knowledge of social structure in order to value, devalue, recommend, discount, accuse of bias, applaud etc. what is said by the contributors to that program. They are fully aware and show that they are aware, for example, that knowledge is socially distributed. They are also fully aware of the institutional and social contexts of knowledge and knowledge-claims. They are fully aware that what is to count as knowledge is in significant part institutionally determined. They are fully prepared to treat as opinion, and the product of a point of view, what is presented as knowledge. They are fully aware that the program, and others like it, are directed at particular audiences, and that they, as viewers, may not be the "proper" audience of any particular program, and on that basis to discount their own view of it. (We are not concerned at present with whether we think some or all of these claims and responses are correct or not. Our intention is to show in them the perspicuous use of "common sense knowledge of social structures.")

The issue of media bias has already figured in Morley's and in our account. The very fact that a news-type program might be construed as biased is predicated on the fact, already assumed, that the public world both in which it is institutionally situated and on which it reports is one that may be represented as politically divided, where that division can be presented as one between "Left" and "Right." We have already noted its relevance in the context of a question of whether a presenter can be seen as putting "a slant" on items. It further provides the context for asking, for example, the following question of (working class) print management trainees:

> Q: Would you say that the discussion in the program is evenly balanced between management and union interests? (Morley, 1992: 105)

First, we note that in their answer the trainees make it clear that the question is an intelligible one: that management and union might have different "interests" and that those "interests" might be opposed is a commonsense feature of the social world:

A: ... the guy from the union said everything, then they asked something
from the man from Rolls Royce and immediately the guy from the
union had the last word ... (Morley, 1992: 105)

Second, we note that in their reply, the trainees can be heard (from the
point of view of Morley's agenda) as displaying bias in favor of management which, their being working class, might allow their response to be
heard as displaying "false consciousness."

Morley's subjects are fully prepared to treat as opinion and the product
of a point of view what others may consider and present as knowledge,
and they are tied to social location. Asked a question about where they
thought *Nationwide* stood politically, shop stewards provided a very
different response from that of the print management trainees. In the view
of the former, the program expresses the politics of the Right, in which the
media are "all saying to the unions 'you're ruining the country...'"
(Morley, 1992: 110). Compare this to what was said by the group of print
management trainees when asked the same question:

It's basically socialist. I mean it's BBC and ITV. ITV can't be socialists
because it's private enterprise. BBC is a state-owned thing so it's socialist
... on Nationwide they're very subjective ... the people on it are very
pro-Labor ... they're always biased. (Morley, 1992: 105)

This particular definition of the institutional (with regard to ownership)
can be heard as being used by them to justify their view of the program's
content:

I have seen people being pulled through the mud there, just because they
have too much money ... now *Nationwide*, for them, those people are "pigs,"
the "pigs" of this society who rob all the money ... they really drag people
through the mud because they're businessmen. (Morley, 1992: 105)

That knowledge is socially distributed and known to be socially distributed is shown in "the self-evident fact" that the program is intended for
particular sorts of viewers (qua sorts-of-persons). Morley's researchers
make it evident in the very questions asked of the subjects (as is seen below), and the subjects make it evident in their responses. Both questioner
and respondee demonstrate their commonsense knowledge of the ties between program content, presentational style, and the presumed viewer.
(Incidentally, this effectively undermines any notion of ideal reader; it is
clear that texts are intended for particular audiences.)

Q: What kind of audience do you think the program is aimed at?

A: It's for women, housewives ... they're the only people home at 6 o'clock ... all those bits about budgeting ... housekeeping, it's surely all directed towards women. (Morley, 1992: 106)

This, again, nicely exemplifies commonsense knowledge of social structures, this time qua temporal routines. Asked the same question as the above, teacher training college students answered that:

Nationwide's for general family viewing ... like the mother rushing around getting the evening meal ready ... it's for people who don't listen to current affairs programs really, and if *Panorama*'s on they switch over to *Starsky and Hutch* or something ... (Morley, 1992: 106)

A "kind of viewer" is made evident with economy. When further education students are asked if they think the program is made for people like them, they reply:

No way, it's for older people, middle class people ... affluent people ... if it's supposed to be for us, why didn't they never interview Bob Marley? (Morley, 1992: 107)

Such a response is intelligible on the basis of the, not unreasonable, assumption that older middle class people are not interested in Bob Marley. The same group was asked about what they thought of the way the Budget was dealt with, concerning its implications for different sorts of families:

Q: What did you think of the bit in the program where they said that "everyone in Britain should fit into one of these three categories" and they showed you some families they said were typical?

A: It didn't show one-parent families, nor the average family in a council estate - all *these* people they showed seemed to have cars, their own home, property ... don't they ever think of the average family? (Morley, 1992: 107)

And this as tied to the comments that preceded it vis-á-vis middle class people: These are not people like us, and the program is not made for people like us. They – middle class people – are, because they own property etc., interested in these things, we in other things. To be, for example, middle class may be said to unthinkingly make certain assumptions and to express certain attitudes. What those assumptions are and in what they consist will depend upon the location of the person making the judgment. Here, for example, is a response from one of the apprentices:

... the people we see presenting, they all seem snobs to me ... I don't say upper-class, but getting that way ... you wouldn't think that anyone actually worked in factories - at that time of night: to them, teatime's 6 o'clock and everyone's at home ... a real middle-class kind of attitude. (Morley, 1992: 108)

The middle-classness of the presenters and their presumed audience can be directly read off from the program itself. These things are visible, evident. There are people like us and people like them. Morley's subjects see themselves as incumbents of social categories related systematically to other categories of person.

When we turn to what Morley writes under the heading "Interpreting the Transcripts," the occupational categories are used to show how responses are tied, and tied intelligibly, to the category "occupation." Thus, bank managers: "It seemed as if they shared the commonsense framework of assumptions of *Nationwide* to such an extent that what was said on the program was so non-controversial to them as to be almost invisible" (p. 111). Morley contrasts this response with that of trades unionists, "to whom the program appeared to have a very particular and highly visible content – a 'theme' ... Because this 'theme' was unacceptable to the trade union group it was highly visible to them" (p. 111-112). It is perfectly intelligible to contrast bank managers and trades unionists: What is "acceptable" for one may well not be for the other – and what those issues are will, again, in very large part be uncontroversially intelligible.

Morley writes of the responses made by print management trainees as:

so far to the right of the political spectrum (espousing a hard-line free market version of "radical conservatism") that they might be said to be making a 'right-wing oppositional reading' of *Nationwide* – which they take to be a 'socialist' program. (Morley, 1992: 112)

As readers of Morley's text, it is conceivable that we might take exception to his construal of these or other responses (and in doing so unwittingly reveal our own positioning in social structure). It is certainly possible to read this and an earlier comment regarding the response of trade unionists to the program's term of address as a rejection of "*Nationwide*'s ideological formulation of the 'issues'" (p. 112). But more to our present point, construing the response of print management trainees in this way (a way which is certainly a plausible one, if one reads their responses) allows Morley and hence his readers to situate "print management trainees" socially, to grant them a socially structured position.

We must remember that what Morley appears to be doing is determining independently of his categories the various "codes" they use to interpret the program's content. These codes, it will be remembered, are "dominant," "negotiated," and "oppositional." That is, it may appear as if the codes have but a contingent relation to social structural location of his subjects. But he uses their known social structural location, elaborated by means of reference to their responses, to formulate the idea of "code" which remains an artifact of his own devising, and it is entirely spurious to suppose that it, in some manner, accounts for the differential readings. Thus, Morley argues that the very different responses made by managers and trade unionists are the products of "the interpretive code which the audience brings to the decoding situation" (Morley, 1992: 112). But this would seem to indicate that (a) there are persons (managers, trades unionists) who are differentially located in social space, but that this fact alone is insufficient to suffice for the differences in their responses. What is required (it would seem) is that (b) they also each possess a "code." But how they are to acquire this code, a code, moreover, appropriate to their social positioning, is entirely unclear. It is peculiarly absurd, too, given that the notion "appropriate to class position" already requires that they respond, not randomly, but in a very particular fashion.

Morley makes use of (as he has to) the inevitability and naturalness of responses, namely, that they are rightly regarded as intelligible and un-problematic. Morley uses this fact in his allotment to decoding schemas. So, for instance, we see it in the way he deals with the responses of university arts students:

> Like the bank managers, these students dismiss *Nationwide*'s style and mode of address. Like the teacher training college students, this group's commitment to the discourse of education leads them to assess *Nationwide* according to criteria of "relevance" and "informational value" .... However, when it comes to more directly politico-economic affairs, and in particular *Nationwide*'s presentation of unions and management, their decodings are consistently less oppositional. (Morley, 1992: 113)

It is the very unsurprising character of these responses that allows Morley to write of how "decoding will also vary depending on a group's relation to different kinds of subject or topics" (p. 113). Of course differences between "readings" are not randomly distributed. But this, on its own, is no evidence for their being produced by different decoding schemas. Morley mutually elaborates that which is seeable as (a) typical of the different categories and (b) their social location, and it is this that enables him to advance and elaborate the idea of "code." Thus elaborated, the idea of "code" goes to reaffirm "the facts" that it supposedly makes evident, as when Morley writes (concerning the response of apprentices - "these working class groups") that:

..their decodings were, on the whole, "in line with" the dominant or preferred meanings of *Nationwide*. This seemed to be accounted for by the extent to which the lads' "common-sense" ideological position was articulated through a form of populist discourse which was quite compatible with that of the program. (Morley, 1992: 115)

Further, differences in responses within, rather than between, groups leads Morley to argue that "patterns of decoding should not be seen as simply determined by class position, but by the way in which social position artic- ulates with the individual's positioning in different discursive formations" (p. 116). This secondary elaboration thence allows Morley to retain the idea of "code" but at the cost of economy. Yet it allows us to see Morley's use of commonsense ideas of social structure, in that, in the case of the views of trade unionists, insofar as their remarks can be treated as intelligible, that is, as typical of trade unionists, then differences can be explained (or explained away).

It is not without interest that Morley subsequently, in returning to the *Nationwide* study some ten years later, rejects the decoding model, as well he might ("The *Nationwide* Audience: A Critical Postscript," Morley, 1992: 119-130). The purpose of our present remarks, however, is not to engage in further inquiry into the meaning and use by sociologists of the notion of "code," or other notions of similar sort. Our present interest is in the way that Morley seeks to, or presumes to, explain (to the reader, to himself, to sociology) different audience's responses to media output by appeal to social structure as causal (whether or not mediated by "cultural codes"). But this is actually a most curious way of thinking; and it is evident from the transcript samples he presents, and in his own categoriza- tion and commentary on them, that neither he nor his subjects regard the connection of persons, their attitudes, opinions, prejudices, point of view, and class position in this way. On the contrary, both Morley and his re- search subjects evidence the fact that they see these matters as internally related and mutually elaborable.

Conclusion

Our larger point (and this sums up the sociological thrust of our remarks) is that (a) the relationship between category and the person to whom it is applied, (b) the relationships between categories such as to enable us, sociologist and non-sociologist alike, to speak of "social structures," and

(c) the attributes (of all kinds) seeable as appropriate to and applicable to categories are all relationships of a conceptual and normative sort. In displaying the logical grammar of these ties and relationships we are at the same time displaying the grammar (call it "the structure") of a "society" or "form of life." Sociologists and ethnomethodologists both address themselves to "social structures" yet each conceives them very differently. The difference can be seen as one of description (ethnomethodology) versus explanation (sociology). What ethnomethodological inquiry makes evident is that the knowledge common to all society's members, what we have glossed as "commonsense knowledge of social structures," is also drawn upon by media sociology, but in seeking to theorize it, misrepresents it.

Notes

1. Among sociologists' representations of "social structures" can be included the following: kinship structures as depicted by anthropologists; the Registrar-General's list of occupational classes; the structural oppositions of Levi-Strauss; Durkheim's contrast pair, "mechanical" and "organic" forms of social solidarity; in Marxist analysis, the relationships between social classes, and between the base and the superstructure; Weber's "ideal types"; Schutz's "typifications"; the formal schema of "dominant," "negotiated" and "oppositional" codes as derived in the first instance from Frank Parkin (1972) and used by David Morley (1992) in the *Nationwide* study considered in this paper. Each may be seen as being related to that from which they abstract in such a manner as the structures they make evident can be seen in it. They may thus be thought of in terms of what Wittgenstein has to say concerning the seeing of aspects, for each constitutes and displays an aspect of that which they may be taken as representing.
2. Because ethnomethodologists are careful to avoid the conflation of formal and substantive inquires, they are not led to make this assumption; likewise, "the problem" of the social actor passes them by, for it is not their problem.
3. A further option might be to treat intentions etc. as external to social structure, yet, at the same time, deny them the kind of effectivity here discussed. In this case they would figure simply as that which dis-orders the smoothly running system, namely as noise (in the information-theoretic sense of the term). Yet to do so would of course mean radically reconstruing the sense of such terms as "intention" and "motive," and even should we wish to, it is hard to see it being done in any intelligible fashion.
4. The parallels between these concerns and sociological debates over the status of "social structures" should be obvious.
5. The terms "media messages," "production" and "consumption" are Hall's: we find all three deeply problematic, but for the present we let them stand.
6. We have not, in our argument, given separate attention to the notion of "ide-

ology." But we note, here, that if "ideology" is to figure as an intelligible notion, "agents" must have a degree of scope for independent thought and action. For ideology is a normative notion (bound up, in the case of studies of the media, with notions of misrepresentation, bias and deception), and insofar as it can be recuperated within the structure/agency split it appears as a division between objective structures and subjective perceptions of them. The mass media would then function as reinforcers of misrepresentations of those structures. Yet, as we have shown, as soon as "agency" is granted an independent role, so the structure/agency dualism is undermined. That is, the notion of "agency" requires that "agents" behave, not randomly and incoherently, but in an intelligible manner, viz., in socially structured ways. What we are left with is a notion of "agents" as a little bit structured, a little bit determined. The sociologist must therefore choose to recuperate "agents" to structures; but in doing the notion of "ideology" will become unworkable. Either that, or the notion of "social structure" has to be radically rethought. We just note that this never seems to be done.

Chapter 2

Critique and Analysis in Media Studies: Media Criticism as Practical Action

Paul L. Jalbert

Introduction

The concern over what counts as analysis in communication studies in general and mass media studies in particular has generated mixed commentary on the part of several reviewers of work which is informed by ethnomethodological insights and which simultaneously explicates the critical expressions intelligible therein. My analysis of the U.S. network television coverage of the Lebanon War in 1982[1] can serve to demonstrate this concern. The informal treatment of that work by critics both positive and negative has been peculiar. The negative assessments almost uniformly complained that I had produced a "polemic" regarding the coverage and not an "analysis" of it. The positive comments indicated that I had been successful in "exposing" media partisanship, while also arguing that, in so doing, I had transgressed the boundaries of the analytical project and crossed over into the "critique" of ideological positions. While it is true that critical assessments along ideological lines could emerge as a by-product of the explication of the meaning-options made available to members[2] in the reports I analyzed, such critical assessments (e.g., of "bias") were ascribed to *me* as *my* assessments of the coverage rather than to *possible members with certain specifiable background commitments*. This was a curious situation and it encouraged me to become clearer about the methodological, conceptual and analytical enterprise in which I am engaged. The result is this essay.

What Should Analysis Look Like?

The task of analysis of media reportage is to attempt to explicate, to unveil the social constructions that allow people to make sense of the world. The access that I seek to do this, the medium through which I seek to make this available, is through the study of mass communication media representations of events and states of affairs. I am *not* trying to uncover *which* "meanings" particular members actually discern, but to elucidate such meanings as *could* intelligibly be achieved. These meanings can logically be argued to inhere in actual texts in virtue of their organization etc.; the issue is what is available to be grasped from them. While we do not know how many possible understandings could be derived from a particular text or communication, we can nonetheless make arguments of the *kinds* of understandings that *can* be achieved, and, in many instances, for *very specific* understandings which can be derived. To make such arguments does *not* mean that the analyst is "instructing" people as to which meanings are actually achieved or *should* be achieved; although, much of media "analysis" does exactly that (see Anderson and Sharrock, 1979).

If, in the logic of the explication, it so happens that certain renditions, certain versions of the world, become elucidated and, in so doing, the results look like, have the appearance of being, a critical formulation, *that should not be seen as a departure from the analysis. The "critical edge" is itself an achieved phenomenon on the part of a possible recipient and the analyst.* What ends up looking like a critique *a fortiori* emanating from the explicative analysis should not be cast aside as undercutting an *analytical* program. Why should the analyst be accused of engaging in a polemic because some of those critical factors emerge in the analysis? Aside from the very real possibility that the analyst may himself[3] be critical of a text he is analyzing – one of the goals of the analyst could be to be critical – the critical implications attendant upon the analysis are not necessarily the product of a diatribe or a polemic. For example, media analysts obviously will adopt any one of the range of existing ethical positions concerning the abortion controversy. Consider the case of one such analyst who characterizes the logic of categorization embodied in the dispute in the following way: Wherever a protagonist in the controversy speaks of abortion as a matter of "murdering babies," he obliterates the conceptual distinctions between "babies," "fetuses," "embryos," "gametes" and "zygotes," along with their very different ethical and even theological implications. Moreover, the available categorizations of anti-abortion activists as "pro-life" can be argued to postulate an implicit contrast to a derogatory construction "anti-life," i.e. what would it mean to be "anti-life"? Surely, this would beg the question. It may very well be argued that such an account of the logic of the controversy already embodies elements of *"pro-*abortion" reasoning. However, there is absolutely nothing which precludes an analyst trading upon his own *critical* resources for the production of an analysis of meaning-options: After all, these are not idiosyncratic to him but rather elucidate exactly the parameters of *a* critical interpretation, just as an ethnomethodologist has no choice but to draw upon his practical knowledge as commonsense resources in an elucidation of the *logic* of any such resources. As Turner (1974b) argues:

> At every step of the way, inevitably, the sociologist will continue to employ his socialized competence, while continuing to make explicit *what* these resources are and *how* he employs them. I see no alternative to these procedures, except to pay no explicit attention to one's socialized knowledge while continuing to use it as an indispensable aid. In short, sociological discoveries are ineluctably discoveries *from within the society.* (p. 205)

This also applies to media analysts in terms of their deployment of "socialized competence" or commonsense resources, not excluding their *critical* faculties. The issues here are: to avoid explicit *advocacy* of a contending position within the analysis itself; to be able to identify succinctly the parameters of socially distributed points-of-view with which one may be in personal disagreement as well as those with which one may be in agreement; and to argue for an analysis without presupposing the validity (or otherwise) of the critical viewpoint being advanced. Often, those best able to elucidate the structure of a particular argument may well be among its most committed protagonists. However, rather than construe this as a defect, it should be appreciated as a potential advantage. Unless all we wish to read, study and analyze are treatments of matters sympathetic from the outset to our own commitments and presuppositions, in which case we will forever shield ourselves from an elucidation of our *own* taken-for-granted ways of reasoning, arguing and using the language in general, the only way we can have analytical access to the cultural phenomena by which the concept of "criticality" can be measured is to recognize its character as *an emergent feature* of the actual analysis. Moreover, the analyst engaged in such explication should not be accused of *distorting* analysis for the sake of a "critique" or a "polemic." On the contrary, insofar as a critical posture can itself *facilitate* analysis of some contested position, argument or text, why should we impoverish the domain of analysis? Max Weber

(1949) made a similar claim in different historical circumstances in his essay "The Meaning of 'Ethical Neutrality' in Sociology and Economics":

> One of our foremost jurists once explained, in discussing his opposition to the exclusion of socialists from university posts, that he too would not be willing to accept an "anarchist" as a teacher of law since anarchists deny the validity of law in general – and he regarded his argument as conclusive. My own opinion is exactly the opposite. An anarchist can surely be a good legal scholar. And if he is such, then indeed the Archimedean point of his convictions, which is outside the conventions and presuppositions which are so self-evident to us, *can equip him to perceive problems in the fundamental postulates of legal theory which escape those who take them for granted.* (p. 7; emphasis added)

Weber was not endorsing anarchism as a political philosophy in this comment; he was taking stock of the kind of intellectual insight which can be won by adopting such a (critical) vantage-point as a methodological device, whether or not the one who adopts it does so for more than a methodological purpose. I propose that our earlier example pertaining to the use of categories taken from a consideration of the abortion controversy is exactly analogous.

Within the context of ethnomethodological inquiries, a related issue has arisen which requires some comment. Ethnomethodologists are required to analyze practical actions, including (centrally) communicative action, without any commitment to their adequacy, correctness or otherwise. This policy of "ethnomethodological indifference" is then sometimes held to preclude the kind of methodological device under discussion whereby adopting a *critical* standpoint toward some phenomenon can enable us to obtain access to aspects of its organization, logic or structure otherwise not readily available. According to Garfinkel and Sacks (1970):

> Ethnomethodological studies of formal structures are directed to the study of such phenomena, seeking to describe members' accounts of formal structures wherever and by whomever they are done, while abstaining from all judgements of their adequacy, value, importance, necessity, practicality, success, or consequentiality. We refer to this procedural policy as "ethnomethodological indifference." (p. 345)

In the course of analytical practice, however, such a policy has its own logical limitations: In what sense could it be considered "indifferent," for example, to conceptualize the practice of "water divination" as a *reasoned* procedure as distinct from, say, mysticism or irrationality? Could ethnomethodologists "indifferently" treat astrological or phrenological judgments as "achievements" of reason in contrast to "defects" of reason?

Garfinkel and Sacks themselves actually include "divinational reasoning" alongside legal and psychiatric reasoning as if they were un-problematically equivalent:

> Persons doing ethnomethodological studies can "care" no more or less about professional sociological reasoning than they can "care" about the practices of legal reasoning, conversational reasoning, divinational reasoning, psychiatric reasoning, and the rest. (1970: 346)

I do not deny the importance of striving to bracket off assumptively theoretical treatments of reasoning and activity as far as is possible. My only point here is to draw attention to the fact that some phenomena are *constituted* by "judgements of their adequacy, value ... success or con-sequentiality," such as memory, the achievement of gender, making a scientific discovery, or arriving at a determination that someone has committed suicide, all of which phenomena have been investigated ethno-methodologically. After all, a recollection is not an *apparent* recollection, a scientific discovery is not a failed attempt at one, etc. Given these inherent limitations to the implementation of a strict policy of "ethno-methodological indifference," and given Weber's argument in favor of adopting a critical standpoint as a methodological procedure for identifying and elucidating fundamental assumptions in a domain of human behavior, I see no reason to limit ourselves as analysts to orientations exclusive of *critical* ones. The only caveat is not to transgress the boundaries between explication and advocacy under the auspices of analysis.

In dealing with media representations of controversies, political phenomena and similar areas of investigation, analysis is not to be understood as *intentionalist*. It is, rather, *conventionalist*. There is neither the evidence nor the argumentation provided to support ascribing to actual reporters intentions to bias, to under-report, etc. The only issue is, *using the texts and only the texts, the communicated reports and only the reports, as data,* how to provide for whatever viewings such materials can be claimed to make available to viewers. Naturally, to a critical recipient, bias or neutrality can be determined, whereas, to a non-critical or counter-critical recipient, these dimensions of assessment do not become relevant. Whatever dimensions of assessment can be made are intelligible/invocable *only if these are logical options in the first instance.* That is, some reports cannot logically be determined in any way, for any recipient, to exhibit bias of a particular sort, just as other reports for any recipient cannot possibly (i.e., logically) be found to exhibit neutrality in respect of some position. In my work on the coverage of the Lebanon War, I frequently encountered the objection from reviewers that I had tried to demonstrate bias. This is not the case: What I had tried to demonstrate was that a recipient *could have logical grounds for discerning bias within a communicative object.* Whether he does, or should, is not my concern. *Whether he could* is the issue, and the only issue, I address analytically. Moreover, if we are looking at what could be understood, and one such understanding has a critical character, then what does it look like? How is it achieved? Surely, this is as worthy of analysis as any other comprehension option.

The methodological issue at stake here is this: A member may view "bias" etc. in a report only given his background knowledge/belief(s), moral orientations and like commitments. However, against any such background (which can be described as a possible – even a conventional – background for viewing a report), how could this inform an orientation to a text? Surely, we can analyze the options for a characterization any text embodies, *along with a description of various backgrounds (e.g, historical knowledge/belief, political perspective, etc.) for its reception,* and arrive at a conclusion such as: Against background *B*, text *T* can, in virtue of its analyzable intelligibility structures/devices, be heard as, *inter alia,* biased (for or against position *P*) or neutral. Other dimensions of assessment available to members include: balanced/unbalanced; accurate/inaccurate; partisan/non-partisan; complete/incomplete; objective/subjective, etc. It takes logical, ethnomethodological and linguistic analysis to show "the how" of any such achieved understanding that members may arrive at.

This approach proposes that the "text" (the embodiment of categorization practices and conceptual arrangements through them) be the object of inquiry. While this is not a new approach in principle, there have been some orientations to texts which have created problems. For example, due to a Kantian prejudice, a traditional conception has been to think of texts as *passive,* inert phenomena, requiring the activity of the mind of a viewer to impose structure, intelligibility or otherwise upon them.[4] Against this, a more recent argument has proposed that the text itself is *active* (Smith, 1982) in organizing whatever orientations a member *can* logically find in it. However, we should not take this position to mean that we are substituting a model of an active text and passive mind for the Kantian one of an active mind and a passive text: Rather, *both are active!* In this sense, we have outlined a methodological procedure to elucidate conjointly the structures of textual organization and design with respect to the analysis of available backgrounds for orienting to them. (By "mind" here, of course, we are not involving any Cartesian category of a *res cogitans* – we could just as well say "member," "viewer," "reader," "listener," etc.)

The Matrix of Criticality and Its Permutations

There are many interrelated levels at which the concept of "criticality" can operate in our domain of interest. Consider, as a first approximation, the following distinctions (often conflated or overlooked): The *non-theoretical* recipient of an text can be critical of (a) the text, (b) the producer of the text, (c) the organization for which the producer of the text works, etc. The *theoretical* critic can be critical of (a) the text, (b) a given non-theoretical characterization of it, (c) a given background commitment on the part of a non-theoretical recipient of it, (d) the background commitment of a rival theoretical recipient of it, (e) the producer of it, (f) the organization for which the producer works, etc. The analyst, *by contrast*, who restricts himself to that form of analysis which begins and ends with the *text*, which locates the *text* at the center of his analytical attention, is *never* interested in criticizing producers or recipients, their background commitments or organizational affiliations. He is interested only in portraying as faithfully as possible the intelligibility structures and devices inhering in the text as well as the background commitments which interact with any such structures or devices so as to generate a given possible understanding and assessment of it. Insofar as some such assessments can be demonstrably critical of a text (and, by transitivity, of its producer, his affiliation, etc.) they also need to be grounded in the possibilities made available by the analysis of the text. To provide for the logical option of criticality of a text is not *eo ipso* to concur in that assessment as one that *should* be adduced. Should we discover, for example, that a given text makes available for someone of a given background commitment the determination that X is the case whereas X is not the case *in fact*, must we, as a matter of *analytic strategy*, state that X is not the case in fact lest we be taken to concur in its facticity? Surely not. (The converse can also be proposed: Namely, that when a text makes available that X is not the case, whereas in fact *it is*, the analyst must say so as a part of his analysis – again, surely not.) To claim that this is essential *for analysis* is to commit the fundamental error of arguing that an analyst must be *complicit* with one specific account of text and viewer *as a condition of analysis*. The fallacy involved in this, however, should not be confused with the perfectly reasonable proposal that, given a text T, its analysis and a description of background commitment(s) B, position P can be found as generatable by T in its interaction with B, where B may very well be defensible, conventional knowledge (or indefensible, conventional ignorance) of a particular sort, or where P may well be indefensible (or defensible) from other points of view.

Just because an elucidation of some P given some T and B may make some fellow analysts *uncomfortable* (politically, ethically), this is insufficient reason (a) for their refusing to grant, on *technical grounds*, the claim that P was indeed a generated option from the interaction of T and B and (b) for discrediting and/or rejecting an analyst's work. For example, it can be shown that, given a specific background:

B^1: Acceptance of an historical account of the West Bank and Gaza Strip which depicts it as an unjustified occupation of other people's territory.

a specific text:

T: "The new arrivals from the Soviet Union were taken to their new homes in Judea and Samaria to enjoy their new-found freedom from anti-semitism."

can generate position:

P^1: "T is biased in favor of the Israeli official position."

Now, consider the *gestalt* opposite. Holding T constant, but varying B, T can generate a different P. Thus, with background:

B^2: The West Bank and Gaza Strip were historically and rightfully Jewish under the biblical names of Judea and Samaria.

text

T: "The new arrivals from the Soviet Union were taken to their new homes in Judea and Samaria to enjoy their new-found freedom from anti-semitism."

can generate

P^2: "T is simply a factual account of the situation being described."

Both positions[5] can intelligibly be generated from the same text given the difference in background commitments. How is this possible? That is a matter for analysis to reveal. It can proceed to do so by explicating the internal structure of the text. For example, given that any location can be described with more than one set of categories, what procedural basis can be found to animate any given selection? Correctness is not enough, since many alternative depictions can have a claim to correctness (e.g., "West Bank and Gaza Strip," "the (Israeli-)Occupied Territories," "Judea and Samaria," etc.). Thus, any given selection can be found, *varying B*, to have been *differentially* grounded. The analyst does not have to be *complicit* with one or another of these positions or their associated background commitments to explicate it and to connect it to the broader theme of categorial logic in account production.

From the above argument, the following corollary may be drawn: It is not permissible to ascribe the deliberate production of any *P* and *T* by an author (*A*) or reporter (*R*). Although commonsense would tell us that there are some reporters who can determine the possible range of background assumptions on the part of their constituency in order to manipulate or manufacture their consent to some particular position in virtue of the way in which they design their account, nothing in the above argument could warrant any such determinate attribution.

"Criticality" is as much a part of commonsense reasoning as "conformity," exercised or not. Members routinely engage in commonsense *critical* appraisals of wide varieties of ongoing perceptual phenomena. Their criticality can be achieved at both the *tacit* and *witting* levels. One legitimate objective of analysis is to demonstrate how critical viewings are achievable. In order to clarify the distinction between what I shall call partisan commonsense critics, on the one hand, and the explication of "options for criticality," on the other, I have selected to contrast the treatment by Joshua Muravchik of US network coverage of the Lebanon War with my own analysis of that coverage.

Some Contrasting Conceptions of Media "Criticism": A Case Study

In 1983, Muravchik and I, independently and for very different purposes, had occasion to use the resources of the Vanderbilt University Television News Archive in order to study U.S. television network coverage of the Israeli invasion of Lebanon which occurred in 1982. Muravchik published his report in the journal *Policy Review* (1983), and I presented my (more extensive) analysis to Boston University in partial satisfaction of the requirements for the PhD degree (1984c). Among the many points of contrast between our respective treatments of the same corpus of media materials were the following: My analysis was based upon my reproduced transcriptions of substantial segments of the actually appearing coverage; my analytic effort employed techniques drawn from logic, linguistics and ethnomethodology; and my objective was the elucidation of the meaning structures of the media depictions of the war. Muravchik's study, on the other hand, was an exercise in ideological criticism whose aim was to argue that U.S. network coverage could be generally characterized as having been anti-Israeli in tone and substance.[6] His direct quotations from network media coverage were selected to enable him to make this argument.[7] Among his conclusions was the remark that:

> None of the networks achieved ... [a] rigorous standard in reporting on the events in Lebanon. CBS, however, seemed to be trying the hardest, and it succeeded a good part of the time. ABC's coverage was erratic; NBC's gave the impression that the network was on a crusade. (Muravchik, 1983: 41)

I read Muravchik's discussion with great interest. It was the only serious and relatively thorough assessment of the materials upon which I had been working that I could find in print. My own ideological conclusion, however, was diametrically opposite to Muravchik's. This discrepancy posed for me the following intellectual issue: Was there a methodological procedure that could be used to decide between our competing conclusions? After all, both of us could hardly expect to represent more than a fraction of the materials we had examined: What criteria of "representativeness" could be proposed for our respective "samples"?[8] Was a logic of "sampling" relevant to this issue at all? Were our divergent assessments primarily a function of our different political/ethical starting-points, or, as I continue to believe, were they more a function of our differential sensitivities to the logic of the *detail* of our common corpus of empirical data?

Let us consider the issue of "sampling" from a technical point of view. A parallel consideration has been addressed in connection with conversation-analytic methodology. How are we to treat the transcribed data extracts which analysts reproduce for explication – are they to be construed as samples or in some other way? Coulter (1990) has proposed that:

> The options that are actually adopted in any given conversational interaction cannot be assigned probability frequencies for the simple reason that the universe of possible instantiations of any given sequence class is unknown [and unknowable: it is indefinitely large]. Consequently, the study of any particular instantiation of a sequence class [e.g. arguments] must be motivated not by an interest in empirical generalizations to the class but by an interest in the *a priori* relations between illocutionary actions. (pp. 182-3)[9]

If our interest is not statistical, but "logical," then our reproduced data sets are not samples but perspicuous instances.

> ... I do not have to see *n* games of chess in order to grasp the *a priori* relationship between the two pawns of the same colour in the same column and the act of having used one of them in an earlier move to take a piece. Given a knowledge of the concepts in question, or of the game in question, and the datum that speakers and players are abiding by the rules of proper use, then

one can see that two or more contingent states of affairs are conceptually connected. (Coulter, 1983: 371)

Both conceptual and conversation analyses, then, must invoke a model of "grammatical" rather than statistical inquiry as their epistemological rubrics. Their interests are logical and conceptual, although founded upon instances of actual usage, and not purely empirical in the sense of an inquiry into mere "contingent regularities." Media analysis involving the elucidation of meaning structures is also, necessarily, a model of conceptual inquiry in an extended sense. The rules governing category selections, presuppositions and implications, practical inferences, sequential organization, utterance design and other phenomena of technical interest are derived from, and are answerable to, empirical data in the form of actual cases of, among other phenomena, media reportage. However, the adequacy of such elucidations is, with few exceptions, not decidable with reference to the sheer frequency of empirical instances.

For Muravchik, however, there is no methodological scruple involved in his selection of instances, no sense of the problematics of either sampling or conceptual analysis, and no constraint adhered to (or even recognized) in the derivation of critical inferences. Observations such as the following naturally lend themselves to such scrutiny:

Except for the reporting of Alan Pizey and Bob Simon from Beirut, CBS tended to avoid the tendentious or loaded wording that was used often by Peter Jennings, Barrie Dunsmore, and Mike McCourt on ABC, and by almost everybody on NBC. (Muravchik, 1983: 43)

How does Muravchik *know* (or even claim to know) that CBS "tended to avoid" loaded wording? How often did they "load words" as contrasted to using "neutral language"? What could constitute "neutral language" by reference to which a characterization of "loaded wording" might be justified? According to what evidence are we to hold the entire network accountable for the instances of "loaded wording" putatively detected by Muravchik in *some* reporters' coverage? Did these reporters intentionally, deliberately, set out to load their words, as it were, or is there something else at work which could account for their categorial selections?

Muravchik is perfectly entitled to his "opinions" about US network coverage of the Lebanon War. The question that faces us is to develop methods whereby we can maintain a principled distinction between an "opinion" (or a set of opinions comprising a "polemic") and a critical inference grounded in a logical analysis of the same corpus of empirical materials. In order to give this distinction some flesh and blood, I have selected for discussion a fragment of news reportage from NBC television news on Saturday, 12 June 1982. Remember that, for Muravchik, "NBC's [coverage] gave the impression that the network was on a crusade [against Israel]...CBS tended to avoid the tendentious or loaded wording that was used often...by almost everybody on NBC." Here is the fragment:[10]

> NBC News, Saturday, 12 June 1982 (18:35:30)
> [Paul Miller in Nabatiyeh]
> While Israelis patrolled the streets *looking for terrorists*, they have also looked for the ways of winning over the Lebanese people. In small villages like this, the Israelis and their *Christian* allies are being welcomed. (18: 35:40)

It will not suffice to complain against Muravchik that Palestinian guerrilla forces were frequently categorized as "terrorists," a designation *not once* employed to categorize the Israeli Defense Forces. What has to be shown is *how* such categorial selection was actually used and in what discursive environment. Editorializing commentaries, manifestly direct quotations of Israeli politicians, officials or spokesmen and similar partisan contexts are domains within which such a derogatory character-ization of the Palestinian forces as "terrorists" may be encountered routinely without generating an impression of biased news reportage. (It should, of course, be noted that the sustained and cumulative usage of this category in reference to only one party to the conflict may well have generated prejudicial attitudes on the part of some viewers.[11]) In the extract reproduced above, however, the category is embedded within a live news report by a reporter (not by an editor or network administrator). He is not engaged in direct quotation of an Israeli or anti-Palestinian spokesman. Nonetheless, I claim that his use of this category, according to a logic which I will specify, constitutes grounds for the attribution of bias against the persons so categorized (the Palestinian forces). What is this logic?

Without having to enter into any debate about the correctness or in-correctness of the category selection according to criteria of a moral or political nature, it can be argued that the design of Miller's report affiliates him to the official Israeli (or pro-Israeli) political position.[12] Whether or not the category "terrorist" is, by some standards, a reasonable one to in-voke, is not the issue here. The issue is, rather, that the category is a "disjunctive" one in the technical sense, that while it may be ascribable, it is not self-avowable.[13] Of course, this is not to argue that there is a uni-versal rule preferring self-avowable categories to ascribable ones in cases of conflict. If such a rule were in force, we should all be constrained to characterize Joan of Arc as a visionary and not as an hallucinator and the Stalinist Gulag as a People's Democracy and not as a totalitarian abomination. It is clear that many categories from disjunctive sets are specifically *not* self-avowable by those being categorized. However, a selection from a disjunctive categorial pair (or set) which privileges an extrinsically ascribable category over a self-avowable one (e.g. which selects "hallucinator" over "visionary," "terrorist" over "freedom fighter," etc.) *where the ascribable category is specifically not self-avowable* (irony apart) observably commits the categorizer to a contrastively unsympathetic perspective on those being categorized.[14]

Consider, further, the availability of an option in this instance for marking the categorization as *de dicto* – i.e., While Israelis patrolled the streets looking for *those they call* terrorists ... contrasts with the *de re* characterization actually produced by Paul Miller, i.e., "While Israelis patrolled the streets looking for terrorists ...." Juxtaposing *de dicto* with *de re* categorizations can be consequential for certain contexts and purposes. In this context, neglecting to mark the selection of the non-self-avowable category as *de dicto* presumptively establishes it as *de re*.[15] Such a presumption links the reporter's perspective on these events to that of one side of the conflict at the expense of the perspective of the other. This holds whether or not the reporter intended to display, was conscious of displaying, or would have admitted to, such an affiliation. As I remarked earlier, my analysis is non-intentionalist in character. Muravchik, on the other hand, employs intentionalist and motive-ascribing formulations at every turn.

Although I do not want to belabor my treatment of this fragment, an additional point about it is worthy of mention. Mr. Miller spoke of "the Israelis and their Christian allies..." The category "Christian" was indeed the self-avowed one for those whom Palestinian and their *allied* Lebanese combatants referred to with a variety of non-religious categories, among which were "Phalangist" (the English translation of their political affiliation deriving from their historical relationship to Franco's Fascist party), "Isolationist," etc. It could be argued that the category "Christian" was simply the recognitional preference for an American audience, given the embeddedness of the alternatively correct categories within a relatively less perspicuous political frame of reference. The problem which this selection engenders, however, is that it tacitly projects a religious rather than political-military explanation for the minority Lebanese alliance with the Israelis, and one with which many otherwise disinterested Christian Americans could be expected to identify.

Muravchik singles out John Chancellor of NBC News for special opprobrium, referring to his "crusade" against Israel's invasion of Lebanon (1983: 54).[16] However, it was clear that Chancellor accepted consistently fundamental (pro)-Israeli assumptions in his editorial commentaries. Likening the Palestine Liberation Organization to "Al Capone's mob," he remarked that "It is inconceivable that Israel would deliberately get itself into a situation like that [the siege of West Beirut] .... What is much more likely is that Israel blundered into it and now is stuck with it" (NBC News, Friday, 6 August 1982, 17:51:20). Three days later, Chancellor is explaining to his audience how so many Palestinians came to live in Lebanon. Ignoring the Civil War in Jordan in 1970-1 between Palestinian and Jordanian forces which resulted in a massive influx of Palestinian refugees from Jordan to Lebanon, Chancellor focuses upon the first wave of Palestinian immigration to Lebanon in 1948. Characteristically for this conflict, as for most others, the events of 1948 have already been conventionally articulated in a disjunctive category-pair, "War of Independence"/"War of Conquest." The former is the official Israeli category preference, the latter is that of the Palestinians.[17]

> NBC News, Monday, 9 August 1982 (17:50:40)
> [John Chancellor Commentary in Lebanon]
> Some of these people [Palestinians] came here to Lebanon in the Israeli *War of Independence.* That's how the Palestinians became refugees. (17:50:50)

Chancellor's usage affiliates him to the official Israeli position, hardly the perspective of an anti-Israel "crusader."

D'Arcy (1963: Ch. 1) analyzed a mode of elision in the construction of factual accounts which is pertinent here. For example, I may truthfully say of someone that he entertained his friends at the party, but I will be found morally culpable of misleading my interlocutor if it turns out that the entertainment consisted in torturing someone. I cannot be found to have *lied*: My "sin" is, rather, one of omission. Similarly, were I to describe the Nazi physician Mengele simply as having "conducted medical experiments," it is not that I have lied but rather that I have elided morally significant information. We do not need to ramify such examples in order to establish the validity of D'Arcy's "Non-elidability Principle" for morally consequential accounts. Did Paul Miller, and those other commentators who selected the category "Christian" to describe Israel's allies to Lebanon, violate this principle? Muravchik does not even raise this question. The issues that Muravchik does raise might have otherwise been analytically interesting had he deployed a methodological framework within which to explicate them. I contend that what is unfolding in these methodological discussions and explicative analyses of actual texts is such a methodological apparatus, one which is capable of transforming an otherwise polemical orientation into a critical analytical attitude.

Background, text, position

Among the reasons I have for objecting to Muravchik's style of media critique are: his choice of instances of reportage as a matter of his argumentative convenience alone, his failure to motivate his own readings of his materials by anything beyond his own initial preconceptions about the Lebanon War, and his neglect of the problem of ruling out alternative readings of his preferred instances. I cannot claim that anyone in media studies has yet been able to produce a theoretically definitive account of the structures and devices whereby messages are conveyed, impressions created and inferences facilitated. However, earlier in this paper I outlined a framework for beginning to work out some of these issues, and now I shall try to indicate to what extent it may succeed.

In order to proceed cautiously, I shall consider Muravchik's treatment of a brief fragment from the ABC News coverage supplied by its State Department correspondent, Barrie Dunsmore. Muravchik had earlier characterized Dunsmore as someone "who repeatedly went out of his way to work little digs at Israel in his stories" (1983: 49). Whether or not this assertion can be justified is not relevant here: I include it only as data to illustrate a manifest component of the Background Knowledge/Belief Commitments attributable to Muravchik as a viewer/listener. Here is his treatment of Dunsmore's report:

On 14 July, Mr Dunsmore reported:

> Lebanese police said today that as many as ten thousand people may have been killed in the fighting. To deal with such casualty figures Israel seems to be gearing up a campaign to justify its actions. Israeli sources told ABC news today they had captured hundreds of tons of weapons and documents and have dealt international terrorism an extreme blow.

There were two pieces of news here. One was the Lebanese police casualty figure which deserved to be reported and to be treated with a degree of skepticism. The other was the Israeli announcement of some of the documents and equipment they had captured. Mr. Dunsmore combined the two in a way that negated the second story by implying that it was nothing more than part of an Israeli effort at self-justification. At the same time he implicitly confirmed the fallacious Lebanese police statistic by saying this was the cause of Israel's need for self-justification. (1983: 49)

Using our analytical scheme – *B*ackground, *T*ext and *P*osition – to organize our discussion, we can treat the direct quotation of Dunsmore's report as constituting *T* and Muravchik's commentary upon it as constituting *P*. The main elements of *P* are:

1. The Lebanese police casualty figure cannot be trusted – indeed it was fallacious.
2. Israel's announcement of its capture of weapons and documents was independent of the announcement of the casualty figure by the Lebanese police.
3. Given the dubious or fallacious nature of the casualty figure, Israel's announcement could not have been an effort at self-justification.
4. Israel's claim to "have dealt international terrorism an extreme blow" was correct and not merely a function of some "need for self-justification."

The issue for analysis now is to specify how T and P relate within a structure of reasoning. And the question to be posed is: Is that structure coherent *independently* of B?

Consider first Muravchik's inattention to Dunsmore's use of modal qualifiers: "Lebanese police said ... people *may have been* killed in the fighting" and "Israel *seems to be* gearing up to a campaign ..." Because modal qualifiers *can* be strategically used to protect, by preserving deniability, an account-producer from the fuller implications of a *knowledge*-claim, they can sometimes be challenged by an account-recipient, but not *disattended*. Muravchik must have made up his mind on the basis of other, undisclosed evidence of Dunsmore's anti-Israeli partisanship that he "implicitly confirmed the fallacious Lebanese police statistic." The logic of the text itself provides no confirmation whatsoever of this attribution to Dunsmore. Indeed one could argue that Dunsmore's use of modal qualifiers itself built into his account Muravchik's desired "degree of skepticism."

Muravchik claims that Dunsmore's combination of the Lebanese police report and the Israeli announcement "negated" the Israeli claim. His basis for this way of hearing the report is simply to assert that because Dunsmore had characterized the Israeli claim as a "justification," its status as correct or true had thereby been undermined. This is singularly strange, since presumably things which count as justifications *can* without contradiction be correct or true in their factual status. To say something counted as a justification is not *thereby* to diminish its truth. Of course, people can (and often may well) produce accounts in justification of their actions which are false, but this does not mean that justifications have that property as a universal feature. Quite the contrary: The more truthful the account, the more effective the justification it accomplishes.

On what basis does Muravchik deny the possibility that the Lebanese police statistic (reported by Dunsmore as tentatively given) was accurate? Why does it "deserve to be ... treated with a degree of skepticism"? For some answer to this, we must consult Muravchik's already manifested

Background Knowledge/Belief Commitments. Muravchik is openly pro-Israeli and defended Israel's actions in Lebanon. He expressed misgivings about Dunsmore's attitude to Israel earlier in his article, quoted above. From this vantage-point, we can begin to develop an answer to our question. If we partition the antagonists in the Lebanon War simply as "Israelis" and "Arabs," then, since the Lebanese are Arabs, and Arabs are in conflict with Israel, any Arab – including any Lebanese Arab police officer – who produces a war-related account is immediately open to the charge of exaggeration, lying, self-serving bias, etc. However, Muravchik does not give any basis for his inclusion of the Lebanese police force within the set of actual opponents of Israel. No evidence is given to implicate this police force in fighting Israel's armed forces, in expressing anti-Israel sentiments as a matter of official policy, nor in anything other than a neutral posture. (In fact, from other sources one can develop a view of the Lebanese police force which may tend to align them against the PLO and their Lebanese militia allies.) Thus, Muravchik's critique of Dunsmore's text is based, in this respect, exclusively upon incorrigible commitments already held: After all, if one did not hold such views, the Lebanese police report, however tentatively articulated, might have led one seriously to question Israel's use of such deadly force in Lebanon.

I do not want to be understood here as holding that Muravchik had no right to hear/read *T* in the way he did. From a purely *political* point of view, I am unsympathetic to virtually every aspect of his *Background* commitments. From an *analytical* point of view, the validity of our respective political positions is entirely irrelevant. The issues involved in the critical analysis of media materials are conceptual and methodological: otherwise, the field degenerates into an extension of the very political conflicts whose representations it is trying to understand. In their article "Biasing the News: Technical Issues in 'Media Studies,'" a well-known critique of mainstream media studies, Anderson and Sharrock (1979) comment:

> We are not trying to argue that one *cannot* arrive at the kinds of conclusions that media scholars reach. We argue only that these conclusions are not *necessarily* to be drawn from those [textual] materials, *and* that those conclusions are not the only ones which can legitimately be drawn from those same materials. (p. 367)

In developing the kind of analysis exemplified here, the constraints which Anderson and Sharrock recommend are accepted. Only *logical grammars* can have a necessitarian status. The analyst is precluded from stipulating a *definitive* content to any given hearing/reading/viewing for any given text. The purpose of analysis, including especially *critical ana-*

lysis, is to elucidate the structure of possibilities derivable from the inter-action of any given *B*, *T* and *P* and *thereby to indicate whatever arbitrary contrivances and logical limitations are to be uncovered within the ex-hibited reasoning which links B, T and P.*

Concluding Comments

I have been arguing for wider recognition on the part of professional anal-ysts of media materials of the existence of criticality as a *practical activity* and not just as a theorist's privilege. Ethnomethodology has taught us to recognize the constitutive presence within the social world of pre-theoretical hermeneutics; it has so far had little to say of the pre-theoreti-cal *critical* orientations.[18] This may well be explained, at least in part, by a general adherence to a restrictive interpretation of the policy of "ethno-methodological indifference."

   In the preceding discussion, I have tried to show how an interest in the *workings* of criticality may be investigated in the domain of media studies. This required the formulation of an analytical methodology and a detailed case study involving its application. In order to demonstrate its relative cogency, I sought to specify the results of its application to a corpus of materials and to contrast them to a substantive media critique (that of Muravchik). Further, I tried to show how Muravchik's critique embodied the elements of a proto-methodology which was too weak to sustain his own critical observations. Among these elements were: his reliance upon a primitive mode of sampling selection, his preference for stipulating de-terminate meanings instead of explicating a logic of meaning-options and his penchant for basing critical inferences almost exclusively on what, from an analytical point of view, are arbitrary preconceptions of a political kind. This is *not* to say that preconceptions are avoidable, only that they must themselves be treated as phenomena, as part of the domain of data.

   Just as no ethnomethodologist, linguist or logician can work with mat-erials in a state of amnesia regarding his commonsense resources and insti-tutions, neither can effective explicatory work be accomplished on poli-tical, ethical or other contentious human constructions if the analyst is re-quired to put aside in their entirety his ordinary critical faculties, including his *own* ideological and/or moral commitments. A recurring problem has been to circumvent the criticism which awaits him at every turn, namely, that he has transgressed the boundary between explication and ideological evaluation, or between a critical analysis and a political polemic. I wish to claim that, while there are no guarantees against being systematically misunderstood, the approach being recommended here goes further than others of which I am aware in addressing itself to a resolution of this difficulty.

Notes

1. This ethnomethodological analysis examined the ABC, NBC and CBS reportage of the Israeli invasion of Lebanon. The data were drawn from the Vanderbilt Television News Archive and a detailed explication of the texts elucidated the ideological phenomena embodied in them.
2. By "member," I intend to include all perceptually relevant categories, such as "readers," "hearers," "listeners," "viewers," etc.
3. By employing the masculine gender in third-person references, I am only trying to help establish a convention which would stipulate that male members employ masculine pronouns and female members feminine ones in their discourse.
4. The Kantian-inspired classical tradition of literary criticism and hermeneutic approaches to texts more generally have exhibited this assumption. (For an illuminating discussion of the hermeneutic schools, see Palmer, 1969.) A more contemporary preoccupation with the mind's "assignment of meaning" to cultural objects, including texts, is to be found in the *verstehende* methodology of Weber and the interpretive sociology of the symbolic interactionist perspective in the social sciences. A good reference for these and some contrasting views is Truzzi (1974).
5. I am ignoring here a consideration of the other major inferential option recoverable from the text concerning anti-semitism in the Soviet Union.
6. For a political discussion which argues the opposite, i.e., that the US coverage was pro-Israeli, see my "'News Speak' About the Lebanon War" (Jalbert, 1984a).
7. Note that Muravchik also drew upon print media coverage to construct his argument. For the purposes of the present discussion, I shall restrict myself to an assessment of his treatment of network media coverage. See my unpublished paper, "Media Analysis: On Distinguishing a Polemic from a Critique" (Jalbert, 1984a), which can be obtained from the author.
8. Muravchik complains that:

    > ...a number of commentaries by Bill Moyers ...though tempered by the effort to understand Israel's point of view, were clearly critical of Israel's action, sometimes hyperbolically so. On 15 June, Mr. Moyers said that Israel had waged "total war" and added that "war unbounded follows the logic of hornets – everything in their path is their enemy" (1983: 43).

The contrary can be argued: in a number of commentaries, Bill Moyers can be found articulating opinions hostile to the Palestinian cause. On Friday, 11 June 1982, broadcasting on CBS News at 17:52:30 (See Note 10), Moyers characterized the Palestinian people as "a people displaced and abused, bloodless abstractions and born losers," after having remarked 20 seconds earlier that "the war has improved Israel's security to the north." Two months later, on Monday, 23 August 1982, broadcasting on CBS News at 17:51:40, Moyers castigated "Arafat and his allies" for not having accepted "the reality of Israel," and adds that they had "established within Lebanon a terrorist state sworn to Israel's destruction." This is surely hyperbolic commentary in the reverse direction to that lamented by Muravchik.

My purpose here is not simply to score points against Muravchik's untenable assessment of US network coverage as biased against Israel. Rather I am drawing attention to the dangers involved in playing the sampling game. Perhaps Muravchik could dredge up further examples to suit his purpose and I could reply with a similar volley of counter-examples until both of us ran out of patience. (My own data set consists of hours of video recordings of network coverage spanning all four months of the war; only by subjecting these materials to the most distorting operationalization could it be rendered amenable to sampling of any kind. Muravchik does not even raise this issue, let alone supply a solution.)

9. For a more extensive methodological discussion of this issue, see Coulter (1983).

10. In reproducing in transcript form actual excerpts from US television network news broadcasts, I adopt the convention of *italicizing* words, phrases or larger linguistic units solely for the purpose of highlighting those fragments to be analyzed or discussed. In no case should this practice be taken to signify anything about the original broadcast, e.g., emphasis, intonation, affect or any other endogenous property of the report. In addition, I have included references to the exact time of the broadcast fragments reproduced as data by using EST as the metric. Thus, after giving the date, the reader will encounter a series of numerals as (17:30:40) marking the beginning of the fragment and another at its conclusion.

11. Two years prior to the Israeli invasion of Lebanon, a clear linkage had already become widely established in the United States between the categories "Palestinian" and "terrorist," largely due to media depictions of the Israel-Palestine conflict. A 1980 *Time* poll reported that "30% of the US public think Palestinians are best described as 'terrorists,' 17% regard them as 'displaced persons who will eventually settle in another country,' and 19% think of them as 'refugees seeking a homeland'" (*Time*, 14 April 1980: 42, col.3). One is left wondering, however, what sentiments the remaining 34% of the US public might have expressed on the issue, as this was not reported.

12. As I argued in "'News Speak' About the Lebanon War":

> Miller's use of the category "terrorist" in this way instances a point made by the logician W. B. Gallie (1955-6). He argued that, to the degree that descriptions and categorizations of social phenomena are [uncritically and contentiously] taken to be what those who have an interest in them and who have already described and categorized them assert they are, to that degree one is involved in the use of contestable concepts. To the extent that Miller uncritically takes the categorization of the PLO by the Israelis [i.e., "terrorist"] and imports it into the apparatus of his *own* report, to that extent he is involved in an *ideological enterprise.* (Jalbert, 1984: 27)

For further discussion of the notion of "contestable concepts," see Shapiro (1981: CH. 7).

13. Building upon Sacks'(1972a) notion of "standardized relational pairs" (pp. 38-9), Coulter (1979a) develops the notion of "disjunctive category-pairs":

> At the level of the social organization of their use, we can speak of the categories of "belief" and "knowledge" as forming a *disjunctive category-pair*. We shall mark this by the use of an oblique as follows: knowledge/belief. Other such pairs would include: vision/hallucination; telepathy/trickery; ghost/illusion; flying saucer/UFO; and ideology/science. Where one part of these pairs is involved to characterize some phenomenon seriously, *the speaker's belief-commitment may be inferred, and the structure of subsequent discourse may be managed in terms provided for by the programmatic relevance of the disjunctive category-pair relationship.* Thus, to the nonbeliever, Joan of Arc suffered hallucinations; to the believer, divine visions. To the nonbeliever, Uri Geller is a sophisticated conjurer; to the believer, a telepath and telekineticist, and so on. (p. 181)

In every conflict, disjunctive categorization operates and very often through the use of disjunctive category-pairs such as "government/junta," "mob/crowd," "extremist/moderate," etc. Israeli General Ariel Sharon became highly sensitive to the operation of one such pair in the description of the departure of Palestinian forces from Beirut: during a CBS News report from Jerusalem on Friday, 19 August (17:38:40), he protested "[That is] about the *expulsion* not about *withdrawal*. It is not a *withdrawal*. It's an *expulsion*. It's not a *withdrawal*." (17:38:50).

14. On the logic of disjunctive categorization practices, see Coulter (1979a), Jayyusi (1984: Ch. 5) and Jalbert (1989).

15. *De dicto/de re* conflations were occasionally avoided, as in the following extract from NBC News, Wednesday, 30 June, 1982 (17:36:20), presented by Tom Brokaw: "In south Lebanon, meanwhile, the Israelis presented what they called evidence against the PLO and Rick Davis has that story..." (17:36:30). The use of the explicit *de dicto* marker "what they called" disaffiliated the reporter from the truth value of the object-complement "evidence against the PLO." After all, evidence is to be distinguished from putative evidence: had Brokaw simply asserted that the Israelis presented evidence against the PLO, its status *as* evidence would have been presupposed *de re*. For further discussion of the properties of *de re/de dicto* modalities, see Jalbert (1983).

16. Muravchik even invokes the FCC's "fairness doctrine" against Chancellor on the grounds that his many commentaries on the Lebanon War "were consistently critical of Israeli policy" (1983: 53).

17. For details regarding elision and the categorial phrase "War of Independence," see Jalbert (1994: 143).

18. David Bogen (1989) alerts us to several problems which arise in attempts to reconcile Habermas' "universal pragmatics" with ethnomethodological studies of practical action and reasoning. My own perspective differs from Habermas' while preserving his interest in grounding critical reflections on communication and other social phenomena within the domain of the "lifeworld."

Chapter 3

The Struggle Between Testimony and Evidence at the Iran-Contra Hearings

Michael Lynch and David Bogen

The Iran-Contra Hearings as an Historical Event

In 1987, we began to study the videotaped testimony of Oliver North and John Poindexter at the Iran-contra hearings, focusing particularly on the first day of North's testimony. At the time, the hearings seemed monumental, a major historical event in the making, the cultural significance of which was comparable to that often ascribed to Watergate.[1] Indeed, at the time the scandal was widely billed by various pundits and media commentators as "another" Watergate, and was even referred to on occasion as "Iran-gate" (though, interestingly, this was a label that did not stick). Like Watergate, the affair was said to involve secret government operations, hidden sources of money, and shadowy characters. Like Watergate, when it was initially "exposed" to the press, suspicions were voiced about a "cover up" by the appointed officials who handled the scandal. And, again like Watergate, a number of investigations were undertaken, a special prosecutor was appointed, criminal charges were laid, and broader issues of national security and executive privilege were dealt with on the basis of the Watergate precedent. With annoying regularity, the press cited the key question from Watergate: "What did the President know, and when did he know it?" The transgressions of law and public trust seemed at least as serious, and there were reasons to expect that it would damage Reagan's presidency no less than Watergate damaged Nixon's.

Now, years later, we have a somewhat different perspective on these events. As it has settled into history and become old news, we now recognize the "Iran-contra affair" as events that *might* have brought down a government, but did not. Our sense of what we have been studying has changed accordingly. Where we once figured that we could get at least a minor purchase on the making of an historical event, we now are faced with describing the making of what has become, for the most part, a non-event. It has become increasingly clear that our study has to do with how the Joint Congressional Committees' investigation was successfully blocked, inhibited, or otherwise attenuated by the parties investigated. There are many possible explanations for this: That the administration's efforts to withhold or destroy key documents without being held culpable were, for the most part, successful; that the vigorous efforts of the administration's defenders on the committee were matched by comparatively weak and ambivalent efforts by members of the "opposition" party; that the media's investigatory efforts were less than convincingly aggressive (especially compared to Watergate); and that these investigations were conducted within the generally conservative political climate of the late Reagan presidency. The present paper does not aim to give a comprehensive explanation of what transpired (or will turn out to have transpired) as the "history of the Iran-contra affair." Rather, our focus is upon a few hours of testimony that we figure shaped an especially poignant moment in a public spectacle that brought the affair into public focus.

Background

As soon as it became news in November 1986, the Iran-contra affair seemed destined to be an historic event, although *just how* it would become historical remained to be seen. The affair was widely viewed as a significant foreign policy scandal and a crisis of public confidence in the government. Official and unofficial chronologies of the affair have been written many times over, even though the full scope and historical significance of the events have yet to be determined.[2] These histories report upon how a cast of characters took part in a series of covert operations involving the United States, Israel, Iran, and counter-revolutionary forces in Central America. The broad outlines of the story are familiar, although many of the details remain shadowy and contentious: Acting on Presidential approval, and with the knowledge of leading Cabinet members, officials at the National Security Council (NSC) and Central Intelligence Agency arranged a series of covert arms sales to Iran during 1985 and 1986. The arms sales were authorized with the expectation that they would result in the release of American hostages held in Lebanon by Islamic fundamentalist groups. In 1986, NSC officials arranged a diversion of profits from the Iranian arms sales to aid the contra forces seeking to overthrow the Sandinista government in Nicaragua. Both the arms sales and the diversion contradicted explicit U.S. policy, and by some accounts these actions constituted violations of law of sufficient magnitude to warrant impeachment of the President and/or prosecution of some of the principal White House officials.

Like the millions of other people who were captivated by the Iran-contra affair, we were interested in finding out "what really happened." This was not, however, the primary motive for our study. Instead, we took an interest in the hearings, and in the details of their actual conduct, as a pretext for discussing fundamental themes in contemporary sociology and the philosophy of language. The televised hearings provided a vivid spectacle of a struggle between interrogators and witnesses; a struggle that largely concerned efforts to convert testimony into historical evidence, and reflexively to use the emerging historical record to solicit and constrain further testimony.[3] Like many people who watched the hearings, we noticed that North and some of the other witnesses were asked to testify about events that had been, or may have been, recorded in memos, letters, chronologies, and other written documents. And, like many people, we noticed that these witnesses were often able to disclaim knowledge of particular documents and of what those documents said. We found this very intriguing, and we were attracted by the fact that we could use videotapes of the testimony as a textual basis for examining the vicissitudes of the interrogation. We could imagine that, in however small a way, an intensive study of these videotapes could give us a fresh angle on questions of how testimony related to evidence, or more generally, how speech related to writing. And, we came to believe that this rather academic pursuit could give us some insight into how the official investigation's "spade was turned" as it attempted to dig beneath the "plausible denials" given in the testimonies by North and other operatives.

As we view it, there is no essential point of separation between the history of the affair and the various official investigations through which that history was written. The reflexive relationship between "history" and "investigation" operated with such *density* that the archive of records and testimonies examined by the various fact-finding bodies could not be viewed simply as *data* about the various covert activities at issue. The archive was itself shaped by the alleged covert activities it was used to describe: by the much-publicized shredding of documents by Oliver North and his NSC staff in November 1986; by White House resistance to the disclosure of classified documents; by the admission that documents authorizing covert actions were designed to give "plausible deniability" to authorizing officials; and by "false chronologies" put out by the key actors in the affair. In light of these considerations, we argue that the continuing history of the Iran-contra affair is a history of struggle over the very documents through which that history is being written.

This struggle over the writing of history reached a dramatic high-point during Oliver North's testimony before the Select House and Senate Committee on July 7-14, 1987. The hearings were staged as a *ceremonial of truth*, a public spectacle in which a battery of cameras scrutinized North's every utterance while he recounted his involvement in the Iran-contra affair. The entire set-up was arranged as a conspicuous civics lesson in which the key players expressed an orientation to "the truth" about secret and deceptive dealings.[4] In the words of one of North's interrogators, it was "a principal purpose of these hearings to replace secrecy and deception with disclosure and truth." North, in turn, avowed, "I came here to tell you the truth – the good, the bad, and the ugly" (*Taking the Stand*, 1987: 12-13).

The Ceremonial of Truth

Although their differences are indeed profound, the contemporary tele-visual spectacle at the Iran-contra hearings nonetheless bears an interesting set of resemblances to the 18th century "ceremonial of truth" described by Foucault in the first chapter of his *Discipline and Punish* (1979). In that book Foucault charts the disappearance of what he terms "the great spectacle of physical punishment" and its replacement by a modern penal practice epitomized by the total and anonymous vision of Bentham's panopticon. The book begins with the now famous dramatic recounting of the 18th century "spectacle of the scaffold":

> On 2 March 1757 Damiens the regicide was condemned "to make honorable amends before the main door of the Church of Paris," where he was to be "taken and conveyed in a cart, wearing nothing but a shirt, holding a torch of burning wax weighing two pounds"; then, "in said cart to the scene of the crime, where, on a scaffold that will be erected there, the flesh will be torn from his breasts, arms, thighs, and calves with red-hot pincers, his right hand, holding the knife with which he committed the said parricide, burnt with sulphur ... (Foucault, 1979: 3)

One of the main points Foucault makes about the transition to the more "enlightened" justice of the modern era is that torture and corporal punishment were not de-emphasized simply because of effective opposition to such inhumane expressions of tyrannical power. As he reconstructs the calculative reasoning of the utilitarian philosophers and moral managers, secret interrogations using torture and public executions were ineffective mechanisms for assuring public compliance with state justice. The paragraphs following the passage quoted above include extracts from the diary of Bouton, an officer who witnessed the unfortunate Damien's execution. In Bouton's narrative all kinds of things go wrong: The sulphur is lit, but doesn't burn properly; the pincers prove unwieldy and ineffective; the body does not easily break and pull apart at the joints. What particularly interests Foucault about the spectacle of the scaffold it not the gory details so much as the fact that the civics lesson produced through the public execution was an unstable and equivocal one.

He recites numerous stories of botched executions, rancorous and fickle crowds, wretched criminals who became heroes and martyrs as they performed on the stage of the scaffold. The pre-arranged ritual through which the condemned was associated with the crime, branded with the stigma of the misdeed, and enjoined to confess, provided a set of props and signs which could be dissociated from the pre-ordained civics lesson and recombined spontaneously in the carnival atmosphere of the execution. Foucault describes instances where the semiological excess of the public execution mobilized the crowds to rescue the condemned and turn viciously upon the executioners.

With the rise of the modern penal apparatus, Foucault tells us, all of these contingencies and equivocalities of "truth's enactment" begin to fall away. In the text, first-person accounts, like those in Bouton's diary, are displaced by studies of prison plans and disciplinary manuals. This shift traces a corresponding movement from the populated marketplace of the "public spectacle" to the cool, impersonal architecture of the modern institution geared for carceral surveillance and control. As a result, we are left with a picture of a modern penal apparatus that is "progressive" in so far as it has been progressively successful at articulating and managing the live conflicts surrounding the human subject at the material points of its ritual subjugation. Punishment becomes hidden within the penitentiary, while the previously secret interrogation of the accused becomes a public ritual in which the accused person is examined in the presence of an overhearing public. The "drama" of justice is now enacted through an interrogative machinery through which the accused is asked either to confess to the charges or challenge the accusation (shades of Perry Mason). The "confession" is no longer forced through the instruments of torture (and thereby made equivocal), but is instead extracted from the body through the "rational" instrumentalities of an interrogative cross-examination and an overwhelming presentation of evidence.

The modern tribunal of truth and justice represents a double inversion from the days of torture and public execution. Where interrogation used to be shrouded in secrecy, it is now the focus of a public drama, and where punishment was once a public spectacle, it is now suffered off camera, as a semi-private consequence of the public drama.

The interrogation at the Iran-contra hearings was in significant respects conducted along the lines of a courtroom examination. However, the operations of the "fact-finding tribunal" departed from those of a courtroom trial in several key respects.

First of all, the structure of the interrogation was not strictly governed by a body of courtroom rules and precedents. Many participants and commentators initially treated the hearings as another Watergate, and this mood penetrated the themes, questioning strategies, and programming arrangements. Relative to courtrooms, the genre of "nationally televised congressional hearings" was elaborated as a somewhat more "open" field of discourse in which the interrogator was granted rights to violate hearsay and other exclusionary rules, while the witness and his attorney were able to secure the discursive space for elaborating answers into uninterrupted speeches, while at the same time fulfilling the rule that witnesses respond directly to interrogators questions. The Watergate hearings also provided a variety of televisual themes such as the positioning of John Dean's wife in the gallery, as a silent backdrop to his testimony. While the homespun Betsy North was no double for the impassive and glossy figure of Maureen Dean, her dress and demeanor made a conspicuous "statement" in light of the Watergate precedent.

Second, as a show on daytime television, the hearings assimilated familiar dramatic figures and structures. Narrative figures associated with sporting events, talk shows, war stories, and Western movies were prominently played-up for the media audience. These figures were not only explicitly invoked by North's speeches, his facial expressions and postures also provided a physiognamatic spectacle consonant with the claims and story structures his voice enunciated.

Third, questions concerning the witness' credibility and the plausibility of his testimonies were raised and addressed as thoroughly politicized matters. The addressee of the witness' testimony never encompassed a singular interlocutor, but consisted instead in an explicitly factional audience, which actively intervened in the staging of the spectacle, and threatened throughout the serious, non-partisan pursuit of "disclosure and truth" numerous and continual eruptions of political theater.

Consequently, like the spectacle of the scaffold, the public tribunal provided a "stage" for appeals and enactments that transgressed the anticipated design of the ceremonial of truth. Just as the 18th century "spectacle of the scaffold" provided the condemned with the opportunity to go to his or her death as a redeemed hero, rebellious martyr, repentant soul, or degraded scoundrel, so did the nationally televised ceremonial of truth – arranged to "get to the bottom" of a political scandal – provide North and his allies with opportunities to construct an audio-visual narrative in which he stood as a righteous hero, victim of unwarranted accusations, or martyr. Contrary to Foucault's picture of the modern penal apparatus as a system of total surveillance deployed by a quiet, smooth-running bureaucratic machinery, North's gambit was – at least in part – to mobilize technologies of surveillance in the service of discrediting his opponents within the bureaucracy. By saying this, we do not mean to criticize Foucault's historico-critical method, nor should his failure to account for the contingencies, equivocalities, and everyday disruptions of the modern "ceremonial of truth" be taken as an oversight on his part. Instead, our suggestion is that these omissions might serve as starting points for a history of the present that focuses on those visible sites of action where modern technologies of surveillance and judgment can be seen to mingle with the residues of older forms of rhetorical and performative practice. This openness to the contingencies of its performance was, at least in part, responsible for the *high drama* of such "live" televisual events as the Watergate and Iran-contra hearings.

Speech and Writing: An Ethnomethodological Respecification

In the remainder of this paper, we will focus on one of the major themes arising out of our larger study of the Iran-contra affair. As mentioned above, a prominent aspect of the hearings was the relationship between the witness' testimony and various written documents used as evidence. In the present paper, we aim to analyze that relationship by effecting an "ethnomethodological respecification" (See Appendix I at the end of this chapter, p. 70) of a more general topic: the relationship between speech and writing.

Readers who are familiar with the debate between Jacques Derrida and John Searle will know that their dispute was at least partly about the relationship between speech and writing (Derrida, 1977a, 1977b; Searle, 1977). To put it simply, Derrida argued that Searle, and the tradition in analytic philosophy he represents, subordinated writing to speech by insisting upon the necessity of authorship, intention, meaning and context in the analysis of linguistic intelligibility. He attempted to demonstrate that Searle was unnecessarily privileging a narrow concept of context while shunting aside the possibilities for quoting, citing, or otherwise disengaging speech from an original context and grafting it into an endless play of transformative uses. His key point was that a linguistic fragment or text does not lose its intelligibility when it is divorced from any discernable original situation. Instead, it becomes an item in (and for) an indefinite series of intelligible uses and readings. He did not argue that the fragment retains an original meaning whenever it is quoted, cited, re-stated, or re- read; instead, he attacked the very idea that a static meaning is "attached to" a statement whenever it is uttered, printed, or read.

Derrida argued that writing is autonomous from speech, that its structures of intelligibility cannot be derived from the analysis of spoken discourse, whereas Searle insisted upon the primacy of a discursive situation in which a speaker enunciates an utterance ("seriously") or an author commits an idea to writing. Rather than taking sides in this debate, we aim to show how it frames an interesting practical problem that arose for participants in the Iran-contra hearings. As we view it, the testimony was an instance of speech generated within a dense literary, or textual field. The dialogues between interrogators and witnesses were officially set up as part of a "fact-finding" inquiry, and the House and Senate committees were charged with producing a written report summarizing the hundreds of hours of testimony. Moreover, the interrogators, witnesses, counsel, and committee members were surrounded by notebooks filled with such written records as copies of memos, printouts of electronic mail messages, telegrams, diary entries, letters, and transcripts of previous testimonies. The records were used in the course of the testimony. They were sometimes read aloud, shown on camera, blown up on a display panel, cited, and otherwise used as a basis for soliciting testimony and checking testimony against "the facts." Indeed, the sheer mass of the documents became a strategic issue when, at the outset of his testimony, North and his attorney, Brendan Sullivan, complained that they were given insufficient time to read and study the committee's records. This was initially proposed as a reason for postponing North's appearance, and after that was (predictably) denied, North repeatedly disclaimed knowledge or recollection of what the records documented.

Rather than leading us toward a general theoretical answer to the question of the primacy of writing over speech, the policies of ethnomethodology require us to investigate how the participants in the hearings juxtapose writings and spoken utterances in the course of the testimony. There are at least two general problems that this opens up for our investigation:

(1) The conversion of spoken testimony into a "master narrative" of the Iran-contra affair. By "master narrative" we mean a conventional historical account; a chronology of objective events, complete with a cast of characters and their significant actions. The specifications of a master narrative – calendar dates, chronological times, geographical places,

named characters, and bounded actions and events – contrast point-by-point to the locally organized and biographically relevant stories told in testimony.[5] As we mentioned earlier, the Joint Committees were responsible for a final report, which was published a few months after the close of the hearings. As it turned out, the Committees produced two reports, a majority report consisting mainly of a chronology of events, and a shorter minority report which specified an alternative version on selected topics. This doubling of final reports was an interesting outcome, and an understandable one given the contentiousness of the hearings. In any event, the hearings were framed by the committee's mandate to "hear" testimony as a contribution to an official history they would eventually write. (2) The relationship between the testimony and a written report was not only a linear one, where testimony provided the data base from which an official report was composed. Throughout the testimony, the cumulative "record" of the affair and the mass of committee documents were actively brought into play. Witnesses were questioned in reference to documents, prior testimonies, and the variously contested "facts" which came out of the investigation-so-far. Not only were witnesses' utterances heard by reference to what might be written about them; they were solicited and assessed in relation to available documents, and "the record" of previous testimonies and documented events.

The interrogatory dialogue was structurally framed and intensively negotiated in reference to evidentiary documents. Before the interrogation began, North and his counsel moved for a postponement on the grounds that the committee had sent some thousands of requested documents to Sullivan less than a week before the testimony was scheduled. Sullivan presented a photograph of North standing next to a stack of documents that was taller than he was, and complained that his client was given insufficient time to prepare for an interrogation based on those documents. This request was denied, but it set up a claim that North used regularly throughout his testimony, to the effect that he could not recall particular details because he had insufficient time to study the documents in which they were recorded. Consequently, much of the time allotted to the hearings was consumed by laborious co-readings of particular documentary exhibits, and the claimed lack of "refreshed recall" licensed North's often vague and incomplete recollections.

Despite the mass of documents the committee managed to secure, the documents that were missing were even more notable. North's infamous shredding of an indefinite (but large) mass of documents was a key theme in the questioning, as House Majority Counsel John Nields fruitlessly interrogated North about the contents of the shredded documents. Not surprisingly, North professed not to recall which particular documents he shredded, and whether the documents he shredded were of evidentiary value. But, when Nields raised the obvious connection between missing documents and North's memory, he got the following, rather curt and snappy reply:

Nields: Well, that's the whole reason for shredding documents, isn't it, Colonel North, so that you can later say you don't remember whether you had them and you don't remember what's in them?

North: No, Mr. Nields, the reason for shredding documents and the reason the government of the United States gave me a shredder – I mean, I didn't buy it myself – was to destroy documents that were no longer relevant, that did not apply or that should not be divulged. Part of a covert operation is to offer plausible deniability of the association between the government of the United States and the activity. ... And that's why the government buys shredders by the tens and dozens and gives them to people running covert operations – not so they can have convenient memories. I came here to tell you the truth, to tell you and this Committee and the American people the truth. And I'm trying to do that, Mr. Nields, and I don't like the insinuation that I'm up here having a convenient memory lapse, like perhaps some others have had. (*Taking the Stand*, 1987: 20-21)

Other documents that were not shredded were withheld from the committee by the White House, and many of those that were released contained blacked-out passages for "national security reasons." Some of North's notebooks were used a year later as evidence in his criminal trial, but at the time of the hearings they had not been made available to the committee, and a few committee members complained about this.

These struggles over documents indicate the extent to which the parties to the Iran-contra hearings treated them as crucial items. Put simply, they were treated as actual or potential constraints on what a witness could say (or *not* say) credibly. They were treated as resources for formulating interrogative questions, and as sources of "leverage" for probing a witness, testing his answers, and holding those answers *answerable*. On the other hand, the fragmentary notes, documents, and other writings the committee used were "cut off from their anchoring source in a unique and present intention" (Fish, 1989: 37), and the "live" dialogue with the witness provided an opportunity to fill-in the situational and intentional contexts of those writings. North, like a good deconstructionist, did not always go along with this interpretive program. For the most part, the committee interrogators aimed to use written documents as representations of real-worldly events. North and the other "hostile witnesses" were able to dissociate their testimony from particular texts by, among other things, exploiting undecideable features of the authorship, intention, and original meaning of the "orphaned texts" brought into the interrogation.

Moves in Testimony

At this point we need to consider briefly materials from the first morning of North's interrogation in order to specify those issues we have thus far discussed only in a general way (See transcript in Appendix II at the end of this chapter, p. 72). The transcript includes notations for pauses, in tenths of a second, and in a few utterances we have marked words that are enunciated with emphasis (marked with italics), or stretched (marked with one or more colon). When utterances overlap, the point where the overlap begins is marked with a double slash mark (See Appendix (p. 259) for further description of transcription conventions). The exchange occurs at the beginning of North's interrogation, and it illustrates some recurrent features that pervade his and other witness' testimonies.

In the weeks prior to North's interrogation, stories were circulated in the press about how he was a "loose cannon" whose zealous adventures got out of hand. It was also believed by many that he would stoically accept the "fall guy" role he may have been appointed to play by his superiors. By the end of the first day of testimony, however, North had established a different persona altogether. The character who emerged, in the loudly expressed opinions of many people was an "American hero," although others denounced him as a cunning sociopath. He and his attorney Brendan Sullivan successfully transformed the interrogation of a prime suspect in the scandal into a political debate, and this transformation was evident from the outset of the interrogation.

Formally, an interrogation is supposed to consist in an asymmetric organization of questions and answers, where the interrogator asks the questions and the witness answers each question in its turn. Ostensibly, this limits what a witness can say, since the interrogator controls the initiative. In courtroom cross-examinations, as well as in tribunals like this, interrogators seldom confine their utterances to syntactic questions, as they often present witnesses with series of assertions, often leading to accusations (Atkinson and Drew, 1979). At the outset of North's interrogation, Nields begins with a question (appended with "is that correct?") (lines 3-5, p.72). It is a question of a particular kind that we often find in interrogations. Rather than requesting information from its recipient, the "question" enunciates a statement subject to the witness' confirmation.

Note further that Nields' first question is shaped to solicit North's recognition of the two unnamed "operations of this government of great significance to the people of this country." This is an apt device for enjoining the witness to align with the interrogator's assessment of the situation, but note that North does not entirely comply. When he says, "At least two. Yessir." he qualifies his agreement by suggesting that the two unnamed events (whatever they might be) are part of a larger field (line 7). Now, of course, anyone who knew anything about the affair would know that the two events at issue in the hearings are the arms for hostages trade and the contra supply operation,[6] but we figure that North is not being thick- headed here so much as resisting the way Nields is beginning to put together a story of relevant and significant events in which North's actions will be featured.

In testimony, a confirmation ("Yes" or "That is correct") conventionally allows the interrogator to go on to the next question, and this is what happens here. Nields phrases his next question more fully as an assertion, using a tag question "Is that correct?" to prompt an answer after the lapse of a couple of seconds (lines 8-12). Again, North does not give a "pure" confirmation, since he qualifies Nields' point about "support for the contras during the time of the Boland Amendment" by adding that the operation was conducted before and after that time (lines 14-16). (The Boland Amendment prohibited military or logistic support for the contras by the C.I.A. and other U.S. operatives.) He also rephrases things in an obviously partisan way: support for the contras becomes "support for the democratic outcome." Despite this qualification and minor editorial, Nields again proceeds to build what, by now, has taken the shape of a developing argument; an argument that has accusatory connotations for North's "side" of the case. By reading the series of Nields' utterances, we can infer the line of argument he is building.

(1)   An assertion about two significant government operations in which North was involved.
(2)   A specification of each of the two operations:
      (a)   support for the contras during the Boland Amendment, and
      (b)   sale of arms to Iran.
(3)   An assertion that the two operations were carried out in secret; that they were covert operations.
(4)   An assertion of a contradiction: covert operations are designed to be carried out in secret "from our enemies," but these were designed to be secrets from "the American people."

A witness' confirmations enable the interrogator to use a dialogical structure to build a monologue. In this case we can see the monologue developing into an accusatory argument on how the two covert operations were conducted in a way that contravened their designed purpose. At this point, North steps up the resistance, and far from answering the accusation by confirming it with a confession, he counterattacks by recasting Nields' opposition between "our enemies" and the "American people." He avows that, for all practical purposes, to keep secrets from the Soviets requires that they also be kept secret from the American people.

At this point, North and Nields are into a debate, but this shifts to a new phase, when Nields begins to elaborate a precise (i.e., specifically dated) quotation of what North supposedly said to "the Iranians" in Germany. The quotation mentions a Presidential cabinet officer's explicit reference to the possibility of impeachment if the Iran arms sales became public. This quotation implicates a specific document – a transcript – and Sullivan and North demand to see it. Note how they profess not to know what documents they have. They spend some time rummaging through notebooks, and finding the relevant documentary references. The interrogation is set up to hold North responsible for what the transcripts report him to be saying:

120	Nields:	That's the entire question. Did you say that to the Iranians?
121	Sullivan:	Uh- does it say that on this page, sir?
122	Nields:	Yes, at the very to:p.

After examining the page, North then elaborates an intentional horizon for transforming the "literal sense" of what he admits to saying (and what the transcript records him saying). First, he makes clear that *he* made the tapes and supplied them to the committee so that "there would never be any doubt in the minds of my superiors as to what I had said, or why I had said it." And then, forthrightly, he states "That is a *bald-faced lie* told to the Iranians." This claim entirely transforms the sense of what the evidentiary document is providing evidence *of*. North elaborates that he endeavored to record his utterances, and that it is through his diligence in doing so that his "superiors" (and now the Committee) are able to know about what he said. His lies are accountable *as lies* to the relevant officials (on "our" side), but not to the Iranians. Although North does not contest the transcript's authority as a precise memorandum of what he said, he transforms its evidentiary value. If he is to be believed, it is a record of a lie told for good reason, and not a "literal" statement about what Secretary of Defense Weinberger said at their meeting with the President. Interestingly, here and in North's subsequent editorializing about covert operations ("By their very nature, covert operations ... are a *lie*," etc.), he builds a patriotic rationale for lying and secrecy. The lie told to the Iranians was, in effect, a lie told forthrightly and sincerely for the national interest. In both passages his admissions of lies are justified in reference to "higher" moral and political objectives. The second passage is interesting in the way it invites the Committee to consider their disapproval of "lies" in light of their (ambivalent) approval of covert activities. The invitation is clear: if you want to prevent these sorts of "lies," don't initiate covert activities. This possibility was never seriously proposed in the hearings, to the chagrin of certain critics of U.S. policy (this was one of the numerous sources of dissatisfaction with the Democrats on the committee in leftist periodicals like *The Nation, The New York Review of Books,* and even *The New Yorker*'s "Notes and Comments" section).

The Sincere Liar

North qualifies his admissions of "lying" or "lies" by placing them in an explicitly political context. The lies are told "sincerely" in the sense that they are not concealed (to relevant parties on "our side"), and that they are justified in terms of legitimate objectives ("legitimate" insofar as the Committee did not question the legitimacy of "covert actions"). In these instances, North argues that he knew exactly what he was doing, that he was prepared to lie, did so, and was fully justified in doing so. North's justificatory story is, in Harvey Sacks's (1992b) terms a "fragile" story. Since he admits to lying, and his justification is based on political considerations, one can easily ask whether he's lying *now* in the highly charged political setting of the hearings. In his follow-up questions, Nields disputes whether North's (and the administration's) "lies" were directed only at "enemies" (Soviets, Iranians), in contrast to "the American people."

> Nields: The American people were told by this government that our government had nothing to do with the Hasenfus airplane, and that was false. And it is a principal purpose of these hearings to replace secrecy and deception with disclosure and truth. And that's one of the reasons we have called you here, sir. And one question the American people would like to know the answer to is what did the President know about the diversion of the proceeds of Iranian arms sales to the contras? Can you tell us what you know about that, sir? (*Taking the Stand*, 1987: 12. Corresponds to lines 207-217 in Appendix II,)

An implication to be taken from this is that since North and "this government" lied to "the American people" in the past, they (and specifically he) might do so in the present hearings. Nields associates the hearings with "the American people" and a mandate of "truth" and "disclosure." This asserts a position "above politics." The Committee never fully achieved its claims to be "above" politics. Already, we see that some of the rhetorical force of the condemnation of "lies" is mitigated by not taking up the challenge offered when North identifies "lies" with "covert activities." At the end of the transcript, Nields' question is odd in the way it pivots so quickly from the issue of "lies" about the Hasenfus plane to the question that commentators had marked would be the "key question" in North's interrogation. He even enunciates part of the phrase ("what did the President know and when did he know it") memorialized from the Watergate hearings, and which media commentators cited to frame the "key issue" to be addressed in the hearings. North comments on this *non sequitur* as he begins his reply: "You just took a long leap from Mr. Hasenfus' airplane."

In a subsequent utterance, North addresses the implication of his "fragile story" in one of his most oft-quoted utterances from the hearings:

> Those are the facts, as I know them, Mr. Nields. I was glad that when you introduced this, you said that you wanted to hear the truth. I came here to tell you the truth – the good, the bad, and the ugly. I am here to tell it all, pleasant and unpleasant, and I am here to accept responsibility for that which I did. I will not accept responsibility for that which I did not do. (*Taking the Stand*, 1987: 13-14)

Consider for a moment some of the "literary" features here.
(1) Nields has asked "the" question for which the audience has been prepared in advance by the commentators.
(2) This question was designed citationally, enunciating "the" question from Watergate.
(3) The question abruptly follows Nields' assertion of the committee's mandate – an assertion that linked the committee to "the American people" and identified its purpose with "truth" and "disclosure"; in contrast to partisan interests in concealment (associated with "this government").
(4) North gives "the" answer which commentators prior to the hearings had said he would give (he asserts that as far as he knew, the President knew nothing about the "diversion" of profits from the arms sales).
(5) North forcefully expresses his intention to tell the truth in the present hearings.
(6) North cites the title of a Clint Eastwood film, *The Good, The Bad, and The Ugly,* in which Eastwood (characteristically) plays an ambiguous "hero" – an American who wanders through Mexico, carrying out violent assassinations against swarthy "bad guys." Eastwood retains his heroism in contrast to the unqualified evil of his foes. As in other Eastwood films (e.g., the "Dirty Harry" films) the hero violates legal and moral codes in the service of his violent efforts to eradicate unquestionable evil. Those who stand in his way in the service of legal and bureaucratic standards naively protect evil.

Perhaps we can say that North *enlists* Clint Eastwood's crusade against deeply evil foreigners to combat the historical precedent of Watergate, and in doing so he relativizes the Committee's pretensions about transcendent truth and disclosure (See Der Derian, 1989). *Truth and disclosure* become secondary concerns in the face of the unquestionable threats lodged in foreign lands. The question then becomes one of resolving just when, and in reference to which audiences, truth and disclosure are warranted. With enough force (and in light of the 1980's themes so popular in Clint Eastwood and Sylvester Stallone films) North now has the opportunity to implicate the Committee majority as enemy – as bureaucrats whose legalistic concerns with truth and procedures naively puts them in league with foreign agents.

The paradox of the sincere liar is not so much a question of the liar's statement being false if true and true if false. Rather, in light of this case, the paradox is that *the present circumstance* may come to stand (at least in the speaker's scheme of things) as a "legitimate" occasion for lying – and lying sincerely. Some of North's assertions suggest that he views the Committee as tacitly aiding the purposes of foreign agents and terrorists. Such a connection legitimates lying within the terms asserted by North and (in part) acceded to by the Committee. That is, the Committee did not challenge North's lies to foreign agents and terrorists; only his lies to "the American people." The link between the Committee (and particularly the Committee majority) and the American people proved to be rather fragile. So, North's assurances that he's not lying to the Committee (and his expressions of offence at the very insinuation that he might be having "a convenient memory lapse") can of course simply be heard as "true," despite North's admissions of lies on other occasions. In that sense there is no paradox. But, if one suspects that North is lying, he may nonetheless bring off a justification for those lies by impugning the Committee's mandate. (A *Newsweek* poll suggests he did just that.[7]) In either case the assertions will be made *sincerely* if we treat "sincerity" not in terms of an ideal speech community, but in reference to a "home" community in a politically fractured situation. Once the Committee's mandate is linked to the interests of foreign agents, it no longer counts as part of North's community, and he might as well be meeting with "Iranians."

Conclusion

The administration's defenders claimed that the Iran-contra affair was, in essence, a political dispute, and not the result of the discovery of serious transgressions by the executive branch. We have seen how North and Sullivan worked to legitimate that argument by turning the asymmetric dialogue of the interrogation into a scene where an accused hero confronts the entrenched bureaucrats. This set-up was, in part, negotiated by Sullivan and North before the hearings; but this negotiation space was also used and opened-up as the hearings evolved. We've examined some of the details, but the "space" in which North operated, and was allowed to operate, was not simply a consequence of his conversational virtuosity. The "clearing" for his oft-quoted speeches warning of threats abroad and denouncing enemies at home was secured through aggressive maneuverings by his legal staff and allies on the committees; and, of course, he was aided immeasurably by the quick identification of him as the "hero" that "America needs."

Consequently, the tension between speech and text (or testimony and evidence) that Derrida and Searle try to resolve in their debate became a practical problem and a resource for the participants in the tribunal. There is no settling the debate *in general*, although a pragmatic stand-off worked to North's advantage. He and his lawyers used this tension between evidence and testimony as a resource for problematizing the civics lesson represented by the ceremonial of truth, so that it was multiplied into at least two incommensurable civics lessons. The publication of separate minority and majority reports under the same cover[8] testified to, and gave evidence of, this doubling. By exploiting equivocalities in documents, already designed, erased, or shredded, in order to preserve plausible deniability, and by enlisting the themes of right-wing popular culture, North managed to convert the spectacle of the hearings into a forum for his dubious heroism.

Notes

1. On the "cultural significance" of Watergate see, for instance, Alexander (1984).
2. The official history of the Iran-contra affair is presented in Inouye and Hamilton (1988). This document also includes a minority report (pp. 371-459), elaborating a reconstruction of the key events and a set of recommendations more supportive of the administration's side. Other reports and chronologies include Tower, Muskie and Scowcroft (1987) and Armstrong (1987).
3. This point is elaborated in Bogen and Lynch (1989).
4. The reference to a "civics lesson" comes from Michel Foucault's (1979) reference to the public execution as a "living lesson in the museum of order" (p. 112). One need not read post-structuralist theory to appreciate this point. A newspaper article on the criminal trial of John Poindexter, North's boss at the National Security Council, describes the prosecutor's opening presentation to the jury as follows:

> [Dan K.] Webb, 44, a boyish-looking Chicago prosecutor with flat

> Midwestern vowels and a common-man manner, offered the jurors *a tightly*
> *organized history and civics lesson* for about an hour and three quarters,
> interwoven with accusations of lies, obfuscation and conspiracy on the part
> of the defendant. (Bronner, 1990: 10; emphasis added)

5. See Bogen and Lynch (1989) for elaboration. Our concept of "master nar-
    rative" differs in at least one important respect from the more familiar use of
    the term by Lyotard (1984) and other post-structuralists. Where Lyotard
    treats "master narratives" or "grand narratives" as abstract structures of dis-
    course that tacitly organize the assertions and naturalistic assumptions in a
    culture, we refer to specifically built-up stories about a particular series of
    events. Such master narratives are also abstract, but they are not composed
    strictly of general themes, types of characters, and plotlines; instead, they are
    presented as a factual "record" of times, dates, particular persons, actions, and
    places. The "master" status comes into play as presumed facts of the matter
    to which a particular witness' testimony is held accountable. A master nar-
    rative is defeasible, but since it is built-up through a history of agreements and
    concordances between various records and testimonies, it is not easily dis-
    placed.

6. It may be interesting to consider the interpretive problems faced by the jurors
    at North's criminal trial in light of the clause: "anyone who knew anything
    about the affair ...." The persons who sat on that jury were selected precisely
    because they avowed little knowledge of the much-publicized admissions
    North made during the hearings. It is doubtful that this disengagement from
    publicity guaranteed anything like "objectivity."

7. *Newsweek*, July 20, 1987. The question was : "Is North telling the whole
    truth, is he holding back certain information to protect himself, or is he hold-
    ing back certain information to protect others?" The responses were reported
    as follows: "Whole truth" 19%; "Protecting himself" 23%; "Protecting others"
    53%.

8. See endnote 2.

Appendix I: Methodological Appendix: Ethnomethodology

Ethnomethodology is an approach to the study of practical action and practical
reasoning initially developed by Harold Garfinkel. Garfinkel came up with the
term "ethnomethodology" in the 1950s when he was engaged in a study of jury
deliberations. A jury room had been bugged, and a number of prominent social
scientists wanted to investigate the tapes of how the jurors conducted their deliberations. Garfinkel noticed that the jurors addressed a number of "methodological" issues in the course of their deliberations. He noted that the jurors did not act
as though they were scientists, but that they nevertheless concerned themselves
with making adequate interpretations of the evidence, making use of precedents,
rendering judgments on the credibility of witnesses, and putting together plausible
reconstructions of events outside the courtroom. As he put it:

... you have this interesting acceptance, so to speak, of these magnificent methodological things, if you permit me to talk that way, like "fact" and "fancy" and "opinion" and "my opinion" and "your opinion" and "what we're entitled to say" and "what the evidence shows" and "what can be demonstrated" and "what actually he said" as compared with "what only you think he said" or "what he seemed to have said." You have these notions of evidence and demonstration and of matters of relevance, of true and false, of public and private, of methodic procedure, and the rest. At the same time the whole thing was handled by all those concerned as part of the same setting in which they were used by the members, by these jurors, to get the work of deliberations done. That work for them was deadly serious. (Hill and Crittenden, 1968: 6-7. See also Garfinkel, 1974; and Heritage, 1984)

The jurors did not use the sorts of methods social scientists, jurists, or other professionals use. However, the fact that they did not use professionally credited methods was not necessarily an indication of irrationality, error, ignorance, or bias. Professional standards did not, and could not, apply to the local situation in which deliberations were done.

Consequently, Garfinkel recommended that sociologists could put aside their professional concerns with the methodology of the social sciences, while seeking to investigate the "ethno-methodologies" used in various other settings of conduct. Even though "ordinary" methods may seem to be dim-witted, loose, biased, or otherwise faulty ways of conducting inquiries, they are substantively part of the way routine social scenes are "assembled." Participants in all sorts of lay and professional activities have an interest in getting facts straight, distinguishing truths from lies, finding out how one or another organization "really works" and so forth. To say that they act unscientifically does not address how their inquiries construct and maintain the social settings in which they take place. Garfinkel was not suggesting that common sense "methods" are generally adequate for social scientific purposes, or that we have no right to criticize them; rather, he was recommending that we investigate the constitutive relationship between commonsense methods and the stable social structures in which they take place.

An "ethnomethodological transformation" of methodological topics therefore involves the following sort of procedure:
(1) Take a "methodological" problem (like, for instance, the difference between fact and opinion, the relationship between what someone says and what they "really mean," the question of whether professed reasons should be accepted as adequate explanations).
(2) Treat the problem as a matter of local concern in a particular kind of practical inquiry (such as the jury example).
(3) Describe the way members handle the problem, and how the problem *along with the way it is handled* are embedded in routine courses of action (jury deliberations and their outcomes; coroner's investigations into the causes of death; suicide-prevention center personnel's methods for discerning the difference between a serious and a crank call). (Garfinkel, 1967)
For a discussion of more recent studies that perform various ethnomethodological transformations of methodological topics in the social sciences, see Button (1991).

Appendix II: Transcript: July 7, 1987: Morning Session -- 9:00 A.M.

The transcript (prepared from a recording of a public television broadcast) begins after several minutes of argument over North's request to give an opening statement, and complaints by Sullivan about lack of time to study documents. Begin at p. 8 of *Taking the Stand.* See Appendix (p. 259) for a description of transcription conventions.

```
 1 Inouye:    Mister Nields, proceed.
 2            (1.5)
 3 Nields:    Colonel North, you were involved in two:, (0.8) operations of
 4            this government of great significance to the people of this
 5            country, is that correct?
 6            (1.0)
 7 North:     At least two. Yessir.
 8 Nields:    And one of them involved the support of the contras during
 9            the time the Boland Amendment was in effect, (0.5)  and
10            another one involved the sale of arms to Iran.
11            (2.0)
12 Nields:    Is that correct?
13            (0.8)
14 North:     Ye::s, (ih) it also involved support for:: the democratic out-
15            come in Nicaragua both before an:d *af*ter the Boland Amend-
16            ment was in effect.
17            (2.4)
18 Nields:    And these operations were carried out in secret.
19            (1.5)
20 North:     W:::we *ho*ped so.
21 Nields:    They were *covert* operations.
22 North:     Yes they were.
23 Nields:    And covert operations are designed to be secrets:, from our
24            enemies.
25            (1.0)
26 North:     That is correct.
27 Nields:    But the:se operations were designed to be secrets from the
28            American people.
29            (2.0)
30 North:     Mister Nields, I:'m- at a *loss* as to how we could announce it
31            to the American people and not have the Soviets know about
32            it.  (1.5) An' I'm not trying to be *flip*pant, but I just don't see
33            how you can possibly do it.
34 Nields:    Uh- well, in fa:ct Colonel North, you believed that the Soviets
35            were awa::re of our sale of arms to Iran, weren't you.
36            (2.5)
37
```

38		about that.
39	Nields:	But- but it was designed to be kept a secret from the Amer-
40		ican people.
41		(3.0)
42	North:	I- I think what- what is important, uh Mister- Nields is thet-
43		°hhhh (1.0) we somehow arrive at some kind of an under-
44		standing right here and no::w, as to what a covert operation is.
45		If we could find a way to insulate with a bubble over (0.6)
46		these *hear*ings that are being broadcast in Moscow, (0.4) uh-
47		(0.2) a- and *talk* about covert operations to the American
48		people without it getting into the hands of our adversaries,
49		I'm sure we would *do* that. //But (we haven't)] found a way
50		to do: it.
51	Nields:	//But you (put)]
52	Nields:	But you put it somewhat differently, to:: the Iranians to who-
53		with whom you were negotiating (0.4) on the eighth and ninth
54		of October in Frankfurt, Germany, didn't you. (0.8) You
55		said to them:, (2.4) that- EHHM ((throat clear))- "Secretary
56		of Defense Weinberger, in our last session with the President
57		said, 'I don't think we should send one more screw::'" –
58		talking about the Hawk parts – "'until we have our Americans
59		back from Beirut, because when the American people find out
60		that this has happened, they'll impeach you'" – referring to
61		the President.
62	Sullivan:	*Objection.* Apparently counsel is reading from a transcript of
63		a: tape recording uh- Mister Chairman, °hhhh uh:- uh- which
64		Colonel North may have uh cau::sed to be made. And we
65		have not uh been provided with a co:py of that material, and I
66		think it's inappropriate for questions to be a:sked to the Colo-
67		nel when *coun*sel has a copy of the tape but we do no:t have
68		it. Thank you sir.
69	Nields:	Colonel North does have a //copy of it.
70	(Inouye):	//(yes)
71	Nields:	It was //sent to him-
72	Inouye:	//(the) objection is overruled.
73	Nields:	It was sent to him over the weekend, and it's in a: *notebook*
74		in front of counsel,
75		(1.4)
76	Sullivan:	Well, fine. Thank you Mister Nields, I//-
77	Nields:	//titled- titled "Second Chan//el."
78	Sullivan:	//as I walked in the door at five minutes after I was handed-
79		a:ll these notebooks which I'm now uh: looking at for the first
80		time. Do you want to direct my attention to where it is, sir?
81		(0.6) Which book, and wha//t page
82	Nields:	//(In a)] notebook titled, "Second Channel Transcripts," at
83		Tab Fi:ve.
84		(8.0)

85 Nields: I believe it's the top notebook that you put your papers on top
86   of.
87   (8.5)
88 Sullivan: (Th') Tab *Five,* sir?
89 Nields: Tab Fi::ve.
90   (9.0)
91 Sullivan: And what page, sir?
92 Nields: It's right at Tab Five. On that page.
93   (8.5)
94 Sullivan: (Well)- Would you give us a moment to read it, sir?
95   (0.8)
96 Nields: Yes.
97   (2.5)
98 North: Tab Fi::ve°
99   (2.5)
100 Judy Woodruff [TV commentator]: What Colonel North and his attor-
101   ney Brendan Sullivan are looking at (.) is //copy of notebooks,
102 Sullivan: //(uhm,)
103   (0.8)
104 Woodruff: //Colonel North kept]
105 Sullivan: //Could you help us] out, Mister Nields? Do I begin
106   read//ing,
107 Woodruff: while he worked in the White House.
108 Sullivan: right on Tab Five, or the page behind it?
109 Nields: Right on Tab Five, and my question is simple. Did you tell
110   the Iranians (0.5) with whom you were negotiating on Octo-
111   ber Eighth and Ninth that the Secretary of Defense had told
112   the President at his most recent meeting, (0.5) "When the
113   American people find out that this has happened they'll im-
114   peach (you)."
115   (2.8)
116 (North):   °(Where did he   )° ((paper shuffling)) °(I don't
117   see it)°
118   (1.0)
119 Nields: That's the entire question. Did you say that to the Iranians?
120 Sullivan: Uh- does it say that on this page, sir?
121 Nields: Yes, at the very to:p.
122   (11.0)
123 North: Mister Nields, this is a- apparently, uh- one of thee uh- tran-
124   scripts of tape recordings thet *I* cau:sed to be ma:de, of my
125   discussions with the Iranians. I would like to note, °hh thet
126   for *every* conversation, whenever it was possible, (0.4) I
127   asked for thee (.) assistance of our intelligence services, to
128   trans- to tape record and transcribe every single session.
129   (0.5) So that, when I returned there would be no doubt as to
130   what I said. (0.4) I: am the one who created these tapes °hh
131   plus the seven hours of tape recordings that your committee

132		found yesterday because I knew where they were, and I kept
133		trying to alert you to them, and *I:* am the one who created
134		those tapes so there would *never* be any doubt (.) in the minds
135		of my superiors as to what I had said, or why I had said it.
136		That is a *bald-faced li::e* told to the Iranians. An' I will tell
137		you right now, I'd have offered the Iranians a free trip to
138		*Dis*neyland if we could have gotten Americans home for it.
139		(0.8)
140	Nields:	Question was: Did you sa:y it.
141	North:	I- I s- absolutely said it. °hhhh I said a lot of other things to
142		the Iranians=
143	Nields:	=An' when //the Hasen-
144	North:	//to get the Americans //out.]
145	Nields:	//And] when the Hasenfus plane went down down in Nicara-
146		gua, (1.5) thee United States government told the American
147		people, (0.4) °(tch)° that the United States government h:ad
148		no connection whatsoever (.) with that airplane. (0.5) Is that
149		also true.
150	North:	(Um)- I- (0.4) when I- when (yee) Hasenfus airplane went
151		down, I was headed for Europe. (1.0) So, I do not know
152		what the initial statements were an' I couldn't comment on
153		them.=
154	Sullivan:	=But *who::* in the government and wh*en,* sir? Are you ask-
155		ing him *gen*erally did someone in the government (0.4) make
156		a statement,
157		(1.2)
158	Sullivan:	( )// I- I- I think we'd make-]
159	Nields:	//We've had testi-] We've had testimony that Elliot Abrams-
160	Inouye:	((Off-mike)) Address the Chair if you have any ques//tions.
161	Sullivan:	Yes sir::. I think 'et we'd- perhaps make more progress if he
162		asked, what the Colonel did, what he said, what he hear:d,
163		with respect to his actions, uh- a statement (.) indicating that
164		uh- what someone in the American *gov*ernment had- uh had
165		said, seems to me to be a little far afield, sir. That's my only
166		comment, thank you=
167	Inouye:	=Mister Nields, proceed.
168		(2.8)
169	Nields:	That was not true, was it Colonel North.
170		(1.0)
171	North:	Which was not true, Mister //Nields?
172	Nields:	//It is not true that the United States government had no
173		connection (.) with Mister Hasenfus' airplane that went down
174		in Nicaragua.
175	North:	No it was not true, I had a: (.) indirect connection with that
176		flight.
177	Nields:	Now in certain (0.5) *com*munist //countries]
178	North:	//and many] others, I would point out.

179 Nields: In certain communis:t (.) countries, the government's activi-
180   ties are kept secret from the people. But that's not the way
181   we do things in America, is it?
182   (2.2)
183 North: Counsel, I would to go back to what I said just a few mo-
184   ments ago. I think it is very important for the American
185   people to understand, that this is a: dangerous world, that we
186   live at risk, (0.4) and that this nation is at risk. (0.4) in a
187   dangerous wor:ld, (1.0) and that they (et-) they ought not to
188   be led to believe as a consequence of these hearings, (0.4)
189   that this nation cannot or should not conduct covert opera-
190   tions. °hh By their very nature, covert operations, or special
191   activities, (0.6) are a *lie::*. (1.4) There is great deceit- (0.6)
192   deception, (0.8) practiced in the conduct of covert opera-
193   tions. They are at essence, a lie. (1.0) We make every effort
194   to deceive the enemy as to our intent, (0.4) our conduct, and
195   to deny thee (.) association of the United States with those
196   activities.   The intelligence committees hold hearings on °hh
197   all kinds of these activities, (0.4) conducted by our intelli-
198   gence services. (0.5) °(eh)° (The) American people ought
199   not to be led to believe by the way you're asking that *ques-*
200   *ti*on, (0.5) that (.) we intentionally deceive the American
201   people. (1.0) Or had that intent to be*gin* with. The effort to
202   conduct these covert operations (0.6) was ma::de in such a
203   way (0.5) that our adversaries would not have knowledge of
204   them. Or that we could deny American association with
205   them. Or the associated- the association of this government
206   (.) with those activities. And that is not wrong.
207 Nields: Thee American:: (.) people (0.4) were told by this government
208   (1.4) that ou::r government had nothing to do (0.4) with the
209   Hasenfus airplane. (0.6) °hh And that was false.   And it is
210   a: principal purpose (0.4) of these hearings °hhhh to replac:e
211   (1.0) secrecy and deception (0.5) with disclosure and truth.
212   And that's one of the reasons we have called you here sir.
213   (0.5) °hh And one question the American people would like
214   to know the answer to (0.5) °(tch)° is what did the President
215   know (0.4) about the diversion (0.4) of the proceeds of Ira-
216   nian arms sales (0.2) to the contras.   Can you tell us what you
217   know about that, sir.
218   (0.6)
219 North: You just took a long leap from Mister Hasenfus's airplane.

Chapter 4

Victim, Offender and Witness in the Emplotment of News Stories[1]

Jeff Stetson

"Knowledge is, in the end, based on acknowledgement"[2]

This chapter is concerned with the concepts of "victim" and "offender," the public assignment of which is sometimes problematical. In earlier work, my efforts were primarily focused on the category of "victim" (Stetson, 1989, 1993). In this chapter, I take up matters of the assignability of blame or responsibility to the category "offender" and the expanded notion of "who *really* is to blame" for someone's "victimhood" under conditions of equivocality. The analysis will focus on issues emergent in a specific incident that occurred in the Nishifunabashi railway station in Chiba, Japan. Briefly, as the story was reported in newspapers, an exotic dancer, while returning home by public transportation, was accosted by a school teacher who, at the time, was intoxicated. To ward off his insistent verbal abuse and improper physical contact, she pushed him aside; he stumbled and fell into the path of an oncoming train and was killed.

Newspaper accounts of the event included explanations of who (or what) "really" caused this event to occur; the issue being: Who was the "victim," who the "offender"? Subsequently, various feminist spokespersons objected to the characterization of the woman as an "exotic dancer" which, to some journalists, stood as sufficient explanation for the teacher's behavior. The incident became a *cause célèbre* and sparked prolonged debate.

My interest here is to trace the sequence of events and to explore the "temporal relevancies" in the ascription of the categories of "victim," "offender" and "witness." My assertion is that these events can quite often be story-able and the place where advocates for one side or the other *end* the story is consequential for the final "resolution" of "victim" and "offender" statuses. The fundamental tenet guiding this research is that the use of the concepts victim and offender, as warrantable descriptors of persons, is a matter which is negotiated and assigned in interaction. The "storied" character of the events, (with attendant ambiguities and equivocalities, at the time of the event leading to a death, *and* the legal/moral procedures which followed) was occasioned through a "search procedure" and "category-collection *expansion*" to handle the question: "Who-is-to-blame" for the tragedy? The newspaper articles and editorials which provided the data for analysis are reproduced in the Appendix at the end of this chapter (p. 105).

Sacks' "Rules of Description" Applied to the Analysis of "News"

Lena Jayyusi (1984) establishes the task set before us:

> The structures of, and the practical production of intelligibility are the abiding analytical concern.... It results in the systematic uncovering of various cultural conventions that *enable* the production of sense, of practical actions, and that inform the organization of social relations and the various practices of social life. (p. 3)

Jayyusi calls for "...the investigation of the cultural structures of intelligibility and the practical methods by which they are produced, displayed, understood and *engaged* by members...." (p. 3) Following Jayyusi, the present work approaches the analysis of the concepts of victim and offender through the explication of the "formal properties of culture and the *in situ* production of practical activities" (p. 3). It is in the production of these intersubjective activities that members produce and reproduce an "unrelievedly moral order." Our entry is through the study of the practices of what Harvey Sacks called "membership categorization."

Sacks (1972a) distinguished between the conventional sociological notion of "role" and what he called "categories." Categorizations are ordinary practices in which members are engaged in the characterization of themselves and of one another. Though the term "role" is perhaps quite suitable for the analyses he produced, it suffers the misfortune of carrying some dramaturgical connotations from other perspectives within sociology[3] which take "role" to be a set of activities that an individual is merely "playing at" or "enacting." Sacks' conceptualization of category can be summarized as follows: Who someone *is*, is a function of what one is doing, when, where, and with whom. We are dealing here with a sensitivity to a set of activities produced at some locally relevant time in some relevant context of persons and things. "Categories" are not merely an analyst's typological convenience, for we can readily see that members *need* categories to "hear," "see," etc. That is, by *categories* competent members *know* what is being done by whom.[4]

In the events described at the beginning of this chapter, there were many potentially relevant categories assignable to the parties for purposes of producing a recognizable description of "what went on," for example, "man," "teacher," "kind person," "drunk," "accoster," "insulter," "abuser," "commuter," "woman," "exotic dancer," "irked person," "shover," etc. Sacks (1972b) pointed out that members have resources for making sense of the events around themselves by utilizing what he called "devices" and doing so in accord with their "rules of application." Specifically these are: "membership categorization devices," "relevance rules," and "reference satisfactoriness rules" (Sacks, 1972b: 332). For culture members, who have no time out from making sense, these abstract rules *enable* producing and hearing some description which can be understood, or "seen" as intelligible, rational, sensible, and logical, that is, part of and constitutive of everyday reality.

Here I will provide a brief overview of these rules, to be later followed by examples. One such reference satisfactoriness rule is the "economy rule," which states that the category chosen to describe some member need only be referentially adequate for the purpose of recognizing some phenomenon for whatever it might be. Humans have culturally-furnished, commonsense intersubjective resources for seeing and hearing what is being done and by whom. Jeff Coulter (1979b) puts it cogently in the following:

Commonsense amounts to a set of culturally-furnished *abilities*. Such abilities constitute the doing of any mundane activity, such as transmitting information in various contexts, recommending something to someone, persuading someone about something, enumerating, grading, complaining, insulting, warning, apologizing, thanking, promising, ascribing statuses, and countless other practical actions. To say of someone that he is *able to* do such things means that he *knows how to* do them, and this practical knowledge forms the central core of what is here being described as 'commonsense knowledge of social structures.' (p. 21)

To produce an appropriate, logical, intelligible reference to person(s) and event(s) is to correctly utilize intersubjective resources. By economy rule is meant that even though any person is an incumbent of a large array or set of categories, the seeing, hearing and referring to another is through a selection from among available categories.[5] This selection is quite normally done with the goal of producing the minimum of referents that will enable recognition for the one seeing and to any others being told about persons or events. Also, since events and persons engaged in those events do not occur in some unimaginable, gestalt-free setting, the *who* being referred to is also a function of the *context* in which events are occurring and reference is being made.[6] Sacks (1972b: 334) also pointed out that a great deal of ordinary, as well as technical, knowledge is "category-bound," meaning that we can, for cases of category-bound actions, see *who* someone is along with *what* it is they are doing by dint of the way actions and categories are conventionally bound together. For example,"cops" arrest suspects, "physicians" diagnose medical disorders, "employers" fire persons, "judges" sentence convicted persons to prison and "babies" cry.[7] Moreover, there are things that "everyone knows" about incumbents of categories, whether for good, bad, or indifferent. We "know" categorially that "priests" are religious, "artists" are creative and spontaneous, and "drunks" potentially abusive. Taken to situated "extremes" (itself a moral assessment), such category-knowledge linkages can degenerate into "stereotypes"; however, the existence of such negative forms of a practice of description does not undermine the diverse socio-logical properties and functions of that practice in its non-derogatory modality, most of which, far from being negative in nature, are *necessary* for communicative sensemaking.

A relevance rule proposed by Sacks is the "consistency rule" for the categorization of persons. A corollary to this rule is a "hearers' maxim" whereby if two or more categories are used in describing two or more persons, and if these categories can be heard as being from the same "membership categorization device,"[8] then: hear them that way. "The rule provides for participants' co-orientation to a shared order of relevance when making social reference to persons" (Watson, 1976:62). Finally, Sacks observed that certain categories (e.g., bride and groom) are what he called "duplicatively organized," that is, that certain categories go together like teams (Sacks, 1972b:338).

Sacks' most notable explication of these devices and rules is his analysis of a child's story: "The baby cried. The mommy picked it up" (1972b). Though it may also be *correct* to describe the baby as a boy, it is recognitionally adequate simply to say "baby"; likewise with "mommy," who may alternatively and for other purposes/contexts be correctly categorized as, among other identities, "scientist," "Republican," "granddaughter," "sister," "veteran," etc. It is here where we see "economy" of description at work. Although a "mommy" may also be a "politician," and although it may be factually correct to say "The baby cried, the politician picked it up," the *inclusion* of "politician" in the story calls for explanation, or, at least, conveys an entirely different sense of the scene. This observation reflects an important facet of our commonsense reasoning, one that is entirely relevant to practical determinations of agency, motive, knowledge-structure, and other informational and adjudicatory elements.

Consider the following newspaper headline from an article describing the events at Nishifunabashi station: "Drunk Irks Woman, Killed by Train" (1/16/86). We can see the above rules at work so as to provide for *anyone* being able to understand that which he/she is about to be informed. Of particular note is the issue of duplicatively-organized categories. One need not presume that all, or even most, drunks are men to hear that the drunk in this headline is, indeed, a man. The use of the category "woman" is sufficient to imply, retrospectively, that the contrast class "man" "must" be the gender of the referent "drunk." The terms, "man"-"woman" are relationally paired, mutually constitutive and co-members of a membership category device we call "gender."[9]

Also, because of what "everyone knows" about "drunks," the headline is readable as reporting another case of a drunk's irksomeness, something "typical" of drunks. Note, that if the "irking" had been described as having been committed by a gentle and respected high school teacher (which was indeed what his co-workers and students are quoted as saying) this would be a quite surprising ascription given what is conventionally known about the category "high school teacher." A similar situation obtains for the woman's (Momota's) correct, but, *here*, not relevant incumbency in the category "exotic dancer."[10] A headline such as: "*Teacher* Irks Exotic Dancer, Killed by Train" might lead any reader to form a list of vastly disparate conclusions. In the headline investigated by John Lee (1984) and elaborated upon by Watson (1976), viz., "Girl Guide Aged 14 Raped at Hell's Angels Convention," we might agree that the:

> ...incumbents of the category Girl Guide are conventionally assigned the characteristics of innocence, helpfulness, the pursuit of good works, and that the age-grading categorization "aged 14" underlines the characterization of innocence and naiveté, thus eminently being a candidate for the categorization of innocent victim. (Watson, 1976:63)

In the case under examination, however, one might not unproblematically assign those characteristics to someone who has been described as an "exotic dancer." Nor could one straightforwardly slant the news report about what happened to the "exotic dancer" (irked, bothered) in terms of the traumatic, dramatic nature of the Girl Guide events.

That members can and normally do see and hear matters in this way inspired David Sudnow (1987) to coin the phrase "normal crimes" for specific offenses whose particulars can, for some set of persons, be represented as "typical" rather than unusual for offenses of their class. Sudnow elaborates and provides an example:

> I shall call *normal crimes* those occurrences whose typical features, e.g., the ways they usually occur and the characteristics of persons who commit them (as well as the typical victims and typical scenes), are known and attended to by [public defenders]. For any of a series of offense types, the P.D. can provide some form of proverbial characterization. For example ... child molesting is seen as typically entailing middle-aged strangers or lower class middle-aged fathers (few women), no actual penetration or severe tissue damage, mild fondling, petting, and stimulation, bad marriage circumstances, multiple offenders with the same offense repeatedly committed, a child complainant, via the mother, etc. (p. 156)

A major point to be made here is, whether in newspaper headlines or in everyday explanations,[11] an *ascription* carries with it an "explanation of events."[12] As it relates to crime, "newsworthiness" depends in part upon being intriguing, dramatic, disturbing or threatening (Stetson and Sato, 1996: 118). It was in and through the selection of the category "Drunk" (with a category-bound activity of "Drunks," "irking," that provided the reader with an explanation of the newsworthy event, to wit, "killed." One possible gloss of the headline, "Drunk Irks Woman, Killed by Train," could be: Some drunk acted like an ass in a dangerous environment, as we all know that drunks often do, and got himself killed.[13] However, since most news items of this sort do not remain a matter of single reports (because of newsworthiness, legal time schedules, etc.), the continued relevance of any set of categories chosen for the initial description is open to equivocation and change.[14] I will elaborate on this claim of equivocation later in the chapter.

As in any form of description/storytelling, newspaper stories provide for the proximate co-presence of "victim" and "offender" by treating these categories as members of the device "parties to the offense." It is important to note that another category from the membership categorization device (or "collection") might be "witness." Given that there were other persons present on the railway platform prior to the drunk falling into the path of the train, i.e., potential witnesses, questions were asked by lay and professional commentators as to why the bystanders did not intervene between offender and victim during the course of the "witnessed" assaults. Please notice in the following excerpts from the news accounts and editorial, that the "witnessed" characteristics of this scene remained relevant, storied and consequential over time and across the domains of report of incident, police investigations, and final adjudication of the case.

> Tsuyoshi Sasho, deputy station master of Nishifunabashi Station, quoted Momota as saying that she had cried for help but was ignored by the people around her and she pushed the man. Sasho said there were about 100 people on the platform at the time and at least 20-30 were close to Momota. (1/18/86)

> There were about 100 people on the platform at the time, but none offered to help the woman when she cried out for help. (1/17/86)

> Our criticism, therefore, must fall upon the many people who stood around on the platform ignoring the woman's cries. (1/18/86)

> Momota told police that the man had verbally and physically harassed her at the station that night. She cried out for help, but was ignored by people around her, she said. (1/19/86)

> The defense asserted that the act was in self-defense since bystanders did nothing to help her. (9/18/87)

Coulter and Parsons (1990) point out that for any perceptual claim to acquire the status of *achieved* perception, the claim must, at least implicitly, be ratified by other members. This ratification is based upon "what there is," conventionally, "to be seen." It is interesting to note that once the category "witness" has been "established," a "flip-side-of-the-perception-coin principle" can be applied, i.e., "if you were there and if you were a witness to the events, you *must* have seen X, Y, and Z." As Watson (1978: 106) put it: "These matters may be claimed as noticeably absent and as specially accountable." Mapping this onto the present case, since members are not sovereign with respect to what is intelligibly "seeable," it also stands to reason that, even when *not* co-present to specific events, one is capable of projecting "what was there to be seen." We might refer to this phenomenon as "*post hoc* assessment of perceptual claims."

These inquiries were raised as though by "natural right," as obviously imperative matters.[15] Thus, the consistency rule may be said to warrant a search for a "victim" and "witnesses" to the assault as soon as an "offender" has been introduced. This can also work the other way around.

The categories, "offender," "victim" and "witness" are available together for descriptions and characterizations of the event. These categories can be seen as canonically adequate for the occasioned or *in situ* events. Other categories can, of course, be applied to scenes where actions are deemed "deviant," for example, categories such as "the police," "courtroom personnel," etc. As mentioned above, some newsworthy events are reported upon over an extended period of time, and the journalistic accounts of such events can come to exhibit what I will call *storied category shifts* and *storied category-collection expansions*. Before applying these terms to the events described above, let us examine how these concepts may apply to the cultural evolution of the generic concept "rape."

The crime of rape has, over the last couple of decades, undergone a major cultural transformation. It is now characterized by laypersons, media reporters and many criminologists not as an act of sex but rather has been *shifted* to the class of actions: violence or aggression.[16] What was, only a short time ago, thought to be improbable if not impossible was that a female could rape a male. Though it might be some time before it attains the status of a "normal crime," the event of a female being arrested, indicted, tried, convicted and imprisoned for rape is no longer the newsworthy event it once was taken to be. Further, rape no longer exclusively applies to a crime between strangers but now includes relational *circumstances* of human interaction which, until quite recently, would have seemed irrelevant to rape, namely, marriage, dating, and acquaintanceship (as in "date-rape" and "marital rape," two constructions now readily available in our culture which were alien to the prevailing conceptions of rape of, say, conservatively, thirty years ago). The association with violence remains constant; what has changed is an inclusion or expansion of possible contexts and person categories for which and to whom the concept may be applied.

In the next section I will begin with an analysis of the appropriate place for "explaining" as a members' resource, followed by an analysis of the "search for who is to blame" found in the news stories and editorials concerning the railway platform incident.

Category-Collection Expansion in the Case Under Investigation

Below, I will lay out the rules governing "explaining"/ascribing/avowing. But I first want to make clear that ethnomethodological analysis of the media (or any other domain of human action) does not seek to adjudicate whether the news reports are "right" or "wrong." A great deal of ink has been spilt on the topic of "journalistic bias," "subjective tendencies" and concerns over "the undue power of the few with access to express themselves via mass communication." I propose that those critiques are for domains with goals other than scientific analysis of human action.

[I]t is proposed instead that serious attention be given to the observation that agents' [members'] reason-giving practices are *themselves* kinds of social actions along with the actions for which reasons may be given. Instead of seeking to adjudicate the rightness or wrongness of agents' reasons for some decontextualized purposes, we should attend instead to the elucidation of 'reason-giving' as comprising varieties of rule-governed practices in which we participate. (Coulter, 1989: 5)

Coulter further (1989: 103ff) analyzes the rules governing members' intelligible "explanation" of their own and others' conduct utilizing one set of ascriptions and avowals (from a number of available inter-subjectively, culturally-furnished sets), specifically, personality ascriptions/avowals.[17] That these same rules are applicable to an analysis of media accounts only speaks to the power and generalizability of the ethnomethodological approach.

Intelligible "explanation" (reason giving by use of ascription/avowal, and here, category selection) is a function of: 1) the action done, in 2) a context or circumstance, 3) for an audience with its interests and purposes. An elegant feature of this elucidation is the fact that if we were to change any one of the above formulaic elements of reason giving, the intelligible "explanation" changes. For example, 1) the action of one man punching another, 2) at a party (versus a boxing match) and 3) witnessed by friends, enemies, acquaintances, customers, strangers, or sports fans, etc. would have diverse "explanations" produced for, applied to, and reported about it.

Coulter also points out that ascription and avowals are not an ongoing, omni-relevant activity. As with the criteria of newsworthy crime reports (again, that they be intriguing, dramatic, disturbing or threatening), members do not – as a matter of practice in daily discourse – produce explanations for *normal* activities. The challenge of the "Why did you brush your teeth?" is not in producing an answer satisfying causal sufficiency; the challenge is in making sense of the question. "Stetson Eats Breakfast, Cooked by Same" without contextual particulars making this somehow intriguing, dramatic, disturbing and/or threatening might elicit some doubts within the reader of this "news" about the competency of those reporting such a mundane activity. In the following excerpt, we see that the editorialist saw the railway incident as anything but mundane.

The incident that occurred late the other night at Nishifunabashi Station in Chiba arouses a confusion of emotions. It was altogether a tragic affair, one with such multiple losses that we cannot let it fade without trying to gain something out of it. ... a drunken man ... fell onto the tracks and was killed by an incoming train. ... The tragic element was heightened when we learned that he was a high school physical education teacher and counselor, popular with the students and normally of polite and mild manner. (1/18/86)

Note that the "tragic" character in this news account is framed by the introduction of other categories to which the "drunken man" was also an incumbent: high school teacher, counselor, a popular person, and "as we knew him, a polite and mild mannered colleague."

Having satisfied the criteria of newsworthiness, that is, the conventional "reportability" of some event, the editors might now draw upon intersubjective resources to explain why such an event occurred in the first place.

From the news items examined so far, we have an "assaulter," a "victim of assault," and "witnesses to assault." The witnesses have been characterized as both "unhelpful" and "needed" for the legal adjudication between "victim/self-defender" or "one guilty of manslaughter."

Offender/Victim/Witness are, canonically, the exhaustive categories of "parties to an offense." However, in editorials immediately following and after twenty two months of widespread controversy[18] before the final legal determination of guilt or innocence was made, reference to an additional "party" to the offense was introduced, i.e., "the public."

> From all one hears people comment, the court did right. And not because the reputation of the living is more important than that of the dead. It is because the public generally is sensitized to the common social ill of drunks harassing people.
>
> That being so, what can we expect next? Unfortunately, no letup in such harassment, we are afraid.
>
> It will continue, that is, until the public undergoes a reforming and it becomes the common thing for bystanders to intercede for the protection of innocent targets of anti-social treatment. In the Chiba District Court, it was really the public that was on trial. (9/25/87)

Through this proposal, the collection "parties to an offense" now includes the following categories: Offender/Victim/Witness/*Public*.

The inclusion of the category "public" is, I take it, not an editorial flight-of-fancy or contrivance. It came as an answer to an immanently "natural" question: "Who is to blame?" The question can be seen as answerable only by expanding the category "offender." "Public" was a category "discovered" for the purpose of extending blame – extending blame not only to the "unhelpful witnesses" but, given the now tragic characterization of this news story, a search procedure is expanded to answer the question of how these bad things can happen to such "normally good" persons. Possible support for this observation comes from another newspaper editorial:

A Jekyll and Hyde case? Many people will say that alcohol is capable of making such a transformation of personality. This has been *recognized* especially among [members of our society] - so much as to make for the *accommodation of a traditionally permissive attitude toward drunks.*" (1/18/86, emphasis added)

Category-collection expansion was made possible here by "borrowing" on an element of the membership categorization device "parties to an offense," namely "witness." This expansion is reminiscent of Darley and Latané's (1968a, 1968b) famous account of the 1964 stabbing assault and eventual death of a woman named Kitty Genovese. Despite the extensive time period over which the assault(s) occurred and her many cries for help, none of the 38 witnesses to the crime intervened or even phoned the police. In accounting for this non-action, Darley and Latané ascribed to witnesses and cultural members in general the "malady" of "diffusion of responsibility" or "bystander apathy": Let someone else take care of it, I don't want to get involved. But in matters of such consequence, lack of involvement becomes problematic because just as not answering a question can be noticeable, and not tending to a crying baby by a present mother can be negligent, so can the non-intervention of the persons co-present and "characterizable" as witnesses on the railway platform be seen as *culpable* with regard to the tragic outcome of these events. But note that Darley and Latané's "explanation" for non-intervention provides, in effect, an excusing condition for this behavior, that is, the social psychological "malady" of "diffusion of responsibility" was the "cause" of *morally* inappropriate action. But they cannot have it both ways. As discussed above, explaining (giving reasons) is first and foremost an enormously sophisticated *members'* resource for disambiguating events in the world. However, the in principle assumption on the part of writers such as Darley and Latané is that it requires the special work of specially trained "scientific" analysts to tell the rest of us what causes us to do what we do. This is wrong-headed. Besides reducing humans down to the assumed status of molecules of gas in a balloon under varying temperatures, these writers overlook the fact that they too are humans giving reasons, but alas, "reporting" their conclusions as "causes of human action." There are no causes of human action in the ways that they propose. For if these "causes" were to be discovered, no one would *need* to blame anyone else, seek adjudication in courts of law, be defended by an attorney, etc. In short, the discovery of a cause, in the natural science sense, precludes blame. It would be absurd to blame a falling body for responding to gravity. If the study of human life were constrained by the tenets displayed in Darley and Latané, then it would be senseless for any editorialist to assign *blame* to any witnesses; commentators *could* not rationally hold the *observers* on the platform responsible for their inaction given and *because* of their "culturally accepted and supported tolerance of public intoxication." But, witnesses can act in accord with the *rules* of appropriate behavior and, of course, they can "break" those rules. The analysis of moral action and the pursuit of causal explanation in the natural scientific sense (e.g., the Hempelian version)[19] are incommensurable. This is not merely some theoretical or academic debate; the viability of any philosophical foundation for human scientific research rests upon observations of how the world, indeed, works. In our present case, seeing that the rules for intervening, demonstrating compassion, and maintaining civil order were being "broken," Momota's claim of "self defense" was subsequently tenable and accepted as an excuse by the courts because "no one would help her."[20]

What eventually, for the courts, was a sufficient resolution of blameworthiness given *their* set of relevant categories (assaulter/murder victim, self-defender/accused murderer), remained problematical for the journalistic reason givers – given their continued inclusion and relevancing of the category "unhelpful witnesses."

> "People around Momota did not help her because [our] society is permissive about drunken acts." (1/16/86)

> This has been *recognized* especially among [members of our society] - so much as to make for the *accommodation of a traditionally permissive attitude toward drunks.*" (1/18/86, emphasis added)

The commentators' claims about the public's tolerance of public intoxication is warranted by reference to *other* events of harassment, i.e., it was not sufficient to attempt to resolve the ambiguities and equivocalities in this one event alone. The singular event stands as a representative (or is constituted as a symptom) of a larger phenomenon, namely inappropriately placed tolerance. Having transformed the culpable matter into a behavior-we-all-accept-but-should-not-see-as-acceptable, the commentator was then in a position to call for a legislative change or a moral sanction. This differs from the Kitty Genovese slaying where Darley and Latané – despite their identification of "the cause" of the witnesses' non-intervention – were not in a position to call for legislation banning the witnessing of murders.[21] Note, however, that in the aftermath of such tragedies as the Genovese murder, we see the emergence of a new self-characterization of some members of the public as being, indeed, party to offenses, and efforts are made to reorganize the possible ways that incumbents of the category can intervene. Thus, we see the establishment of civilian groups such as Community Watch and the Guardian Angels riding the New York subway system.

In the data set (9/25/1987) the editorial warns:

[Harassment] will continue, that is, until the public undergoes a reforming and it becomes the common thing for bystanders to intercede for the protection of innocent targets of anti-social treatment.

The charge of public apathy is a claim that the society's members, in general, have abrogated responsibility for the prevention of crime, including a neglect to eliminate the occasional occurrence of such offensive actions. In the case at hand, non-acting witnesses notwithstanding, blame is focused upon the *public's* tolerance of public intoxication.[22] "Reform" in this context is a call for the implementation of constraints and enacted obligation; but constraints and obligation in relation to *future* events. "Future," of course, means that it has not yet occurred; there are no "bodies" relevantly incumbent to the categories of the device "parties to an offense" (offender, victim, intervening or non-intervening witnesses). By utilizing the resource *category-collection expansion*, the editors have, "in one sweep," found "someone" to blame *and* someone to address, i.e., "the public." That the "grounds" for this expansion provide for a "call to change" will be examined below in the section on "revolutionary categories," but first I would like to stop and review, by way of a closer inspection and exemplification, some terms introduced above, namely, *in situ* ambiguity and equivocality.

Ambiguities and Equivocalities

Consider the problematic of: Who was responsible for the death?

Men? Not as a matter of course do the incumbents of the category "men" go about irking "women," at least not in a category-bound sense and definitely not as a category-constitutive element "in-being-a-man." In a burlesqued Gedanken exercise we might imagine parents of a young adult son reflecting upon their achievements in raising him. "He was a good student and now a respected teacher. He is kind and generous to his family, friends, colleagues and students alike. But, you know, I think we failed him in attaining manhood because we never taught him that he should irk women." Besides, this "drunk" in other settings was seen as a gentle, responsible, concerned high school teacher.

Ryota Mori, principal of the Fukagawa High School, told reporters that Kawahara was a health and physical education teacher and was actively involved with the student body and in extra-curricular activities.

> He said that Kawahara, who also served as a guidance teacher, was a polite and mild-mannered man, adding that he was popular with his students. (1/16/86)

High school teachers also do not, as a matter of course, irk women.

Drunks? Sure, inebriated persons X, doing finite sorts of actions, in particular settings, being seen or heard by a limited set of categories as audience members "seeing some X as drunk" *can* be seen as irksome, but to suffer death for drunkenness and being irksome is far beyond any normative balancing of offense and appropriate punishment.[23]

Exotic dancers? Maybe on some occasions, the co-presence of dancers and persons imbibing too much alcohol can lead to overly zealous patrons being rebuffed, by, for instance, categories such as "bouncers." But this, too, hardly counts as justification for a homicidal act. Austin (1970) argues that in circumstances where the one being blamed utilizes justification in an attempt to get out from under that blame, responsibility for some action is accepted but a putative "wrongfulness" of the action is not granted by the one (or their "proxy") producing the action. (See note 20.) For a bouncer to successfully justify the killing of an irksome customer would require the disclosure of further contextual particulars such as the presence of lethal weaponry.

Witnesses? "Witness," like the other categories, is not an *a priori* applicable category, but clearly in this case, it is an *a posteriori* category when viewed in the totality of the ensuing events. From a Saturday, Jan. 18, 1986 editorial:

> Our criticism...must fall upon the many people who stood around on the platform ignoring the woman's cries. *Not them personally*, but the mores of our society that are at the root of this detachment in the face of somebody else's crisis. We need to reform. (emphasis added)

Of course, co-present non-acquaintances saw and heard the events leading up to a person's death, but "what" did they *see*? Coulter and Parsons (1990) propose that all "... human visual orientations are conceptually constituted (concept-bound)..." (p. 251). Competency in seeing requires the acquisition of the concepts of place, person or thing before we can "see" what it, intersubjectively/epistemologically-based/ontologically, *is* we are looking at. For example, a member (let's say, at this time of technological development and distribution of knowledge, a child) must acquire the concept "computer" and what it does and maybe something about how it is used in order to see "that box with a light inside" as, what is taken-for-grantedly seen by contextully competent adult members, *really* a computer.

Presuming all witnessing members on the train platform recognize a "drunk" when they see one, this does not, however, mean that there are not scenic events which are ambiguous, strange, hard-to-figure-out-what-is-going-on. We can see in the editorial the claim that the bystanders did not help because the "mores of our society" do not provide the appropriate concepts for them to *see* the events as ones into which the witnesses *ought to* intervene. The category "drunk" was not selected by observers as the "master category" in this scene and the offense "drunk irking woman" was, putatively, not the event that occurred for *them*. Following the commentators' claim that it is a social malady to accept drunken behavior, the bystanders could not be correctly categorizable as "witnesses to harassment of an innocent victim." To observers on the train platform one possible interpretation available, at that time, was that what was observable was not an act of "irking," but an argument between a "man" and a "woman." Arguments of this sort are neither unusual nor calling for justifiable intervention. Post-facto, the commentators were, however, making room for equivocation of what there was to be seen. But, of course, witnesses too may try to get out from under blame and claim that the equivocation stands as a witnesses' fallback position under post-facto questioning about their not coming to the aid of the harassed victim. "Oh, sure. *Now* I see who did what to whom, with the subsequent result. But at the time, I saw A, B, C as X, Y, Z." The point is not that that specific group of persons constituting "the witnesses" and, say, the newspaper editorialist on his or her way home would see the *in situ* events as they unfolded any differently; as if the true state of perception would be that the commentators see black whilst the witnesses see white. Witnesses on the platform (including the homeward-bound editorialists) saw what conventionally, culturally was there to be seen. In the news accounts and as matters were handled by legal authorities present because of a death, "drunk" and "victim of harassment" are *retrospective* perceptions. For the witnesses, at that time, and with the resources they had for seeing – perhaps an argument between a man and a woman – not unusual occurrences and, as such, do not permit of justifiable interdiction.

To highlight this last point, let me return to Sacks' (1972b) analysis of "The baby cried. The mommy picked it up." A witness to a baby's crying may surely hold the mommy culpable for *not* tending to her baby. But for a passerby – one who is not to be counted within the device "family," or "friend," or "guardian," etc. – to rush over and pick up the baby could be seen as an extraordinarily offensive action. In such circumstances, a "wait-and-see" principle is often used by members as a means of disambiguating the situation; as if to say "I must see more before I can be sure about what I am seeing and I must be wary about intervention lest I become party to an offense of my own making." In our railway death case, the period of "wait and see" was unfortunately sufficient for the fatal events to occur.[24]

In the next section, I will explore how an inchoate revolution in "seeing" as called for by the commentators can "get off the ground" by disambiguating who is doing what to whom, thus obviating equivocal claims of perception.

Revolutionary conceptualization

The following is an excerpt from an editorial published twenty one months after the incident on the train platform (9/25/87):

> From all one hears people comment, the court did right. And not because the reputation of the living is more important than that of the dead. It is because the public generally is sensitized to the common social ill of drunks harassing people. That being so, what can we expect next? Unfortunately, no letup in such harassment, we are afraid. It will continue, that is, until the public undergoes a reforming and it becomes the common thing for bystanders to intercede for the protection of innocent targets of anti-social treatment. In the Chiba District Court, it was really the public that was on trial. We are guilty all right; but there is no retributive justice against an incriminated public, unfair as that may be. In place of the judiciary, we ourselves are responsible to apply sanctions against anti-social behavior, and that is the lesson to be propagated.

Among his many elucidations, Sacks (1979) offered an explication of how it is that social change is possible without being a matter of members constantly coming to blows. Some revolutions "...are attempts to reconstruct how it is that things are seen..." (p. 10). These revolutions are not *officially* recognized nor, in fact, is the structure readily "noticeable" by those promoting such revolutions, yet change can and does occur. Members have stocks of knowledge about, for example, African-Americans as distinct from what we all know about "Blacks," and again as distinct from "Negroes." And the cultural knowledge about "women" is not the same as that about "ladies." That this knowledge is non-trivial is evidenced in the strong form of the theorem: Knowledge is concept bound.

The following is an analysis of the course of one such revolution, a revolution of seeing. Malcolm X was effective in introducing one such novel way of looking at the world, that is, as "Blacks." Malcolm X's success was to have incumbents of the category Negroes look at themselves and their actions and to see how they were viewed by others who were *not* incumbents of that category (ostensibly "Whites"). He also developed within his listeners an understanding of *which* category assumed the right to determine whether or not incumbents of "Negro" acted in accord with the rules of "proper" conduct, that is, of "proper" Negroes. His claim being that the category "Negro" was a category imposed upon them by "Whites." By that, Malcolm was claiming that Whites administered who among them was a good or bad "Negro." The "Black" revolution was a revolution of actions. No longer would incumbents of this category "sit in the back of the bus," allow themselves to be segregated with respect to where their children went to school, where they ate their lunch, etc. Most importantly, this revolution entailed that no longer would any member outside the category Black be "privileged to determine the rectitude of their conduct." And we have a similar revolution with a shift of Blacks in America turning to a perception of themselves as "Americans." Reverend Jesse Jackson, in his formulation of the concept Rainbow Coalition as a political "grouping," intended to assimilate all categories of Americans regardless of skin color. Expanding the category of racial interests to include *all* races effectively eliminates particularistic political interests. What remains is the "super category" American. Operative now are *American* ideals, ideals for what constitutes success for themselves and their children in education, housing, status, etc.

What we have here is not a mere name change. This is a revolution, a shift in *categories*. Again, categories are competent members' culturally-furnished, intersubjective resources for the characterization (including descriptions, inferences and judgments) of themselves and others *and* who someone is, is a function of what one is doing, when, where and with whom. Change any element in the "equation" and we have a change in intelligible characterization. Each of these revolutionary categories was a change in *activities* accompanied by a change in the ways incumbents of those categories *viewed themselves*. The final stage in a successful revolution, one can argue, is when incumbents of categories "outside" of the revolutionary category change the way they see incumbents of that *new* category. The logic of the argument comes full circle with the recognition that what "outsiders" have to see are the actions/activities of those members in the process and achievement of transformation.

The sense, intelligibility, and the very reality of any possible world is *constructed* by members' capacity to see what is going on with reference to the category of person or persons performing some action or set of actions. A social perceptual change occurs, not by physical or biological alteration,[25] but by the way persons are "seen" by themselves and others. Though both categories "ladies" and "women" are composed of females,[26] there is a putative difference between what they each can expect of themselves and what treatment they might expect from those not in that category, i.e., "gentlemen," "men," "mothers," or the culture in general. Revolutionary categories are functions of, or operants in, attempts to change "social reality," which, of course, can be quite consequential.

As a variant of Sacks' formulation, we might see the attempt on the commentators' part as one calling for a reconceptualization of excessive drinking, thus changing the way that drunks are viewed and subsequent constraints enforced. Without this reconceptualization, or, vernacularly, "raising the consciousness of the public," it is implied that continued tolerance can only lead to further tragic outcomes. The commentators' call for an end to the tolerance of public intoxication can be found to be proposing, then, a recommendation for a *shift* in "seeing." Members of society are enjoined to perceive a person's loud, slurred, stumbling, abusive actions as actions *not* of a man against a woman *but* of a "drunk" against anyone else, where "drunk" or "drunkenness" here stand as master categories of actions which "can not and will not be overlooked, anymore than one would not, nay, *could* not, with impunity, overlook the nontending to a crying baby or an act of rape."

The reader might incorrectly derive from this explication a notion that the foregoing demonstrates little difference from Labeling Theory. To head off this impression, I will refer the reader to an example of this latter approach in Scully's and Marolla's (1987) article "Rapists' Vocabulary of Motives" where they sought to determine the forms of excuses and justifications convicted rapists employed in "constructing their identities." The authors posited the source of these excuses and justifications within the culture, a culture which, they averred, holds inappropriate attitudes about the autonomy of women. The convicts' "constructions," then, were reflective of and part and parcel of the problem as the researchers saw it.[27]

In contradistinction to Scully and Marolla, the analysis in this chapter makes no *a priori* claims about the *sources* of a problem, but attempts to elucidate members' *resources* in positing, constructing, or proffering some events, situations, persons, groups, or actions *as a problem*.

Conclusion

It is taken as given that societal members have resources for "making sense" of the objects and events in the life-world. Some of these members *qua* news reporters and editors conduct their affairs, with their purposes, in a particular domain of discourse. "Particular," however, does not mean that their resources are ineluctably distinct or mystified; if for no other reason than that intelligibility is the primary obsession of any competent member, and newspapers exploit the commonsense distribution of knowledge and belief (aspects of which I have elucidated ethnomethodologically here) in order to assure a readership among persons who are, for them (reporters and editors), necessarily *anonymous* others (Sacks, 1984 *passim*). If there were ever a living, practical testimony to the *power of intersubjectivity*, it is the possibility of, the very fact of the existence of, *mass* media. Were they *not* to trade upon analyzable intersubjective resources, this readership would be confused or lost long before it could become hostile! Thus, analyses of media materials can and must illuminate broader, commonsense, practical reasoning which transcends the particularity of a newspaper (or television) account: one can generalize from the analysis of their resources to the analysis of the resources shared by a wider public, because the news media must do this themselves for practical purposes in working up *their* (vernacular) accounts.

This chapter has focused on the construction of descriptions of "what went on," "who did those actions," "with whom," and "who is to blame" under the characterization of an event as an "offense." In a *post facto* context, members, including reporters and the judicial system, were able to come up with "solutions" to these problems, even in the face of considerable ambiguity.

Of specific focus were the procedures not only for category *assignment*, *reversals*, and *shifts* but also for *category-collection expansion*. This last resource, I claim, is particularly utilizable in cases where there exist ambiguity and equivocality. I take it that this is non-trivial in light of the claim that "official" investigations, findings, assessments, reportings, and adjudications are nothing more nor less than the elaborated and formalized counterpart of everyday moral discourse.

The examination of these materials with their "storied" structure is one more perspicuous reminder of the elegant and powerful resources available to members in rendering persons, places, and events intelligible, logical, rational, sensible and seeable.

Notes

1. This work evolved from a chapter in my dissertation, and as such I am grateful to my committee members who provided insightful suggestions and corrections. In this regard, Professors Michael Lynch and George Psathas have my highest admiration for their scholarly achievements, the model they provided for others and for making the academy a vital, energized setting. They can never be thanked enough. Prof. Jeff Coulter was the main reason for my

taking up Wittgensteinian ethnomethodology as the powerful analytic tool that it is and it will ever remain necessary to express my enormous indebtedness to his person and work in the form of texts, articles, lectures, and personal communications.

2.   Wittgenstein (1969: § 378, p. 49)

3.   Most notable among these are Talcott Parsons and early Goffman. For examples of the potential constraints the term "role" can have on the explication of members' practices, see Goffman (1967 and 1971, *passim*).

4.   Kurt Vonnegut, Jr. proposed that: "We are who we pretend to be." I take it that the author of fantastic tales was being at least a bit sardonic. In any case, what it does for us, here, is to highlight a few fundamental tenets of ethnomethodological research and analysis. A) Most basic, of course, is that humans are *social* beings, first, last and everywhere in between – there is no time out. B) Reality is not a reality of Cartesian solipsism; "mind" is not a ghost in a machine. C) Being human is a function of *doing* human activities, which are for the most part, done in concert with other humans. D) Finally, a person is not sovereign with respect to his or her own identity. Now, back to Vonnegut's *bon mot*. Let's say that person Y is pretending to be an X, on some occasion of pretending and, of course, knows ("hidden away in his or her own head") that he or she is pretending to be an X. That X may later be discovered to *really* be a Y, only supports the claim that members utilize a resource that could go something like: *If* a person before me is doing the category-constitutive activities of an X, in relevant contexts of Xs and when Xs may normally appear, with, perhaps, others who can and do see and hear an instantiation of an X, thus satisfying the criteria of being an X, *then* for all practical (read as *ontological*) purposes the person *is* an X – protests from *X* to the contrary notwithstanding. Y may later reveal him or herself, but X is an X – not merely by claiming to be an X – but by doing being an X.

Let me put some flesh on these bones. One day after giving a lecture on "What is a person?," I was sitting in my office when a sophomore knocked on the door; her name is "Susan." She had come "to confess" something that had troubled her for over a year. Susan told me that, on reflection, during her pre-collegiate days she was never known to have a particularly great sense of humor. In fact, she had always thought of herself as being a bit shy and withdrawn. During Freshman Orientation to university, she "just happened" to say something that made everyone laugh and one of the group ("Mandy") told her that she "is a very funny person." For the remainder of the orientation period, whenever Susan was introduced to someone, Mandy would say: "This is my new friend Susan. She's hysterical." Susan told me that, despite her protests to the contrary, most of whatever she said was indeed heard as what a "very funny person" says. After returning home from orientation and continuing into her time at university, she found herself "studying to be funny." She carefully scrutinized comedians on television and rented tapes, she visited libraries in search of joke books, she stood in front of her mirror and practiced voice and timing control, facial and body gestures so that she would "be funny for her new friends who "thought" she was hysterical." Her reputation for humor remained, if not expanded. Susan had come to me to confess that she is a "phony," that she *really* isn't a funny person.

I told her that that was not for her to say because: A) the test of the pudding is in the eating, i.e., "funny" is where (and from whom) you find it; B) "funny" is an honorific ascription, i.e., to be made by *others*. And finally, I informed Susan that she was not "confessing" anything; what she was *now* doing was telling me of the "achievement" of what she had *become* for her friends.

We will later see under the Revolutionary Categories subheading that a pivotal element in the promotion of social change is to exhort all Xs and Ys to become Zs.

5. In theoremic form: *A person = an incumbent of an indefinite array or set of potentially relevant correct categories.* Some emblematic categories (readily available to anyone else by sight alone) to which all members are incumbent are age, race, gender, hair color (if extant), clothing choices, etc. Members are also incumbent to categories contained in religious and political affiliation, personality "types" (cf. "Susan" as an incumbent of the category of "funny persons"), occupation, ethnicity, and so on. A quite frequent protest, even from graduate students, upon first hearing the above is: "Then you are saying that everyone is the same." The primary point in response to this is that the concepts "same" and "different" (just as for any concept) have no meaning independent of their contexts of use (Wittgenstein, 1958: § 20). There is no decontextualized (read as "absolute") "sameness" or "difference" about persons, places, things, events. These concepts are utilized by members in accord with their rules of intelligible use and most generally used as comparators between two or more persons, places, things, events, e.g., "X is the same *as* Y," and "X is different *from* Y." Secondly, the "equation" at the top of this note accounts for the concerns implied by the graduate students' question, to wit, "differences between persons." Identical twin sisters share incumbency in a number of categories: same birthday (let's say), race, gender, parentage, color hair (let's say), clothing style (last one, let's say), and so on. However, at some reasonable, practical point, the two will conventionally be at variance from each other, if for no other purpose than that others may tell the difference between them – in name (I lied, let's say). Returning to the graduate students' concerns, I take it that the question is generated from a Western essentialism distinguishing one person from another. As far as the analysis of human action is concerned, such notions are better discussed in domains of discourse such as theology. Conversely, from Japanese students I have frequently been "informed" that "all Japanese are the same." Though initially surprised by this, I have come to understand who and how this "political *qua* cultural" proposition is utilized. However, the practical encompasses far more than the political. For practical purposes, this "proposition" is obviated by pointing at individual members of a class and in turn saying their name, or gender, or height, quality of voice, sleeping status (and its consequences), etc. I believe the argument I was making became most clear to them when I asserted that it was imperative that I am able to perceive differences between Japanese persons and to utilize those abilities from the first moment of my arrival at the airport. My Japanese wife would probably

have a basis for considerable dismay if I were unable to tell the difference between her and any other Japanese woman (let's say).

6. Elaborations on this claim are to follow, but it might be worthwhile to note the implications of this proposition; it obviates the mainstream social scientific notion of what Garfinkel (1967:68) called the "cultural dope," referring "to the man-in-the-*sociologist's*-society who produces the stable features of the society by acting in compliance with pre-established and legitimate alternatives of action..." *and* what he called the "psychological dope," i.e., "the man-in-the-*psychologist's*-society who produces the stable features of the society by choices among alternative courses of action that are compelled on the grounds of psychiatric biography, conditioning history, and the variables of mental functioning." (emphasis added). By demurring from these "models of man" (Schutz, 1962b:3) as the "basis of our research", we "give up" the search for the "causes exhibited in behavior," whether these causes are supposed to emanate from one's psyche or entailed by class membership.

7. "Category-bound activities" are distinguishable from "category-*constitutive* activities" in that the activities of the latter are essential and componential to category incumbency. "Crying," for example, is a category-*bound* activity of babies. However, crying *eo ipso* does not make any person a baby (though one can "cry *like* a baby"). Conversely, the lack of crying does not make a two-month-old a non-baby. The category "basketball player," however, is *constituted* in the activities of dribbling, passing, shooting a ball at/through a basket and so on. Not to engage in these activities obviates the claim to being a basketball player.

8. A membership categorization device is a collection of membership categories plus rules of application. These insights will be further expanded upon.

9. "Retrospective" interpretation might be a sufficient analysis given that we *do* have the category "woman" in the headline, but, I claim that it *need* not be for all occasions of use. Borrowing from the work of Jeff Coulter (1979a) on "presuppositions" and Wes Sharrock (1974), a reader at reaching "drunk" might be totally justified (indeed, may be obliged) in claiming that "drunk" "definitely referred to a man and not a woman" (again "man" and "woman" filling out the collection of categories in the device "gender"). Without explicit empirical definition, upon what cultural resource can this presupposed claim be made? Sharrock indicated that as part of our incumbency in the category "competent member" we are obliged to display our "category-bound knowledge" of a vast array of categories. What we implicitly "know" about the category "woman" is that they are, conventionally, "sober." Another way of putting it is to do a *Gedanken* experiment using Freud's word association method (though, of course, here, we are not exploring any one person's "psyche"). Before the relatively recent cultural changes due to the feminist movement, "lawyer," "doctor," "thief," "murderer," "rapist," "drunk" were, "of course," referential to "men." Failing to point out the "extraordinary" nature of the lawyer, doctor, etc. may put the describer in a position of accountability for "not making oneself clear," or "what you ought to have told me." Also, these "tags" often come with modalities, e.g., "lady doctor/ lawyer," "male nurse," "intoxicated (vs. "drunk") woman," "a woman who

murdered" (vs. simply "murderer").

Since we are on the topic of culture, I feel quite certain that a number of "anthropologically-minded" readers will wish to point out a substantial lacunae in the arguments being made in this paper, to wit, that these events occurred and were reported upon in Japan. I can hear this claim being made in North America, Europe, Australia and other "Western" lands. Also, from my many years experience of living and teaching in Japan, I am quite familiar with an extant claim here that "Japan is a unique culture." I will not, here, make any more extensive counterargument than to say that what an ethno-methodological analyst is studying is not culture as "divvied up" by politically-based and essentially ephemeral categories of "country," "nation," "race," or any of its cognates. The basis of our research presupposes (supported by the evidence in front of our noses) that intersubjective resources for sense making are universal; that what we are studying is not Japanese, British, American, Australian cultures, but "human culture." My imagined interlocutors might rejoin with: "Then are you saying that there are no differences between – what are at least putatively taken to be – "different cultures?" Sharrock and Anderson (1982) made it clear that what is often taken to be absolute differences between "cultures" is merely the doing of the same things differently. I could not concur more, both as an issue in the philosophy of (human) science and as a correct reflection of my experience living in a "penultimately non-Western" milieu. After living here for many years, there is nothing that "doesn't make sense" or "is so bizarre that I must assiduously examine it to understand it else shrug my shoulders and say: 'Well, it's impenetrably different.'" But – and here is the main point – living here many years does not make my capacity to make sense of my surrounds any better than my capacities were one minute after leaving the airport. The only difference I can see is that now I am, potentially, a "local expert"; meaning that if a newcomer were to point and ask "What's that?" I am in a position to come up with a convincing "answer," "name," "nomenclature," "history," etc.

Having said all that, there are occasions where "cultural differences" might appear and, quite frequently, it is in the "What's that?" that we see something standing out from the "temporally-located" intersubjective, habit-uated ways of seeing and hearing matters (in this case, ascription used in a news report). Some years ago, when I was first investigating these news re-ports, I presented a preliminary report to a group composed of American sociologists and anthropologists. In the interest of ease of reading and to pre-clude any "explaining" of the events in the railway station by way of their "Japanessness," I prepared a handout with Anglicized versions of names and places, e.g., "Momota" became "Monroe," "Chiba" became "Crescent City," and so on. However, after some time had passed there was a rumble of dis-quietude developing within the seminar room. Something was "odd" about these reports. When I asked them to tell me what they found unusual, it took a bit of searching but at last I was told: "It is in the news report of January 16, 1986. Near the end, down at the bottom, it says: "The noted *woman* attorney added:'"

As indicated above, in a post-feminist America with its "post-expansion," contemporaneously well-established categories of incumbency within, say, employment, the very *inclusion* of the tag "woman" preceding "attorney" stood out as an anachronism, an "odd" figure against a ground already covered. In large sum, it is in these so-called "minutiae" where "cultural differences" are commonly "discovered." Due to the current means of transportation and mass communication, we might forego ascribing to some, formerly, distant place the status of being "exotic," "vague," "unique," "inscrutable," or "a paradise on earth." While reading the above news report, and with "cultural difference" in mind, we might more readily resort to temporally-located ascriptions (*qua* political assessment) such as "progressive," "backward," "conservative," etc. The academic and laypersons' grounds for "cultural relativity" claims are rapidly crumbling; in the place of much that we formerly saw as "kinds," we *experience* in "degree." And, of course, much of it can depend upon *when* one is looking. Not even the "difference" of "the same things differently" is carved in stone.

10. The English language reader will note that in none of the news articles is any explicit reference made to "exotic dancer." Native Japanese language speakers inform me that "professional dancer" is a conventional, culturally-embedded euphemism for referring to one engaged in activities akin to bar hostessing *cum* striptease dancing. In the Japanese language, alternative cognates such as "ballet dancer" or "traditional dancer" must be so stated in the description.

Also, it is conceivable that "exotic dancer" could be made relevant to the story. A point to be made in regard to the non-selection of this category in referring to Momota is that "woman" is referentially adequate for *this* headline *and* the reading public. The assertion being made here is that analytical interest must stop at pointing out what referent(s) *were* used or what possible referent(s) intelligibly *could* be deployed, but not which *should* be used. Though often stated it bears repeating, for good, bad, or indifferent it is the analyst's job to find out *how* society's *members* go about "recognizing," "establishing," and "solving" problems.

A final observation on relevancing is that category relevance is a fundamental tool/constraint/study policy in the ethnomethodological examination of any domain of discourse, be it the analysis of media, face-to-face interaction, international diplomacy, etc. However, relevance is not a concern exclusive to ethnomethodologists, as is *implicitly* evident in the following excerpt from the 1/18/86 editorial.

There were two antagonists, a drunken man and a woman stranger.

And *explicitly* on 9/25/87.

He was 47, a high school physical education teacher and counselor, said to be popular with students and normally polite and mild-mannered. All that was *irrelevant, for on this occasion he was drunk.*
    She was 40, employed someplace or other as a dancer - again *irrelevant, for on this occasion she was merely another person also headed for*

a train at Nishi-Funabashi Station late on that night of Jan. 14, 1986. (emphasis added)

11. Logically there *cannot* be "two sets of rules" for making sense: one by which the media representatives conduct their activities and another by which members in face-to-face interaction, *in situ*, for all practical purposes, conduct their "work" of sense making.

12. I put scare quotes around "explanation of events" for a couple of reasons. The first is that it is clear that we (*qua* analysts) are not talking here about explanations, causes, answers to "why" questions. That, putatively, is the goal in the natural sciences. Through experimentation by dropping objects of varying size and weight, Galileo was seeking to establish the cause of the resultant falling, the predictability and nature of that event. Having established the necessary and sufficient antecedent conditions, he could then proffer the Law of Gravity.

    Any such similar attempts within the human sciences have come to naught, because when trying to establish laws for the predictability of human action, it would be more logically tenable to compare the proverbial apples and oranges than to subsume and reduce intersubjectively-learned rule-based human action to the predictability of a falling stone.

    The second reason for setting off the phrase is that intersubjective resources *include* and *provide* for explanation. Being intersubjective means that the resources are available to any competent teller as well as to any competent recipient of that telling. The final point to make about intersubjective tools is that since there is no time out from being human, making sense of the occasional odd event is part of the "job of being human."

13. Sudnow makes the observation on the typicality of "drunks" that: "there is no statutorily designated crime that is necessarily included in the crime of 'drunkenness'.... For drunkenness there is, however, an offense that while not necessarily included is 'typically-situationally-included,' i.e., 'typically' occurs as a feature of the way drunk persons are seen to behave -- 'disturbing the peace.' (Sudnow, 1987:154).

14. Watson (1976:64) observed that "Such imputations can straightforwardly begin when the offender initiated the offense and therefore initiated the ill effect or outcome. However, society-members also possess procedures for mitigating and, on rare occasions, even reversing such imputations."

15. I am indebted to Michael Lynch for this insight. *A fortiori*, we learn from Lynch (*in lecture*, Boston University, 1991b) that: the "natural facts" of life *are* the "moral facts" of life. Though Thomas Huxley (1917:332) may be, arguably, reifying "society", the insight remains the same: "...society not only has a moral end, but in its perfection, social life, is embodied morality."

16. In another paper, I have presented an explication of how it is that the concept of rape, as currently utilized by members, lay and legal, is an act of violence and not one of sex (Stetson, 1989).

17. Where resources other than personality types include: occupation, nationality, race/ethnic group, religious/political affiliation, personal name. The following metaphor I hope may be useful in seeing what we mean by "selecting a set of ascriptions/avowals" in members' explaining some odd occurrence in some

context and for some particular audience. Imagine our ever-helpful Martian anthropologist (on the faculty of the Mars Institute of Human Sciences) coming to Earth to study how humans go about explaining events to themselves and each other. Now since the work of elucidating and explicating Martian life has made tremendous progress, the first place for which he or she would look is the Library of Intersubjectivity. He or she would hope to find a section equivalent to their own which is under the rubric "explaining." Here, if he or she were so lucky, would be a collection of texts entitled: "Explaining by Use of Occupation Ascriptors and Avowals," "Explaining by Use of Nationality Ascriptors and Avowals," and so on. In the "Personality Ascriptors and Avowals text, our anthropologist would find entries such as: industrious, cheerful, jealous, mean spirited, compassionate, psychotic, fearful, and all the personality characterizations that we here on Earth share in common.

Of course, no such library, in fact, exists. But what is important in this imaginary example is that members possess such resources for making sense of any and all events. It is from these human culturally-furnished, intersubjective "texts" that logical, intelligible, sensible, reasonable assessments are drawn. Just as a child goes to school to learn the times tables, so the child learns how to produce reasons for X occurrence, in Y setting, for mother, father, sister, brother, teacher, friend, teddy bear, strangers, and all the categories of persons that inhabit their world.

18. The "controversy" that ensued is not immediately evident in the news reports reproduced here. Most of these discussions took place in weekly journals and in reports of meetings of Tokyo-area office workers, students and feminist organizations. Minor reference to these activities was reported on 9/18/87.

> A group made up of more than 20 office workers and students was formed to support Momota.
> The group has held rallies and collected signatures for a petition claiming Momota's innocence.
> Momota's supporters also charge responsibility for the case to men on the scene that night who failed to help the dancer. They maintained that the bystanders had forced her into the act by their inaction.

19. Philosopher David Hume defined "cause" as: An antecedent condition that brings about a subsequent effect. Hempel's contribution was in the following formulation: Cause is an antecedent condition (necessary and sufficient) to bring about a subsequent effect. For example, the existence of gravity is a necessary and sufficient condition to bring about the falling of a rock from the Tower of Pisa. Contrastively, though it is necessary for one to be a sexually mature female in order to give birth, *being* female alone does not *cause* one to give birth.

20. Below is a table of potential responses to allegations of blameworthiness for past, present, and/or future actions. Listed to the right of Confession, Excuses, Justification, and Entitlement is how the act is viewed by the one being censored. To the right of that is the culpability accepted or not by the one accused (or their proxy). Confession and Entitlement are pretty straight forward. It is in Excuses and Justification where we find matters relevant to

Momota's defense. J.L. Austin (1970) characterized these forms as "attempts to get out from under blame," or ways to avoid being held culpable for one's actions:

Confession	"Act is wrong"	"I am responsible"
Excuses	"Act is wrong"	"I am not (fully/ at all) responsible"
Justification	"Act is not wrong"	"I am responsible"
Entitlement	"Act is not wrong (nor especially right)"	"I did it and it is not wrong (nor especially right)"

Excuses, according to Austin, are defined as involving an *admission that a given act was bad*, (i.e., fell below a standard of conduct, or entailed ill effects), but as also involving a denial of full, or any, responsibility for the act.

Justifications involve an *acceptance of responsibility for a given act*, but also involve a denial that the act itself can be judged as "bad." As if to say "since no one came to my aid, and allowing oneself to be harassed is a bad thing, I was left to my own devices." To see how this intersubjective logic works in domains as putatively disparate as, for example, suicide, see Sacks (1967, *passim*).

21. Of course, here, I am making a logical argument. Certainly, as private citizens, Darley and Latané can turn their efforts to initiating any legislative proceedings at their disposal. However, as positivists "discovering the laws of human behavior" they are logically constrained by the very meaning of "natural law", i.e., invariance. No amount of *moral modification* can affect the movement of the planets.

22. An interesting referential issue arises with the wedding of "the public's tolerance" and "public intoxication." John Dewey (as cited in Molotch and Lester (1974)) defines "public" as "a political grouping of individuals brought into being as a social unit through mutual recognition of common problems for which common solutions should be sought." I wish to disagree with this "operationalization" by pointing to some problematic upshots of this formulation:

1.) We are not looking at *properties* of "individuals" but category-bound *activities* of categories. As elaborated upon in endnote 5, from Harvey Sacks (1972a and 1972b) we learn that "a human social member is an incumbent of an indefinite set or array of potentially relevant correct categories." With no priority over any other category, "individual" (with its cognates: group, race, occupation, age, height, etc.) is *a* category which may relevantly apply in specific contexts of use. Any member, in any given context, can "see" themselves, and be "seen" by other members, as *instantiating* some relevant category.

2.) Even the most cursory examination of the combinatorial tolerances of the use of the concept "public" demonstrates a usability which supersedes Dewey's limited definition. As a grammatical modifier of concrete entities we have, e.g., "public toilets," "public baths," and "public transportation." We can also use the concept "public" in the abstract, e.g., "public opinion." Some uses are a combination of concrete action and the abstract, e.g., "public display of affection." Though both are typified categories, with "the public's tolerance" of "public intoxication" we have the abstract "explaining" the concrete. A member is not sovereign even to the contents of one's body; in the context of a bar or party, the ingestion of alcohol and subsequent behavior within normative constraints, is normally seen as quite appropriate behavior. For that person to take a step into "the public" opens him to, at best, "tolerance."

23. This is one more instantiation of what was discussed above, namely, rules for the intelligible, logical action of ascribing and avowing to oneself and others some characterization; "drunk" is one such ascription. The point being made here is that it is not *merely* biological status which "determines" what or who is doing what there is to be seen and explained. A volunteer in a study of the effects of alcohol, admitted to a clinic and having an IV solution of alcohol administered to attain the same blood level as the drunk/teacher/dead person in our news reports, could most reasonable be seen to be of a "character" quite at odds with the ascription "a drunk." Given that alcohol is a soporific substance and the volunteer is reclining on a bed, it would not be too grand a risk to predict that the ascription most likely to be made would be: "sleepy."

24. That ambiguity and equivocality can be powerful constraints on social behavior can be seen in a conversation about airplane safety between Oprah Winfrey (talk show host) and John Galipault, a representative of the Aviation Safety Institute, a "watchdog" of the airlines. NBC, April 16, 1987.

Oprah W.: "I was on this flight once and the plane lost an engine, the plane shook, but no one spoke, we just looked into each others' eyes for like five minutes. The crew wouldn't give us any information. Looking back on it, I thought it was odd that there was no screams like in the movies."

John G.: "They wanted information before they made their scream decision."

N.B. I take it that the humorous quality of John G.'s rejoinder is in its disjunctive character, i.e., we do not normally consider the act of screaming as one we "decide" to do. Coulter (1989), in his elucidation of emotions, provides the grounds for the reasonableness of Galipault's response to Winfrey. "Emotions" are not endogenous components of a person "causing" them to do anything. Emotions are contingent upon appraisals of events or situations. The passengers in the above anecdote had to wait for more information given the relative technical complexities of airliners and their possible malfunctions. Once they were able to render the situation as what "it ordinarily is," (Sacks, 1984) that is, a "crisis situation," grounds were provided for the reasonable, intersubjective, culturally-furnished response of screaming.

25. This, of course, does not obviate the possibility that incumbents of revolutionary categories may not choose to make such alterations by such measures as: dress, hairstyle, diet, physical regimen (or not), tattoos, etc. These alterations may be, putatively, "category-bound activities" of participants in cultural change. The point here is that these alterations are not, by themselves, "constitutive" of a successful revolution.

26. However, because of another cultural revolution, viz., Gay and Lesbian Liberation, reproductive biology itself is no longer an inclusive/exclusive "determinant" for either "woman" *or* "lady."

27. For a fuller ethnomethodological treatment of these issues in the domains of police interrogations/interviews and in face-to-face interaction, please see Watson (1978 and 1983).

Appendix: Newspaper accounts of the incident at Nishifunabashi Station.

(1) The Japan Times, Thursday, January 16, 1986 (page 2).

Drunk Irks Woman, Killed by Train

CHIBA (Kyodo) - A drunken man verbally and physically harassing a woman on the platform of Nishifunabashi Station shortly after 11 p.m. Tuesday was pushed off by the woman and killed by an incoming train.

Police arrested the woman on suspicion of causing injuries resulting in death. She was identified as Misuzu Momota, 39, a professional dancer from Kitakysuhu, Fukuoka Prefecture.

The station is on the Sobu Line of the Japanese National Railways.

According to investigators, the man fell onto the railway track and died after a train bound for Ochanomizu Station dragged him about 20 meters. Some people on the platform tried in vain to save him by pulling him up from the tracks.

Police reported that the man died due to severe rupture of his internal organs.

Investigators said the man had persistently followed the woman after he entered the station. He reportedly poked his elbow into her side and yelled at her, "You idiot!" When he touched her body, she pushed him away and he fell off the platform.

The man was identifies as Kunimitsu Kawahara, 47, a teacher at the Fukagawa High School in Tokyo.

Tsuyoshi Sasho, deputy station master of Nishifunabashi Station, quoted Momota as saying that she had cried for help but was ignored by the people around her and she pushed the man.

Sasho said there were about 100 people on the platform at the time and at least 20-30 were close to Momota.

Police said that Momota, who was upset, said during initial questioning that the man had poked her on the head a few times.

Police sources said the case was being investigated closely with the possibility considered that her act may have been in self-defense.

Meanwhile, Ryota Mori, principal of the Fukagawa High School, told reporters that Kawahara was a health and physical education teacher and was actively involved with the student body and in extra-curricular activities.

He said that Kawahara, who also served as a guidance teacher, was a polite and mild-mannered man, adding that he was popular with his students.

He said he could not believe what had happened and did not know why Kawahara was in Funabashi.

Because of the accident, two train runs on the line were canceled and nine train runs were delayed up to one hour.

Hiroshi Itakura, professor of criminal law at Nihon University, asked to comment on the case, said that generally speaking it depends on how much the man harassed the woman whether or not she had acted in self-defense. He declined to discuss this particular case, saying he did not know the details.

He said that he felt it would be unfair to say the woman over-reacted if she had felt physically threatened while people around her did not try to help her whatsoever.

Lawyer Mariko Awaya said that she would do the same thing as Momota if she found herself in the same situation.

"I have not heard every detail of the case yet. But based on what I heard so far, I feel that her act should be justified in self-defense."

The noted woman attorney added: "People around Momota did not help her because Japanese society is permissive about drunken acts.'"
[Reprinted by permission]

(2) The Japan Times, Friday, January 17, 1986 (page 2).

POLICE CONTINUE PROBE OF TRAIN DEATH INCIDENT

CHIBA (Kyodo) - Police Thursday sent to the Chiba District Public Prosecutor's Office a woman who allegedly pushed a drunken man off a station platform after he physically and verbally harassed her Tuesday. The man was killed by an incoming train.

The incident occurred shortly after 11 p.m. Tuesday at Nishifunabashi Station in Chiba Prefecture. There were about 100 people on the platform at the time, but none offered to help the woman when she cried out for help.

Police Thursday quoted the woman, Misuzu Momota, a 39-year-old dancer from Kokura Ward, Kitakyushu, Fukuoka Prefecture, as saying, "On an impulse, I pushed the man back with both hands in order to break free of him. Then he reeled and fell off (onto the train track)."

The man, who was crushed between the platform and the train, was identified as Kunimitsu Kawahara, 47, a teacher at Fukagawa High School in Tokyo.

Investigators have not ruled out the possibility that the woman acted in self-defense. They have questioned eyewitnesses to the incident.
[Reprinted by permission]

(3) The Japan Times, Saturday, January 18, 1986 (page 14)

Editorial: A TRAGEDY OF MULTIPLE LOSSES

The incident that occurred late the other night at Nishifunabashi Station in Chiba arouses a confusion of emotions. It was altogether a tragic affair, one with such multiple losses that we cannot let it fade without trying to gain something out of it.

There were two antagonists, a drunken man and a woman stranger. From all that has been reconstructed with credible verification, he was harassing her persistently from the time they passed through the wicket. On the platform, he shouted verbal abuses at her and poked her body - until she responded with a shove. He fell onto the tracks and was killed by an incoming train.

From this much, it appears that the woman acted in self-defense. How to describe the man's actions is a more complex matter.

The tragic element was heightened when we learned that he was a high school physical education teacher and counselor, popular with the students and normally of polite and mild manner.

A Jekyll and Hyde case? Many people will say that alcohol is capable of making such a transformation of personality. This has been recognized especially among Japanese - so much as to make for the accommodation of a traditionally permissive attitude toward drunks.

If that is to be continually justified, however, we must also make some accommodation for the victims of the drunken Hydes. And that, of course, means taking some measures to prevent the victimization.

Our criticism, therefore, must fall upon the many people who stood around on the platform ignoring the woman's cries. Not them personally, but the mores of our society that are at the root of this detachment in the face of somebody else's crisis. We need to reform.

Some, at least, tried to rescue the man from the tracks. But then it was too late - both for him and for the distressed woman.

[Reprinted by permission]

(4) The Japan Times, Sunday, January 19, 1986 (page 2)

STATION INCIDENT WITNESSES SOUGHT

CHIBA (Kyodo) - Police have put up signboards at Japanese National Railways' Nishifunabashi Station seeking persons who witnessed a platform incident that occurred late on the night of Jan. 14 in which a man was killed, it was learned Saturday.

According to police, the man, Kunimitsu Kawahara, 47, stumbled and fell onto the tracks when he was shoved by a woman he had been harassing and instantly killed by an incoming train.

The woman, Misuzu Momota, a 39 year old dancer, was later arrested on charges of inflicting bodily injuries resulting in the death of the victim, police said.

Police said they put up the signboards to collect more evidence in their investigation of the case because there is a possibility the woman had acted in self-defense.

The signboards were placed at three locations in the station.

Momota told police that the man had verbally and physically harassed her at the station that night. She cried out for help, but was ignored by people around her, she said.

Momota said that after putting her bags on a bench in the middle of platform No. 4 she tried to shake him off by pushing him from behind with both hands.

The place where she pushed him was around the center of the 8-meter wide platform and four to five meters away from the edge of the platform where the man fell onto the tracks, police said.

The man, who was a physical education teacher at Fukagawa Senior High School, was killed caught between the train and the platform, according to police.

Police questioned persons who tried to pull the man up from the tracks, but they were not able to provide evidence as to what extent the woman was harassed which would determine whether the woman's act was in self-defense or not, police said.

Police hoped persons who had actually seen Momota push the man would contact them.
[Reprinted by permission]

(5) The Japan Times, Friday, September 18, 1987 (page 2)

COURT ACCEPTS PLEA OF SELF-DEFENSE, ACQUITS WOMAN OF CAUSING MAN'S DEATH

CHIBA (Kyodo) The Chiba District Court on Thursday found innocent a 41-year-old dancer charged last year with causing the death of a drunken man who insulted her and started a quarrel.

Misuzu Momota, of Kitakyushu pushed the man off a railway platform onto the tracks, where he was hit by an oncoming train.

The court ruled that the dancer's act had been in self-defense.

According to the ruling, the dancer who worked in Chiba Prefecture, was verbally and physically harassed at around 11 p.m. on Jan. 14 last year on a platform at Nishi-funabashi Station of the Sobu Line in Chiba Prefecture.

The drunken man, later identified as Kunimitsu Kawahara, a high school teacher, was caught between the platform and the train. He died as a result of internal injuries, according to the ruling.

The dancer was charged with inflicting bodily injuries resulting in the death of the man. Prosecutors asked for a two-year prison sentence.

The prosecution maintained, based on evidence given by witnesses, that her act was not in self-defense but was intended.

However, the prosecutors admitted that the man's harassment triggered the incident. As a result, they demanded the relatively light sentence.

Momota's defense counsel contended she had only pushed him in an attempt to free herself.

The defense asserted that the act was in self-defense since bystanders did nothing to help her.

The defense also maintained that it would not have been difficult for the man to get out of the way of the approaching train.

A group made up of more than 20 office workers and students was formed to support Momota.

The group has held rallies and collected signatures for a petition claiming Momota's innocence.

Momota's supporters also charge responsibility for the case to men on the scene that night who failed to help the dancer. They maintained that the bystanders had forced her into the act by their inaction.

[Reprinted by permission]

(6) <u>The Japan Times</u>, Friday, September 25, 1987 (page 20)

Editorial: **INCOMPLETE JUSTICE**

He was 47, a high school physical education teacher and counselor, said to be popular with students and normally polite and mild-mannered. All that was irrelevant, for on this occasion he was drunk.

She was 40 [sic], employed someplace or other as a dancer - again irrelevant, for on this occasion she was merely another person also headed for a train at Nishi-Funabashi Station late on that night of Jan. 14, 1986. It will never be known why he chose her as a target for verbal abuse and physical harassment, which he began at the wicket and continued with growing force on the platform.

No one could have imagined this encounter of strangers would end in a death, least of all either of the antagonists. It was to free herself - an act of self-defense, as the Chiba District Court ruled recently - that she gave him the shove that sent him staggering, eventually off the platform.

From all one hears people comment, the court did right. And not because the reputation of the living is more important than that of the dead. It is because the public generally is sensitized to the common social ill of drunks harassing people.

That being so, what can we expect next? Unfortunately, no letup in such harassment, we are afraid.

It will continue, that is, until the public undergoes a reforming and it becomes the common thing for bystanders to intercede for the protection of innocent targets of anti-social treatment. In the Chiba District Court, it was really the public that was on trial.

We are guilty all right; but there is no retributive justice against an incriminated public, unfair as that may be. In place of the judiciary, we ourselves are responsible to apply sanctions against anti-social behavior, and that is the lesson to be propagated.

[Reprinted by permission]

(7) <u>Asahi Shimbun</u>, Shimbun Friday, October 1, 1987 (page 31)
[Translated from the original by Mikako Sato. The syntax remains as close as possible to the original.]

FALLING DEATH OF A TEACHER AT NISHIFUNABASHI STATION PUBLIC PROSECUTOR ABANDONED THE INTENTION TO FILE AN APPEAL

On 30th, Chiba District Prosecutor's Office decided not to appeal† the case of ex-dancer, Ms. Misuzu Momota, 41 years old, of 1-Chome Ima-machi Kokura Kita-ku, Kitakyusyu City. Chiba District Court made the ruling of not guilty for the reason of self-defense against the charge of *shogai chishi zai* †† regarding the incident in which a drunken high school teacher died after falling from the platform of Japan Railways' Sobu Line in Nishifunabashi station in January, last year. Therefore, Ms. Momota's not guilty has been practically finalized.

For the reasons for abandoning the intention to appeal, the District Prosecutor's Office considered the following: 1. The motive of this incident was that the teacher harassed††† Ms. Momota.†††† 2. The way of Momota's action was only that she pushed him away once. 3. The teacher's family expressed the wish that they do not want the prosecutor to continue the case, and the Office also said that they discussed the matter with Tokyo High court and came to the conclusion.

[Reprinted by permission]

To the Reader: The following notes are "For Your Information" purposes only. Make of it what you will. However, the inclusion of some "particularities" of a country's jurisprudence practices should not be seen as an endorsement of "cultural relativity" claims. If this analysis is to succeed at even the most minimal level of scientific validity, it must, in principle, be universally relevant and applicable regardless of "nation," "culture," "race," "native language" or any of their analytically delimited, operationalized or reductionist cognates.

† The Japan jurisprudence system provides for prosecutory appeal if the defendant is found not guilty in a lower court. I am informed by Japanese scholars that prosecutors as well as defense attorneys "refuse to lose," consequently such cases as this can continue for many years.

†† The literal translation of this legal term is "harm which resulted in death" [Translator: Mikako Sato] Compare this with the English version in The Japan Times, Jan. 16, 1986: "causing injuries resulting in death."

††† Note: the verb used here is *karamu*, it is a word used often with drunken behavior of "not letting people go from conversation or interaction," it usually refers to the behavior of being a sort of selfish person (usually used in the case of one under the influence of alcohol) by not being considerate to the others but continue to do what you want to do. However, it does not have as strong a connotation as "harassment" especially when used with the word "drunk," because a person who is doing *karamu* does not necessarily necessarily have bad intentions, but is insensitive or acting that way because of alcohol. *Karamu* is seen as a "bad way" of being drunk. [Translator: Mikako Sato]

†††† The phrase "motive of this incident" is used. I am not sure whether this "motive" is the legal term meaning "the starting point" or the "cause" I take it that what they are emphasizing here is that it was all started by the drunken teacher and not by Momota.

Chapter 5

"The Soccer Game" as Journalistic Work: Managing the Production of Stories about a Football Club.

Liz Marr, Dave Francis and Dave Randall

This paper seeks to apply insights from the ethnomethodological studies of work program to a study of the ordinary, mundane, day-by-day work of a football journalist. In so doing, contrasts are drawn between the analytic orientation drawn from this program and the characteristic concerns and theoretical assumptions of sociological studies of the media, and, in particular, studies of the "occupational culture" of journalism. Our interest lies in the examination of the ordinary and practical work done by the journalist both within the newspaper and within the football club concerned, and suggests both that "commonsense" views of the journalist as intrusive and "story-seeking" are far from accurate, and, further, that some typical sociological approaches to journalism are a gloss on an elaborate set of practices. A more nuanced perspective, we argue, lies in the examination of the processual character of story production through a fragile and accomplished "complicity of practice" between football club, newspaper and journalist, based on known-in-common features of the football world. This paper takes as its topic the ordinary, day-to-day working of a journalist who reports on the affairs of one of England's football clubs. The football club concerned is one of the best known clubs in the English Premier League. The data reported are taken from an "occasional" ethnography, that is, a study of journalism which, while lasting a number of years has only occasionally taken football as a specific topic of inquiry.

Ethnomethodology, Work and Culture

Much has changed in the world of soccer ("football," in the UK). By virtue of ever increasing media coverage, it and other sports have become arguably the primary area of interest for newspaper readers and television viewers. As Real (1990) has suggested, "Sports pages are the first-read pages of the print media for many. A vast amount of resources, technology, money, energy and time ... is given over to mediated sports" (1990: 349).[1]

Television coverage, along with the general increase in reportage by newspapers and magazines of various types, has both made the soccer match available to a greater audience than ever before and used ever more sophisticated techniques relating to viewpoint, analysis, and "color," all of which provide the fan with ever more information about the game, its players and so on. As Real further points out, "Sports pages today examine the heroes in minute detail, warts and all, outlining details of greedy contracts, after-hours drug abuse, and undisciplined sex lives, but sports heroes and their motivating power over others live on" (1990: 351). That is, sport has become an arena which is extraordinarily familiar and mundane to the "fan," and is now arguably a major source of identification, pleasure and emotional satisfaction for large numbers of people. In few other environments can participants to the game be so regularly offered up for wholesale public scrutiny, both on the pitch and seemingly in their private lives. Equally, it seems more or less obvious that much of the knowledge available to the fan is "mediated" knowledge, acquired through viewing and readership.

In this respect, it is hardly surprising that sociology has focused increasingly on sport as a topic of inquiry, for sports like soccer have evidently become extremely fashionable. Those of us who have taken the ethnomethodological "turn," however, are accustomed to some cynicism over the way in which sociology, like a circling vulture, descends to pick the flesh of each new fashionable body, and yet does so in strangely familiar ways. Our particular concern, and we do not propose to re-open old and largely fruitless discussions, is the consistency of the analytic devices used by sociologists, regardless of the topic in question. To paraphrase Graham Button (1991) the business of sociology, whatever the topic opened up for investigation, is the business of theorization and theorization, moreover, which exhibits some astonishingly stable properties. Ethnomethodology, in contrast, has explicitly rejected the theorization of "foundational matters." This distinction between sociology as the business of theorizing and a sociology which is concerned with the examination of practice is contrastively available as much in the study of sport and the media as elsewhere, and in this paper we seek to examine the day-by-day work of a football journalist to establish just such a contrast. We seek in other words to draw attention to the "just what" of *soccer* journalism.

We do so from an analytical point of view informed by the program of inquiry known as "ethnomethodological studies of work" initially proposed by Garfinkel and others (Garfinkel, 1986). We take the distinguishing concerns of this program to center around description of the local, *in situ* organization of activities, that is, the ways in which any sphere of practical action is produced and managed "from within" as a recognizably and reliably orderly social environment. Associated with this central concern is a methodological commitment involving rejection of "sociological irony," that is, any attempt to explain or account for such recognizable orderliness in terms which assume a distinction between order as a sociological construct, on the one hand, and order as members' experience, on the other. With reference to these commitments, "ethnomethodological studies of work" investigate selected social settings for their "accomplished orderliness" as socially organized environments of practical conduct. The studies of work program has included investigations of the work of laboratory scientists engaged in neurophysiology research (Lynch, 1985), mathematicians engaged in the work of constructing a mathematical proof (Livingston, 1986), computer programmers engaged in writing and reading computer programs (Button and Sharrock, 1995) and schoolteachers and students engaged in the daily round of classroom activities (Macbeth, 1990). We believe that one of the major strengths of this program is to collapse the distinction between work activities and culture.

We are, then, concerned with how members in a given setting "get the business done," and with the resources of knowledge, skill and competence they employ and require of one another in so doing. More than this, though, in focusing upon such competencies they seek to topicalize the setting-specific "sense of order" that the members of a given setting "take for granted" in conducting their affairs. In any sphere of activity, participants conduct their affairs in ways which realize what one might call a "principle of economy"; that is, they develop recipes and routines which make possible the doing of many activities with a minimum of focused attention and exhibited effort. Such recipes and routines contribute to the members' sense of the daily round of work as "life as normal," in which much that occurs thus has the character of being "seen but unnoticed," in Garfinkel's (1967) famous phrase. It is against the background of this expected and expectable order that particular events are recognizable and properly treatable as "noticeables." Members' "sense of order," then, comprises an ability to recognize such events as "events" to be remarked upon, which are "problematic" and demand attention and effort. It is this focus upon the "taken for granted" and on the "noticeable" which most clearly distinguishes ethnomethodological studies of work from conventional sociology.

The theoretical inspiration we draw from the ethnomethodological studies of work program provides a perspective upon the phenomenon of sports journalism which contrasts decisively with conventional sociological approaches.[2] A principal theme of studies of journalism has been the socially determined nature of media content. Specifically, it is argued that journalistic decision making is socially shaped; that is, judgements that are made about such things as what constitutes a "newsworthy" story (and thus what should be included in a newspaper or news program, reported more fully rather than less fully, should be followed up with "follow-on" reports, and so forth) are all responsive to "wider" social forces and interests. Thus, in theorizing about these matters, sociologists of the media most frequently assume a "gate keeping" conception of journalism.[3] According to this view, the news media act to screen events such that what appears in print or in television news programs comprises a selective and "biased" representation of what has actually occurred. In this way, news media content can be understood as a crucial ideological mediator between society and its ordinary members. Variations on this theme include, on the one hand, an argument which suggests that journalists themselves are victims of a complicity between large commercial concerns, which include the media industry, and, on the other, an alternative view which has the media taking a more predatory role, in which "innocent victims" are pursued to the exclusion of coverage with a deeper analytical focus, and through which the reader is constructed as obsessed with the trivial and the salacious. From this latter point of view, complicity exists within the profession of journalism rather than across broad structural interests.[4]

To a greater or lesser extent, analyses of the kind we have sketched above presuppose some process of "boundary maintenance," which trades on notions of "insider" and "outsider," whether conceived as a relationship between the messages which media personnel produce and media consumers receive, or as complicities between journalists and other professional insiders. In what follows, we provide an alternative, not because we wish to problematize "typical" sociological accounts of journalism but because we wish to understand "how," rather than "why," stories, in this case stories about football, are produced. That is, we do not wish to suggest that the stories that arrive in newspapers are not subject to various kinds of interference from parties with an interest in assuring that a particular "spin" is placed on accounts. Instead, our argument relies on questions concerning how it is that sociological accounts of the relationship between commercial interests, the media, and the audience can unproblematically portray them in insider/outsider terms. That is, the "gloss" provided by sociological accounts relies on commonsense distinctions between those in the know and those who rely on media accounts, which ignores the very production of those relationships. From the ethnomethodological standpoint adopted here, our interest is in the "practical, member managed character" of distinctions such as that between "insiders" and "outsiders." It remains, of course, possible, given this general lack of sociological interest in the detailing of practice, that these accounts may misrepresent the ways in which "insider" and "outsider" relationships are produced, and may underestimate the fluidity of these boundaries.

Returning to the issue of work activities and culture which we mentioned earlier, we can further explicate our ethnomethodological approach to football journalism with reference to the idea of "enacted culture." The conventional sociological literature on journalism (see, e.g., Ericson et al., 1989; Fishman, 1980; Gans, 1980; and Tuchman, 1978), along with the literature on other occupational groups, is characterized by a "transcendent" view of culture, where typically journalistic decisions are made explicable with reference to an "occupational culture" which is learned and operated by journalists in and as the routine order of their daily work. However, while studies have emphasized the significance of this occupational culture, descriptions given of it leave much to be desired. The prevailing tendency is for description of a generalized and idealized kind, one which gives little sense of what such a culture is like as a "lived reality." Thus, it is asserted that a central component of journalistic culture is a conception of "news worthiness"; a shared notion, or set of notions, in terms of which journalists decide what information is worthy of being treated as "news" and what is not. However, in study after study one is presented with representations of "news worthiness" as consisting in a set of maxims or rules which guide or direct journalists in making such decisions. In their operation, it is argued, such rules, when mapped onto a collection of possible news items, produce a "preference order" of stories. For example, according to Gans (1980), one such rule is "Prefer items which will "balance" other selected stories over items which will unbalance the program/newspaper" (p. 173-176).

Thus the descriptions of the professional culture of news journalists presented by Gans and others exemplify what we are calling the "transcendent" view of culture. In representing this culture as a set of maxims or rules which journalists follow, and explaining journalistic decisions as motivated compliance with these rules, studies presuppose a conception of culture as a system of rules which stands over and exists independently of activities, and thereby directs them. Culture "explains" activities because it has a decontextualized character – the rules are abstract in form and general in scope and application. Particular occasions of their use thus are described in terms of their "conformity with" or "deviance from" the abstractly formulated statement of the relevant rule or maxim. It is this transcendent abstraction which "constitutes" the culture.

The notion of "enacted culture" which we propose contrasts with the transcendent conception at all points. Thus, rather than conceiving common culture as something which stands over against activities, we prefer to view it as "realized in and through" activities. In other words, it is in the ways by which members treat their knowledge as known in common with relevant others that a common culture is made manifest. Similarly, it is in and through the ways that members treat activities as rule related that rules are made socially available and thereby constituted as cultural facts. It follows that culture is always "contextualized"; there can be no context independent description of it, since all such descriptions, including those proffered by sociologists, are practical actions responsive to their particular context. Even to speak of "it" arguably is, from this point of view, to commit a "fallacy of misplaced concreteness" to borrow Whitehead's (1925) phrase. Viewing culture as "enacted," therefore, means that the task of the sociologist is not to explain but to describe; where description consists not in constructing abstracted and quasi-definitive idealizations but rather accounts of the practices by which members accomplish the local relevance of shared knowledge. By representing journalistic culture as an explicit decision making process, governed by rules, such accounts as Gans' fail to convey the experiential character of journalism as a daily round of work within a "known-in-common" environment, the features of which can be treated as transparent and reliable.

We not only wish to step back from the theoretical assumptions contained in these sociologies, but to "get behind" the gloss to the situated practices and "lived work" which they make invisible. We prefer to ask how the sense "members" have of their "worlds" is produced and sustained. Our interest centers around the ways in which "stories" are produced out of what is "known in common" by football professionals, football journalists, and football fans, and thereby realize the "world of football" as a lived phenomenon. To avoid any misconception, we emphasize that this is in no sense an argument which seeks to reformulate how "consensus" is managed. As we endeavor to show below, disagreements arise and conflicts occur between members of the football club and the journalist reporting on the affairs of that club, between the club and its fans, and indeed sometimes between journalistic representations of events and the fans who read their stories. Rather, and following Wittgenstein

(1968, § 241, p. 88), we seek to distinguish "agreement in opinion" (or disagreement), and agreement "in the form of life." Put very simply, in order for journalists and football clubs to agree or disagree, there must be foundational agreement which allows them to mutually explicate what they are agreeing or disagreeing about. It is this fundamental issue, the issue of what doing the work of producing football stories is like and how it both depends on and defines mutual understandings of the business of football that is of interest to us.

The Demand Conditions of Football Journalism

We borrow the concept of "demand conditions" from the work of Roy Turner (1969: 4) on the local organization of policing as routine, daily work.[5] Turner points out that in conducting his daily work, the beat police officer orients to a number of features of his work situation as constraining circumstances, conditions which cannot be ignored or "wished away," conditions which comprise defining parameters of his environment. Like police work, the daily work of the football journalist involves a number of demand conditions. In the case of the journalist, these conditions are all concerned in various ways with the production of journalistic copy. We mention three such conditions.

The first involves the fact that, over and above all else, the work of the football journalist involves the production of "match reports." The shape of his work environment is conditioned by the scheduled program of matches involving the club to which he is assigned. His readership essentially comprises fans of that club, and his paramount task is to provide these fans, and anyone else who reads the newspaper, with accounts of the matches played by the team. Thus, much of the routine work of the football journalist might be characterized as "descriptive." That is, it concerns itself with ordinary descriptions of events at football matches, descriptions which might include the ordering of the match according to goals scored, chances missed, controversial moments, who played well and who played badly, tactical and strategic changes and so on. These reports are temporally constrained: They must appear in the newspaper on the same day (if there is an evening "sports edition") or the day immediately after the match. Such reports, temporally situated as they are, enable the fan to "follow his team"; to read the match account as "news"; such a reading being independent of whether the fan has been present at the match, already knows the match result, who scored the goals, and so forth.

A second demand condition involves reports which are news of a different kind, the production of "revelatory" rather than "descriptive" reports. Nowadays, football journalists increasingly are involved in the production of what is sometimes called "investigative" material. Not surprisingly, perhaps, the only access the fan has to the inner workings of the football club, its disputes, the transfer speculation, changes in the fortunes of individuals and so on is the "story" available to him or her as presented in the media.[6] In England, at least, "news" stories concerning footballers and managers, and particularly stories which appear to contain investigative elements, revealing to the fan what had previously been secret, is the province of the press. Television, hitherto, has not substantially engaged in this work. As part of this revelatory process, the journalist appears to "speak" for the fan, representing their views, and "discovering" aspects of the life of the professional footballer that will be of interest. The language of the journalist when covering such issues must further be a language that is intelligible to the fan. From the point of view of the journalist, however, these things are not "givens." Football writers are, and must be, sensitive to what it is that readers are likely to find interesting. Part of the "skillful work" of the journalist is assessing what is of interest. When the journalist we observed speaks of "a good story," or "too good a story to miss" he is exhibiting precisely that judgement. Lest it be thought that such "stories" speak for themselves in some way, it should be remembered that a large part of published material would often, to the neutral observer, be trivial and banal. Equally, and less obviously, a developing feature of the modern game in England has been the progressive organization of groups of fans. This has become manifest, for instance, in the production of alternative "fanzines" which purport to represent the fan's perspective, and the existence of a number of "independent" supporters groups or associations that are in various ways distanced from the interests of the club they support. Representatives of such groups now appear with some frequency on British television when news stories concerning individual clubs break, and they are not infrequently given a forum when issues relating to football in general are discussed. Further, as the Public Relations Officer of the club remarked to one of the authors:

> In the old days, people used to just discuss what the manager should do in the pub or at work. Nowadays, they're more likely to ring the club up ... you wouldn't believe how many phone calls we get telling us where we're going wrong ...

This increased activity on the part of organized fans is reflected again in the fact that representatives of these organizations would regularly ring the journalist, at work and at home, both to elicit information and to express opinion. In sum, the notion of a passive audience for media output is increasingly problematized by organized fans' developing knowledge of media practice.

The third "demand condition" of football journalism follows from the preceding two. A fundamental aspect of journalistic work, and one that is as true of sports journalism as any other variety, is that copy has to be filed every day. In other words, whether or not decisions about "what" story to print have to be made, "some" story must appear. The routine work of the sports journalist is above all the work of "space filling." The newspaper takes its shape around various parameters. Advertisements are placed first, for the simple reason that they are a large part of the newspapers' revenue, and stories must be fitted to the spaces that remain. Secondly, and as a feature of a regional newspaper where most readers will support one or another of the local clubs, material must be fitted to a general editorial expectation concerning the amount of space typically devoted to sports stories. In the case of the newspaper in question, this will mean that four or five pages every day will be devoted to local and regional sport, a large part of which will concern the local professional football clubs. Such material is usually referred to either as "back page," or alternatively as "inside page" material, because it reflects readers' expectations of what is to be found in those locations.[7] In addition, however, material will have to be provided for "special" events, such as Cup Finals and important League matches and would typically be located in "Pull out" sections or in dedicated editions of the newspaper. Moreover, there will frequently be, because of the strength of local interest, front page stories, over and above these regular pieces, which cover "breaking" news. The imperative of the regular production of "news," it should be pointed out, is produced not only from the expectations of editors and fans, but also from those of the football clubs themselves. The clubs might be expected to intervene in the journalistic process only when problems over stories arise, but our observations suggest that clubs themselves expect the newspaper to provide this regular level of coverage and that in many respects it suits their interests that it should do so. These combined expectations are an encountered phenomenon for the journalist, manifest in editorial demands for copy at short notice, in fans' complaints over non- or mis-reporting of events, and above all in the insistence of the clubs that the journalist maintain regular, daily, contact with their operation.

One consequence of the demand conditions we have outlined is a universal expectation that the work of the football journalist requires daily and close contact with managers, players, and other officials at the football club. The routine, mundane, work of the journalist is in large part the work of spending time with professionals, eliciting opinion on various matters, and gaining a sense of feeling about both trivial and controversial matters. In terms of the relationship between this particular journalist and the club he reports on, this is institutionalized in a daily phone call to the manager, and more or less daily visits to the club. The point again is that, if we can speak sensibly of complicity here, complicity does not consist in conspiracies by one group or another to prevent the production of particular news items, or the selection of others, but in the recognition that the work of "doing football" professionally is in part the work of mutual elaboration by professionals and journalists of material which can form the basis of published stories. This is reflected in assessments of football professionals in terms of their ability to play this particular game. Thus, as our contact reported,

> The worst manager I ever worked with was *X*. .... I used to ring him up every morning and say, "Got anything for me?," and he'd say, "No, nothing's happened yet" ... I mean, come on, I'm supposed to be writing stories ...

In this instance, castigating the manager as "the worst I ever worked with" is not a reflection on the manager's technical competence but on his inability to understand, as most managers do, the mutually explicative nature of routine story production.

The Production of Football Stories

Having provided this general account of the socially organized character of football journalism, we move now to a more detailed level of analysis, concerning the production of particular stories. We seek to explicate the daily work of the football journalist in and through some observations of interactions which take place around story production. Our data are taken from ongoing ethnographic observation of journalistic practices. The primary focus of our interest here has been the collection, structuring, and use of information resources. Nevertheless as part of this work and for reasons which include long personal acquaintance with a football journalist on the part of one of the authors, and an abiding interest in the game on the part of all of the authors, we have had ongoing access to data relating to football journalism, and it is that data we use here. Thus, and as a methodological note, although our interest in journalism is sustained and intensive, our interest in football journalism has been more occasional. For this reason we call the study we report on here an "occasional" ethnography. Even so, we were in a position to observe the work at first hand, to hear private exchanges and telephone conversations, to conduct informal interviews and listen to a vast fund of anecdotes and stories which constitute a fascinating personal history touching constantly on a rapidly changing public game. The data, we should stress, consists of examples which are sometimes contemporary and sometimes occurred some years ago. The common thread is the journalist who was one party to the production of the story. The journalist concerned works for a regional newspaper in England, and has the specific task of reporting on the affairs of one football club.[8]

We made reference in our introduction to the phenomenon of "events," that is occasions upon which the routine, taken for granted course of things is seen to be disrupted and a circumstance generated which members perceive as "out of the usual" in some way. Such occasions are marked by their storyable character. The members of a setting can and do recount such occasions in the form of stories, sometimes termed "war stories" both between themselves and for the benefit of "outsiders." This phenomenon provides the ethnographer with a way to do ethnography – "getting the natives talking" invariably involves eliciting such storyables. Football journalists are no exception; they have a fund of storyables which provide insight into the routine and non-routine features of their work situation. We begin this section of the paper, then, with a story recounted by our principal informant, one which illustrates something of the "enacted culture" of the football journalist by virtue of a disjuncture it makes available between that culture and the wider occupational culture of news journalism generally. The story was told, at least in part, to exemplify the contrast between "what any football journalist knows" and "what outsiders know," where "outsiders," in this instance, include among their number other journalists working for the same newspaper. With reference to this "members' contrast," then, we can begin to identify the "haecceity" (Garfinkel & Wieder, 1991) of football journalism.

The event the story tells about concerns a noted international footballer (*A*) who was known to be "unsettled" at the club. Our football journalist explained the story to us as follows:

> The reporter from the news desk rang me to say that one of the girl reporters had gone round to *A*'s house, basically to do a birthday photo of their new baby. The thing is, a friend of hers was at night school with *A*'s wife and it seems that *A*'s wife had told her how *A* was really unhappy cos the manager didn't like him ... he wanted to leave but the manager wouldn't let him go. *A* had already been fined once for talking to the press without permission. Anyway, the girl went round and over coffee, out of the blue, the pair of them just spilled the beans about how miserable *A* was. The girl and the news desk wanted to run the story ... let's face it, it was a good story ... but I rang *A* and he was dead worried about what would happen if we did. I told them not to run it because it would cause problems, but they insisted. There was nothing I could do, but I said they should get a quote from [the manager] so I rang him ... unfortunately he wasn't in so I worked up something around something

he'd said about *A* on an earlier occasion and we ran that. I rang him up later and told him what the situation was and what I'd done ... he was quite philosophical about it, really ... he basically accepted there was nothing we could do.[9]

The storyable character of this event resides in the fact that, rather than the story arising from the normal work of the football journalist, it arose, as it were, by accident, during a routine news assignment. What is recognizably unusual in this case is the very fact that the footballer should talk this way to a journalist whose known in common purpose is merely to provide some trivial "color" for the inside pages. That what happened is untoward is evident from the fact that the sports journalist rang the footballer in effect to check what had in fact been said, and the footballer's expression of concern during the course of this call. What is particularly interesting about these events is the sports journalist's "hearing" of the event in a quite different way from that of the news reporter and indeed the editor. For the former, regardless of whether a "good story" may be produced from this happenstance, the events occasion a problematic situation. He, and he alone, recognizes the need to do "work" around the need to get an "official" view, a view which for contingent reasons is not immediately forthcoming. The journalist then engages in a practice which is often assumed to be widespread in the newspaper world, which is simply to invent a quotation from the manager. Our somewhat naive reaction to this was a degree of shock. It seemed that "putting words in mouths" of innocent victims was indeed a common practice. The following extract from a subsequent conversation gives something of the flavor of our misunderstanding:

(*L*: ethnographer; *D*: football journalist)
L: That's disgraceful, really, isn't it? ... I mean you've just gone
      ahead and invented what he said.
D: Well, what else could I do? ... I needed a quote from [the man-
      ager] about this ... and I couldn't get hold of him ... it was just
      one of those things, he was away. So I wrote what I thought he
      might say and then I rang him up the next day and told him what
      I'd written.
L: You don't think that's a bit immoral?
D: Why? ... no ... I wrote what I knew he'd say and checked with
      him afterwards.

Our account of this story might also be said to trade on distinctions between insider and outsider but, and to re-iterate, it is the member's contrast that is of interest to us here. That is, the problem for the journalist here is the management of "what outsiders know," which in this case is what constitutes a "good" story, against "what any football journalist knows," which is to do with understanding the ramifications of the story within the club and in terms of the club's relationship with the press. As we have stated above, the work of the football journalist entails day-to-day meetings with football professionals, meetings which rely on mutual understandings of what can be reported and what cannot, and in what circumstances and which can be sustained only through the ongoing maintenance of those understandings. This particular story arises from the work of someone who was unambiguously doing journalism as a "news" rather than a "sports" reporter. In other words, and for the football journalist, the "news" reporter is an "outsider" who is not party to the rules of the game. Whether or not it is the case that the footballer concerned was talking under the misapprehension that the conversation was "off the record," the fact is that talking in this way on the part of a professional footballer is recognizably unusual and problematic to the sports journalist. This is not to say that footballers do not wilfully break rules and attempt to manipulate the media to their own ends, for our own data suggests they sometimes do. What is unusual is precisely that such issues should be raised during the course of an otherwise trivial exercise in reporting. Indeed, one of the striking features of the above example is the way in which, from the point of view of the journalist, the routine and the unusual are more or less the reverse of what one might anticipate "from the outside." Doing the work of the story has routine elements, of course, and they are to do with, in this instance, managing a recognizably inadvertent outburst by the footballer concerned into a "fair enough" story. Part of this work involves what for the observer is a startling act, that of inventing a quote. The point of course is that this invention is utterly routine, and is predicated precisely on what is known in common between the journalist and the manager. The most interesting question to be addressed here is not whether journalists might, as a matter of routine, invent quotes, slant what is said, or make public private exchanges, but how it is in this instance that in so doing, the apparent "victim" reacts philosophically and demonstrated no subsequent ill feeling. The point is that "putting words into someone's mouth" in this case does not literally mean writing whatever one might like the person to have said, but rather means the imaginative re-creation of what one thinks they would have said. The absence of any ill will is testimony to the skill of the journalist in representing the views of the manager without having spoken to him. That this is possible is precisely a feature of the skillful practice of a sports reporter. After all, versions of what was published have indeed been said on other occasions, as both parties know, and the journalist is manifesting an insider's "good faith" in reporting not "any old version" but the version which he believes would reflect the manager's opinion. That he subsequently rings the manager to check that this is indeed so, and that the manager is evidently content with the published version evidences the fact that what for the naive ethnographer is a dramatic fabrication is for the journalist and for the manager an ordinary and mundane event. In contrast, the storyable character of this event comes precisely from a distinction that the observer would not find remarkable, to whit, the distinction between a news reporter and a sports reporter. They are, after all, both journalists working for the same newspaper. Yet for the sports journalist it clearly does matter, in that news reporters and their sub-editors are not party to the ramifications of this story, and the fact that it matters occasions the work that he does in this context. That is, and for us, what is of interest is not just that the distinction between insiders and outsiders is problematized in this account, but how it is made manifest in the activities of the sports journalist. It is the very fact of his recognition that a "breach" has occurred in the normal workings of the football world, a realization that is to do with his instincts as a sports journalist rather than a journalist at large, that occasions his "mediating" work here.

As we have tried to make clear, our descriptions of routine working are not intended to dispute the notion that interest groups will not attempt to control story output. Our data is replete with both trivial and rather more serious examples of attempted interference, accompanied by what could be construed as precisely the kinds of threat that the likes of Chomsky (1969) use as evidence of the "managed consensus." After all, our source has remarked to us at various times, apropos of the football club:

> They're paranoid about anything that appears that looks like criticism. They hate criticism.

and,

> They want the stories that suit them when it suits them – not when anyone else wants them if it doesn't suit. But you can't turn the publicity machine on and off.

In referencing his relationship with a particular ex-player (*W*), he commented:

> It's like *W* ... he hated me and made it obvious. He finally told me, after he'd retired, that it was because I wrote more than anyone else about his bad disciplinary record. But he couldn't have it both ways. I wrote more about him full stop than any other reporter. I wrote about his goals and I wrote about his bookings. He can't just pick and choose what is reported about him.

As a further exemplification, the reporter indicated something of the tension that can exist between club and media:

Football clubs never change. They always want to control the critics, especially the media. Look what they've done lately ... they're even thinking of banning local radio from matches. They've had a few run-ins and now they've got their own radio station ... they reckon they can do without outsiders sticking their noses in. It's the same with T.V. They're talking about setting up their own T.V. station, but do you think that ITV and BBC would take it lying down? They'd have an even bigger problem with Sky, because they put an immense amount of money into football. Perhaps they'll see sense and accept that it's swings and roundabouts with the media.

"Swings and roundabouts" is a formulation that refers to the way in which the work of the journalist is inevitably the work of managing tensions between football clubs' expectations and the expectations of editors and readers. Clearly, football clubs, much as any other commercial interest, will try to control stories which appear because they perceive it as in their interest to do so.

At the same time, however, editors (who themselves may have little or no understanding of the workings of the football world) also induce tensions through their insistence on news value to the exclusion of considerations relating to relations with the club. Thus, in the context of one story we mention below, the editor, insisting the story should run, and against the advice of the journalist, said:

I'm running this paper, not [the football club] ... They can't tell me what to print and what not to print. If they stop talking to us, well tough ... they won't get anything in the paper.

What is evident here is that the somewhat cosy notion of a complicitous relationship between the commercial interests of the media and football clubs barely recognizes the way work is done which can result in either consensus or in conflict. Our point here is that outcomes that can be construed as "complicitous" and outcomes which might be viewed as "conflictual" are precisely the outcomes of work done by the journalist with editors, with footballers, with managers, and so on. They are the accomplishment of members rather than the logical outcome of either dominant ideologies or the dominance of economic interest groups. The point is best made by reference to some relatively recent events in which the club concerned was implicated. In the first of these, it came to the attention of the reporter that an employee in the ticket office had been sacked as a result of widespread, systematic, and long-term corruption in the selling on of tickets to "touts."[10]

The first reaction of the reporter, on hearing from a source that these "storyable events" had taken place, was to ring the club to get a response to this allegation. As he later commented:

> Well, they made no comment, as you'd expect ... but they also put a lot of pressure on ... they threatened to withdraw cooperation.

These actions by the football club are probably not in the expectation that the subsequent story can be kept from the pages of the newspaper, but "damage limitation" exercises in which it is anticipated that the tone of stories subsequently produced will perhaps be more "balanced." In this instance, the story was not printed, but the reasons had little to do with the pressure applied by the club. Rather:

> The problem is, they've denied everything and they're sticking to another story ... and we've got no proof except the word of a ticket tout ...

In the next example, the complex relationship between the interest of the club, the practices of the journalist, and the perceived interests of the fans who read the newspaper are all interwoven. The end result was a series of reports which, from the point of view of the club were variously received as "fair enough" stories, that is, essentially correct, or as "mischief making." In this instance, the manager of the club had some weeks previously given an interview to a national newspaper in which he had mused on his own future. In effect, he had indicated that he saw his future at the club in terms of "moving up" (perhaps to a seat on the board of directors) and further had suggested that a previous player with the club, an ex-International player who had been extremely popular with fans could be "brought in." Leaving aside questions of the manager's own motivations for giving such an interview, the initial reactions to this event were prompted by the evident fact that inferences had been drawn about his intentions. In this case, inferences were clearly drawn by both the assistant manager of the club and by the Chief Executive of another club in the area (club *B*). That this is so is revealed by the fact that the interview occasioned a telephone call from the assistant manager (*K*) to the local reporter (*D*).

> *K:*   Uhhh, *D*, hi, it's *K* ... uhhh, listen, can you give me some advice in confidence? The thing is, I've been approached ... you know *F* [the manager] gave that interview? ... well, I've been approached by [Chief Executive of club *B*] ... he wants me for the job at [club *B*] ...

D: this is off the record, *K*, yeah?

K: What? Yeah, Christ, yeah ... I'm trying to work out what I should do cos I don't know what *F*'s plans are and I don't know what it means for me ... listen, *D*, can you find out what's going on for me?

He reveals that an approach had been made to him from Club B in which the Chief Executive of club B had stated that it was the intention to sack the current manager of club B and wished to establish whether the assistant manager would be interested in the shortly to be vacant post.[11]

He further asks the reporter if the latter will give him some advice. Such an appeal would hardly be a common event, but is indicative of at least some level of trust over what is after all a strong story if published, and one which would have consequences for both clubs involved. This bears some further examination. After all, we have established that the interests of a football club cannot be said to dominate decisions about what to publish, and it is on the face of it quite remarkable that a club official should ask a reporter for advice in a confidential matter which all parties except the reporter might wish to remain private. The point is that assumptions are made here by the assistant manager as to what might constitute "likely" practice by the journalist in this context, assumptions predicated on the belief that confidences can and will be kept. Equally, the journalist draws inferences concerning the situation on the basis of what he knows about the assistant manager:

> *K*'s a diffident character ... really nice bloke but a bit shy and quite self-deprecating. Don't get me wrong, he's very capable and he could easily do the job at [club *B*], but basically he's worried that if he moves he might get the sack after a year or two. After all, they've got through a lot of managers. Really, he'd prefer to stay, but he needs guarantees.

The reporter's (*D*) response to this somewhat delicate situation was to raise the matter in his daily call to the manager (*F*):

> Hi *F*, *D* here ... I wanted to ask you about the story in [the national newspaper] ... the thing is, I can't see what's going to happen to *K*. ... after all, he's very popular with the fans ...

For the reporter, again using knowledge of the world of professional football, the salient question is what was going on such that the manager had made public statements which appeared to overlook the career interests of the assistant manager. As he put it to us:

> I think he forgot ... I genuinely think he was so busy pursuing his own interests that he forgot that it put K in a rather difficult position.

Later in his daily call, therefore, he raised this point with the manager, asking him:

> Does this mean that K will always be an assistant if he stays here?

eliciting the response that this was not the intention. He subsequently also, using his regular contact with the players, ascertained that many of them were surprised and disappointed at the apparent lack of support for a popular member of the management team. The result was a strong story on the back page of the newspaper, with the headline:

> K NEEDS [the club's] SUPPORT.

Following on from this, the club Chairman then asked that the matter be held in abeyance until after an important Cup match. Perhaps unfortunately, the incumbent manager at the other club in question was sacked and national press speculation began as to who would be likely to take over. At this point, the name of the assistant manager was mentioned in one such story as a possible target. The assistant manager (K) rang the journalist again, repeating his request for advice. He also raised his fears concerning action the club might take if it became apparent that he had spoken to the press. During the telephone conversation, he mentioned that:

> My lad's been running around telling all his mates that [the chairman of the other club] has been on at me about the job ... I can always blame him, I suppose ....

The journalist wrote a second piece in which he argued that the assistant needed guarantees and suggesting that the club could obviate press speculation by a public declaration of support for the assistant. On the same day, the club secretary rang the journalist and accused him of "mischief making and speculation." Given that, since the source of the information on which the story was founded was the subject of the story, such an accusation is inaccurate. That is, there is available to the journalist a ready-made defense, namely that the story is true and that he has evidence to that effect. Interestingly, however, the journalist declined to defend himself in these terms because to do so would have consequences for the assistant. Indeed, to our knowledge no mention was made of the approach either to other members of the club or on the printed page. There can be little question that such a story, if it had appeared, would have been "big" news for the readership of the football pages.

In this instance, then, we can identify all of the elements that conventional sociologies would cite as evidence of "managing consensus," including several attempts at pressuring the journalist by members of the club. The parties to this particular "event" ultimately do produce what for most of them is a "fair enough" story, one which both meets the needs of the newspaper and at the same time avoids raising detail which might be troublesome for the club and one of its members. Regardless, our point is that understanding, describing and explicating the play of interactions that take place during the course of the unfolding story is foundational to any subsequent sociological description of journalism in insider/outsider terms. The parties to this latter story, in other words, have *achieved*, in and through their knowledge of each other and their mutual concerns, some kind of consensus over the boundaries of acceptable work on the part of the journalist. Notions of consensus are not, and cannot be, external to the work.

Conclusion

Our necessarily brief introduction to sociological work on journalism referred to conceptions of media production which variously rely on arguments concerning the way in which political and economic relationships underpin story production, on the "gatekeeper" effect of the media, whereby the flow of information from "insiders" is mediated and controlled by journalists with common interests, or on "preference analytic" stances (Gans, 1980). All of these approaches rely on some conception of structural interests and/or "occupational cultures." As we have pointed out, such theories (and we make no attempt to adjudicate between them) show a singular disdain for the haecceity or "just thisness" of journalistic work, and our task here has been to rectify this by providing a flavor of just how the work of football journalism is encountered. In so doing, we are not attempting to theorize the relationships formed as a consequence, but are concerned with the contingent ways in which members of different groups play out their interests in ways which are specific to the story in question.

What our small vignettes suggest is a complex and shifting pattern of loyalties, members' knowledge, personal ties, manipulations and usages, which work in many directions. Insiders and outsiders, rather than being preordained features of the "occupational culture," are accomplishments of members, depending on the story in question. Such boundaries, that is, are endlessly shifting, produced out of a set of "known in common" practices. "Known in common" here refers not to complicity between the interests of the football club and the journalist who is subject to the play of those interests, nor to complicity between the investigative journalist and the salacious interests of his or her readers, but to the way those who "know about football" and who, moreover, know about football in ways that are deeply implicated in the work of "doing" football, must manage their interactions on the basis of what they know about each other. That is, the fragile web of relationships on which journalistic access is possible is formed from a close "members" understanding of the mutual job of work to be done. Disagreements, of course, arise not only between club and journalist, but between journalists.[12] Disagreements may also arise from within the ranks of football professionals who may then seek to manipulate press attention, or otherwise innocent mistakes may be made with much the same results. Nevertheless, and in keeping with our use of the concept of "demand condition," they must be "managed." Observation of the moment-by-moment work of the journalist suggests it could hardly be otherwise. After all, the work is characterized by ongoing, routine, and personal contact between the journalist and the object of his or her attention. Nonetheless, sporting journalists are journalists. The demand conditions of their work, as mentioned above, include the temporally ordered production of both descriptive and "revelatory" copy. In the latter instance, although sometimes the journalist may happen on stories, on other occasions the need for this kind of copy can be generated by colleagues or indeed by media competition. Our point is that footballers must treat with sports journalists according to their knowledge of what it is that sports journalists know and do, and vice versa.[13] That is, it is their mutual apprehension of situations as being "like this" that allows the intelligibility of the football story. In characterizing work this way, the notion that journalists in their relationships with football clubs are simply "insiders" who report those matters which clubs wish reported, and any countervailing idea that journalists are predatory investigators on behalf of the fan, where the members of the football club are, so to speak, "innocent victims" is clearly problematized. Notions of the complicity of "insiders" must, given these conditions be a gloss on the relationship between the journalist and, in this case, the football professional – a relationship which is founded on a "working collaboration" between football club and journalist, based on known in common features of the footballer's world.

A second and related conclusion is that decision-making, or "preference," in turn, is not an individualistic process but the outcome of the deployment of various concerns and interests. Although football professionals provide sports journalists with a large part of the descriptive material that fills the back pages of the newspaper, the journalist must *somehow* deal with matters arising. As the example below makes clear, where, for instance, competitors are engaged in investigation, or have placed a particular spin on a story, then the issues they raise must be addressed:

> There was one time in [Europe] when the paper just changed my whole intro and made it sound really bad because of the last time but in fact the authorities had really tightened up and there'd been welcoming parties at the airport and they put flowers around [the manager's] shoulders and things. There were about two signs saying "Welcome to Hell" but they were miles away and they didn't compare with the welcoming party. Anyway I wrote my piece and sent it over but the radio and T.V. people had focused on these two banners and beefed it up for their angle. So the desk said, "what are you playing at?" – and I tried to explain to them that there was no problem but they said "you've got to beef it up." Sometimes they say "beef it up" and you know that if you don't then they will, so it's better to do it yourself, so I gave them another version. They obviously still weren't satisfied, so they changed a few of the words and shifted the emphasis to make it sound like the radio and T.V. reports. It's more of a process than a decision because of the number of people involved. The news desk will have put in their stuff in which it gives their view, and the sports desk will want it to coincide and the editor will think it needs beefing up so at every stage someone puts a bit more in until it's completely different. So it's not as if it's a decision, it's a process.

Events must, as soon as they enter the public realm, be reported. Moreover, when stories arise, the manner of reporting will, as our examples show, not be a matter for the sports journalist alone. In this example, demand conditions are established by reporting in other media, and the final story is the outcome of work done not only by the journalist concerned but by the "sports desk," the "news desk," and the editor. In sum, the idea that journalism can be understood simply in terms of decision making, then, ignores the processual character of work. While this work might be glossed as "negotiating the relations between two worlds," it is the detail of that work in its local and processual accomplishment that this chapter has sought to describe.

Notes

1. Anecdotally, there are more subscribers to the Sky Sports Channel, a satellite television service, than to any other service they provide.
2. See, for example, Rowe (1992) and Bourgeois (1995). In Bourgeois' article, the work of the sports journalist is examined in terms of a "conflict of interests" which impacts on the "narrative" that is constructed. In so doing, it fails

to examine the *in situ* practice of sports journalism, focusing instead upon the "product" on the basis of unexamined assumptions about practice.

3. Criticism of the gate-keeping model has pointed to its over-simplification and neglect of the complex variety of influences to which journalists are exposed. It has been critiqued for its overly determined conception of news production; journalists and other news workers are conceived as decision-makers who make choices among a range of potential news information in an essentially "pre-programmed" fashion. Thus the gate-keeping model takes little account of the "active" ways in which news journalists generate news in the first place. Thus, Schudson (1989) remarks that:

> The term "gatekeeper" is still in use and provides a handy, if not altogether appropriate, metaphor for the relation of news organizations to news products. A problem with the metaphor is that it leaves "information" sociologically untouched, a pristine material that comes to the gate already prepared; the journalist as "gatekeeper" simply decides which pieces of prefabricated news will be allowed through the gate. (p. 265)

4. More recently, and in a more sophisticated vein, sociologies of the media have concerned themselves with such notions as "textuality," and audience reception (Jacobs, 1996). Regardless, the force of such analyses is typically to separate communities of interest according to their positioning within a complex of economic, political, and ideological determinants.

5. Turner (1969) says:

> By demand characteristics I mean to refer to those situational and contextual features which persons engaged in everyday routines orient to as governing and organizing their activities.... (p. 4)

6. Leaving aside the production of "gossip" and "rumor" which is characteristic of the talk of football fans.

7. Typically, English newspapers give sports coverage at the back of the edition with the lead story or headline news appearing on the back page and more analytical, in-depth treatment on the inside pages.

8. For obvious reasons, we can neither name the journalist concerned, nor the club. We have taken steps to disguise various stories in the earnest hope that the protagonists cannot be identified.

9. All football clubs in England have rules concerning the conditions under which players may officially talk to the press. These normally include a requirement that there be prior permission from the manager.

10. The source of the information was a ticket "tout" involved in selling match tickets at prices considerably higher than the official price, a practice familiar to sports fans all over the world. The fact that a "tout" might wish to have such an issue publicized, however, raises an interesting question concerning the "official" stance by football clubs over these practices. The practice has recently become illegal in Britain.

11. Such approaches are illegal under Football Association rules, but are believed to be common practice.

12. Space forbids similar data which analyzes the relationship between the sport

journalist and organized groups of fans.

13. This is institutionally recognized in the annual Professional Footballer Association media courses which are run for would-be managers. The journalist we followed lectures regularly on these courses and has referred to the work of lecturing as "training [would be managers] in how you'd like them to behave."

Chapter 6

Glances, Trances, and Their Relevance for a Visual Sociology[1]

Douglas Macbeth

I. Introduction

I want to lay out a very modest domain of inquiry into the coherence of non-fiction film and video.[2] It has to do with the work of the continuous shot as a course of analysis, and with the resulting record as a produced coherence. The work of the shot is the mark of *verité* film-video making, amateur and professional. It furnishes what we see between-the-edits of documentary and ethnographic films, and is thus a constitutive feature of what we find across them. It reminds us that someone is at work, producing a first witnessing of the affairs we find on the screen.

Film is a profoundly expressive and formative cultural medium with a rich analytic and critical literature. The history of film studies is punctuated by treatments of the directed achievements of the *cinematic* shot, meaning those highly crafted sequences of continuous action that are the laminations of scripting, direction, acting and equipmental virtuosity. The baby carriage careening down the palace steps in Eisenstein's *Battleship Potemkin* (1925), the action shots of John Ford westerns, and the corpus of Hitchcock's films are marked by their high achievements in organizing and recording compelling courses of action, presented to the viewer in the brilliant temporal and audio-visual detail of a distinctive field of view. Hitchcock's *Rope* (1948) is perhaps the summary expression of the discipline of the shot in feature film: It is a film consisting of approximately 10 edits. In its day, motion picture film was available in reels of approximately ten minutes, and *Rope* was produced as eight continuous shots, each one meticulously crafted to assemble and display a synchrony of action unfolding before the camera.

Though there are awards and recognitions for cinematography, in cinema the shot is the director's medium, and an enormously complex aesthetic, technical, and practical order of activity. Within the literatures of non-fiction film, however, the shot is an object for which the familiar terms of theory and criticism have had little to say. The reasons are, in part, matters of a technical history, and a more abiding intellectual history. Following a brief review of those histories, I want to propose that both the work of the shot in non-fiction film and video, and the record it yields, are indeed available to analysis, but not by the prevailing terms of film theory or criticism. In the long run, I want to propose that a sociology of a kind is the apposite analytic discourse for recovering the practices and achievements of camerapersons in the field.

Non-fiction film has from the outset, and especially at the outset, been a meditation on the spectacles of ordinary things and the powers of their representation. Lumière's *L'Arié d'un Train en Gare* (1895) produced a spectacular record of the mere arrival of a train.

> In 1895 the citizens of La Ciotat observed the arrival of a train with indifference, but those who watched (the film) reportedly dove under their seats in terror. In one sense this was the purest non-fiction film, the least compromised representation of "reality"; the passengers walking blankly by Lumière's camera, not knowing that they are being filmed ... (Weinberger, 1994: 4)

The account offers us a virtual origin story for two of the central topics of non-fiction film study: the meaning of film for its audience, and the relationship of filmmaking to the world it records. At this peculiar moment in filmmaking, Lumière was indeed able to record "people doing precisely what they would have been doing if the camera were not there" (Goldschmidt (n.d.), in Weinberger, 1994). It required the utter novelty of the occasion to achieve this separation between the work of record-making and the character of the records made. However we might imagine a discourse on subjectivity or social location, Lumière's early record-making was relieved of the camera's "gaze," and with none to return, the world "walked blankly by." Filmmaking thus began with an exemption from reactivity, and though lost now, Goldschmidt, and much of film theory, remembers it, in discourses on objectivity, bias, and "researcher affects." The possibility of recovering a semblance of Lumière's circumstance has been a regular topic, even for those who have no use for it.[3]

As for the meaning of *L'Arié d'un Train en Gare* for its audience, the audience for Flaherty's (1924) first rushes at Hudson Bay witnessed them in much the same way. They too were confronted with seeing again the spectacle of their life-world in a darkened room, and learned whatever these devices and alchemies were doing well enough to suggest still other things that Flaherty might look at with his apparatus (and thus offer their assessments of what things were worthy of seeing again).[4] Though we don't know how they discussed it, they too were among the first to take up the warranting questions of non-fiction film analysis and criticism: What of everyday spectacle shall be represented, and what does its representation mean? Ours is yet a third topic. It focuses on filmmaking as a practical order of witnessing that has developed without need for a theory of film, and owes instead to film's technical history, the professional practices that have grown up around it, and the domains of social life that then came into view.

Some Technical History[5]

The shot we are interested in emerged at a formative time in non-fiction filmmaking, where the first portable synchronous-sound film systems were used, and whereby documentary filmmakers came into possession of a novel circumstance. Portability and film speed had already uncoupled the portrait camera from the studio, and opened the world to the work of Reis, Sanders, Weegee, and the family album. It was opened as well to newsreel and travelogue, but not yet to the moving-language spectacles of the social world. Intertwining temporal duration and synchronous sound, portable film would produce records of social action in its audible-visible detail. It opened the world to documentation in a way and in places that had not been seen or heard before, and presented camerapersons with a distinctive task and field: finding the continuous course of locally meaningful action as could be found, for example, in the course of a conversation.

Vaughn (1992[1979]) describes the development of portable synchronous-sound filmmaking as an opening onto hitherto inaccessible realms of "domestic life," realms that show a fragility to observation, and a non-repeatable indifference to direction. Portability alone afforded some order of access, but synchronous sound transformed the intelligibility of domestic life. The technical development of documentary equipment provided for entirely new fields to interrogate in the construction of its continuous records, and the spectacles found by Flaherty (1924) or Bateson and Mead (1942) were other than what we find in Wiseman, McElwee, or *COPS*.[6]

(See also Barnow, 1979; Kozloff, 1979; and Nichols, 1991 on the transformations of portability).

It was then not only portable systems, but portable synchronous systems that permitted a new order of record making. And the fullness of the technical achievement was not only that the hand-held synchronous system could now "hear." Motion picture sound was not itself a problem, and television was already in place when documentary film developed synchronous sound in the late 1950s. The technical problem for documentary film was rather an organizational problem first: how to free camerapersons and sound persons from the cables and tethers that constrained their range of movement. The portability of the new equipment reorganized the work of field production, by permitting new ways of moving through the social world to assemble its documentation. (See Fauman (1978) on organizations of the crew.) With the development of synchronizing signal generators, each medium (audio and visual) was now attached to a body that could navigate within the very affairs it was seeking, recording them in synchronous detail *as* their coordinated navigations. The camera and microphone became enfolded in moving bodies, and what could then be seen, approached, heard and recorded was an order of spectacle novel to film representation. The possibility immediately began generating footage of a kind that had not been seen-heard before. The "footing" of the record-makers was transformed by the hand-held, synchronous sound technology, and so were their records.[7]

Of course, I am trading on wavy distinctions when I speak of the "shot" as a creature of hand held cameras and synchronous sound – it is not only to be found there. Bateson and Mead (1942) recorded hand-held 16mm film in the field, and weren't the first (see MacBean, 1994). Flaherty reportedly had a remarkable capacity for holding cameras in odd places and positions (Weinberger, 1994), and motion picture film technology was available to the public for a price in the 1930s. And in looking for the organization of the shot, we will examine Asch's footage of a Yanomamo *Ax Fight* (1975), though it was recorded entirely from a tripod. Yet though the continuous record is variously produced, it is distinctively recognizable as a singular and contingent course of inquiry behind the view-finder, and a first exhibit hopes to show this on the page.

"Primary"

Rouch (1975) and Marshall and de Brigard (1975) cite one of the distinctive first expressions of synchronous documentary film in the Drew Associates production *Primary* (1960), documenting the 1960 Wisconsin state Democratic presidential primary campaigns of Hubert Humphrey and John Kennedy. It was among the first to use a cableless synch-sound system, of their own design. Both Rouch and Marshall and de Brigard refer to a

Image Set 1
Primary (1960)
by permission of Robert Drew, Drew Associates

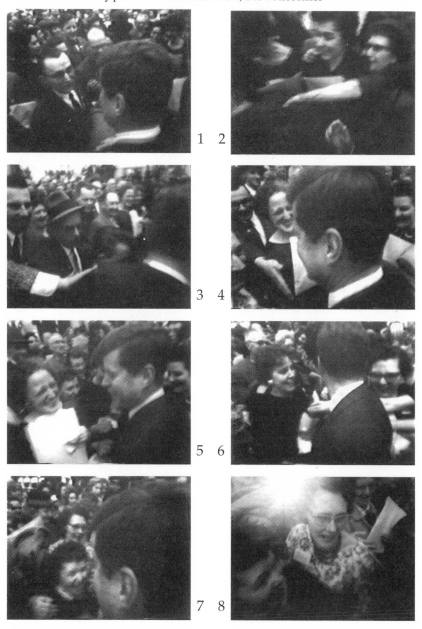

particular shot in which the cameraperson, Albert Maysles, follows Kennedy's exit from his limousine, and entrance into a campaign hall filled with supporters.[8] There is an edit as Kennedy enters the hall, and then we begin a continuous shot of his walk from the rear of the hall, to the stage. (See Image Set 1.) He is walking down a pulsing aisle of supporters extending hands, glances, remarks and shouts. It is a remarkable passage, tinged with celebrity. Maysles walks directly behind the candidate, and the image is from an elevated angle, as though of the tallest person in the hall by nearly a head.[9] Throughout, the view-found is of a singular witnessing, in the course of looking for the developing affairs he finds.

The record is built as the viewfinder's work of finding his way, second in the lead, seeing only what he can. We see Kennedy's walk-through as Maysles pursues its unfolding course, and the Image Set attempts to exhibit the shot as a temporal course of action. Finding his way not unlike a vehicle within a traffic flow (bumper to bumper is more apt), he records the pulse and cadence of Kennedy's walk-through, finding it just after its production in the world.[10] Thus, at times the camera nearly stumbles into the candidate, at other times loses, and then recovers, its exposure to flash bulbs, house lights and dark fields, to find again the paced array that yields a recognizable course of Kennedy making *his* way. Punctuated by turns, pauses, engagements and rejoinders, the viewfinder's task is to see and find the order of the procession in its unfolding production, an order that is sensible only in the witnessing, for Maysles and for us.

We find the occasion as Maysles' equipmental witnessing, and find it not only as the affairs to which the camera was oriented, but as those to which the occasion was too. In the talk, looks, queues, and co-orientations of the persons assembled, the occasion "itself" was oriented to its own production, and the camera was near its focus, relying on the ordered social trajectories of greetings, pace and gesture for the organization of its technical production. For us, and for Maysles, the scene possesses an endogenous intelligibility – in Jayyusi's (1991b) lovely phrase to which we will return, a "scenic intelligibility." In these scenic orientations, in the developing coherence of an entry underway, both the occasion *and* its record were assembled. Though we may understand them as documentary shards of still larger fields of meaning, planning and action (or of power and gender), at the edges of the frame the record yields a cogent world-in-action. How the camera finds and frames a world for the record from within a world for the witnessing, is the interest I find in "the shot." To recommend further ways of speaking about those practices and achievements, I want to turn to the more familiar terms of film theory and criticism, and ask whether and how the work of documentary record-making can be found there.

A Semiotic of Film: The Visible and the Invisible

Semiotic analysis is the most mature and productive program of film study, possessing a distinguished intellectual history, and pointing not to logics of classification, but to structures of signification. The first achievement of semiotic analysis, structural linguistics, offers an analytic program that both attacks and re-affirms one of the great recurring formal analytic puzzles: the ordered relationship of visible and invisible worlds. The systematics of order and meaning are promised for the relationship. Expressed in Saussure's (1966) speech-language pair, *parole* displays in indefinite iterations the masked structuration of *la langue,* in the operations of a sign. Meaningful communication is achieved in the ordered relations of the signifier and the signified, and the play of meaning and language is then on a field of signs and syntagmatic structures. The sense and reference of *parole* is thus assembled as a signed-sense. What is also to be seen is that of the foundational objects of semiotic analysis – the sign as the relations of signification that join signifier and signified – two thirds of them are shrouded from view; only the signifier is in evidence, standing on behalf of the structures and relations that give it expression.

Borrowed from the promise of structural linguistics, the formal structures of signed-relations have become the prevailing program for the analysis of film sense and sequence, and disclosing the operations of film signification has become the central analytic task (cf. Eco, 1976; Metz, 1974; and Wollen, 1970). By Burgin's (1982) account, the semiotic analysis of the photographic image developed oppositionally, to counter a prior foundationalism in photo criticism and analysis. This foundationalism was not in the first instance a matter of theory. It rather owed to the compelling, naturalistic spectacle of the photo-image itself. The realism, naive intelligibility, and material detail of the image not only sent Lumière's audience under their seats, it invited

> a metaphysics of interpretation through which an attempt is made to reconstitute the missing "presence" which is felt to be the source of a singular and true content of the empirically given form of the text ... [a] logocentric longing which is expressed in the "window-on-the-world" realisms of the great majority of writers on photography. (Burgin, 1982: 55).

We can usefully say that Magritte's caption announced the semiosis of the image, whose first move was to bracket the naive realism of the image and suspend its naturalistic accountability for those who see it.

Semiotic analysis thus disrupts the grounds of image sense and meaning, and the image becomes an object formatively embedded in shifting chains of signification. At the same time, however, the semiotic move preserves the mystery and primacy of a "presence" elsewhere. Image-signs are always other and more than can be seen or shown, and the meaning of the image becomes an object removed from its mere visibility. By some accounts, what is evident in the image is consigned to what is "accessory, and more or less accidental" (Burgin, 1982: 51). The organization of visible-invisible relations can be seen in Eco's (1976, 1985[1967]) "codes of recognition," as the play of un-seen binaries and conventions within systems of "valid expectations in the world of signs" (1985: 593). In this fashion, the first move of semiotic analysis is to render the intelligibility of the image opaque, and then organize a program that will clarify it. Even there, however, the posit of structures of signification relies on the intelligibility of the image, evidently. The *evident* sense of the image provides for an analytic field that already possesses its prize.

Narrativity

For Metz (1992[1968]), the development of film as a semiotic exercise is tied to its development as a narrative, and editor's, medium. He formulates the difference between feature and documentary film as a matter of "dialect" within a narrative language that owes to the early history of the film invention:

> The merging of the cinema and of narrativity was a great fact, which was by no means predestined ... a fact that in turn conditioned the later evolution of the film as a semiological reality ... *(I)t was precisely the extent that the cinema confronted the problems of narration* that, in the course of successive groupings, it came to produce a body of specific signifying procedures. (1992[1968]: 170; emphasis in original)

By this account, filmmaking found its conventions of signification as it became a narrative program and narrativity not only formulates film's task and animates technique. It embeds film in a social and material space: The *cinéma* – the theater of the narrative telling – became the institutional site for the play of film's signed-signifying assemblages. It is the place and occasion of the telling, and the analytic setting for much of film theory and criticism. In the *cinéma*, we encounter the full complement of the relations of film-semiosis, and the puzzle-parts of semiotic film analysis – the full play of the narrative ensemble of texts, readers and authors, signed structure and interpretation – comes to rest there (cf. Silverman, 1983; Martinez, 1992; Metz, 1992[1968]; Stoller, 1994).

Within the plenum of the *cinéma*, the "shot" we are interested in – the shot as a practical course of action – becomes a formal analytic object. Filmic sense begins with the image, as an iconic "resemblance," code or technique of composition.[11] The image plays in semiosis as a first cogent thing, whose cogency is already implicated in syntagmatic operations

(Barthes, 1981; Eco, 1985[1967]; Metz, 1985). Metz (1992[1968]) places the image in the denotative "plane" of film's semiology, "represented by the literal (that is, perceptual) meaning of the spectacle reproduced in the image," whose sense is (re)presented without notice on condition of its place within constellations of other signings (1992[1968]: 171). Montage, or image transition, is then (re)affirmed as the analytic focus. As for the shot and how it is different than the image, and for the difference between photography and film more generally, the denotations of the shot are themselves produced "articulations." Thus, filmic denotations are already syntagmatic, and the shot is to be appreciated as the "smallest unit" of filmic signification.

> The shot is therefore not comparable to the word in a lexicon; rather it resembles a complete statement ... already the result of an essentially free combination, a "speech" arrangement. (Metz, 1992[1968]: 173)

Notwithstanding Metz's caution and ambivalence for the notion of a "cinematographic language" (1985: 583), the place of the metaphor in film theory is evident in the passage above. Language structuralism encounters not only problems for its extension into film, but solutions within its own metaphor. Film may not show us a language-system – a *langue* – and yet still show us an expressive language. If so, film semiosis becomes evidence not only of structure, but of un-seen subjectivities living beyond the frame, "speaking" the image and/or producing its articulations:

> Jean-Pierre Oudart refers to the spectator who occupies the missing field as the "Absent One." The Absent One, also known as the Other, has all the attributes of the mythologically potent symbolic father: potency, knowledge, transcendental vision, self-sufficiency, and discursive power. (Silverman, 1983: 203-204)[12]

To this account, we can agree that the image implicates the work of an "other." But by our account, it is an other really, and without transcendental credentials. Produced by camerapersons in the field, the non-fiction record offers second-sight knowledge of first-seen affairs. How the one affords the other is the achievement of the shot, and we can more reasonably look for the work of this achievement in non-fiction film studies.

Non-Fiction Film

The literature of non-fiction film studies – visual anthropology and sociology – tends to show a double movement to structuralism, in its debts to film theory and its attachments to social science. Ethnographic film study assumes the discourse of formal analysis by its first attachments to social science, and the obligations of a disciplinary discourse have produced the identifying topics of the literature (see, e.g., Heider, 1976; Hockings, 1975; and Nichols, 1991 on what makes ethnographic film ethnographic).[13] Formal analysis also affirms the puzzles of visible-invisible relations, and the extraordinary visual-temporal detail of the film record only thickens them. Weinberger (1994) finds in the puzzle the identifying questions of ethnographic film study. He credits the MacDougalls in the early 1960s for producing the first ethnographic films to introduce an order of native interaction (or "domestic life") into the record, by filming ordinary conversations and using sub-titles to show their sense and coherence. But this move in opening their records to organizations of local action and knowledge is then re-considered in light of a familiar analytic problem. Speaking of a trilogy of the MacDougalls' films among the Turkana of Kenya, Weinberger concludes:

> As a record, its style is unusually inventive; but it never solves the perennial questions of the genre: When there are not individuals, who speaks for the people? ... When there is an individual, to what extent can she or he represent the group? (1994: 19)

The good sense of the questions is overwhelming. They trade on the received paradox of ethnography: Though accountable to formal knowledge, it can only and unavoidably collect quiddities – collections of just these things on just these occasions. Alternatively, Weinberger's questions also ring fundamentally of a tourist's question, asking for more than we can have of the world in view. The "realism" of this analytic-tourism stipulates a field larger than can be seen at all, and thus grounds an irremediable complaint for whatever actual ethnographic record can be produced. What lies out of view organizes a dissatisfaction – and a skepticism – for what lies within. The problem is formulated as though it were peculiar to filmic records and their realism. But it is the same as the unachieved program of formal analysis, namely, to organize a systematic documentary method that will assemble a field, a field of view of distal order and local meaning, the likes of which no native could achieve.[14] To find some relief from the complaint, we could recommend a paraphrase of Weinberger. We could ask instead: When there is an individual, what is she *doing*? This is the actual-practical task the view-finder routinely finds.[15]

Though sometimes critical of the linguistic analog, the literature of ethnographic film just as often returns to signed-systems for its analytic coherence (cf. Bellman and Jules-Rosette, 1977; Crawford, 1992; Ruby, 1982; and Worth, 1981).[16] Ruby (1982) and Worth (1981) furnish our exemplars. For both, the turn to a semiotic of ethnographic film begins with an ambivalence that becomes reconciled to itself.

Ruby (1982) is working to position ethnographic film as a disciplinary exercise, between Realist and Formative film theories. The former treats film as a "transparent" document of the world as it appears to be; the latter treats film-sense as the province of emotion, art, and recursively inferred structures of intention. Though he is doubtful about a semiotic that could deal with "all sign systems," Ruby provides for both Realist and Formative frames within a field of "sign-events."[17] This common root in signed-objects allows the rabbit of the dialectic to be pulled from the hat of opposition:

> Film semiotics and cine-structuralism with all of their limitations ... provide a basis for the development of the synthesis of Realist and Formative into a theory of film as communication ... Such a theoretical structure would allow for the construction of an ethnographic *trompe l'oeil* for film: the development of filmic codes and conventions to "frame" or contextualize the apparent realism of the cinema and cause audiences to "read" the images as anthropological articulations. (1982: 129)

The ambition is substantial: To discipline the image to the service of a disciplinary discourse. Filmic codes and conventions would yield a syntax for anthropological ways of "seeing," and offer the further promise of a synesthesia:

> Once constructed, it will be possible to explore the consequences of transforming abstract thoughts, such as theories or models, into images. (1982: 129)

The ethnographically constructed film then becomes an alternative, visual discourse for delivering the formal objects and knowledge of the discipline.

"Pictures can't say ain't"

Worth (1981) is also taken with what is different, but also continuous, between image and text, and I want to use his title phrase "Pictures can't say ain't" as emblematic of the formative role of language structuralism in ethnographic film study. The phrase shows its own double move: The negative observation organizes an invidious assessment, and by producing the observation as a play on speaking, it affirms the primacy – and measure – of language signification. And indeed, pictures *can't* say "ain't." Though images belong to the family of signs, they are of a kind that "cannot deal with what is not" (1981: 173). But Worth is not only returning to Magritte's inscription. Bereft of powers to signify negation, it follows that film's powers to show "what is" are similarly bracketed, and continua of truth-falsity are therefore "useless" for understanding the sense of images. The image is only existential, and unavoidably interpretive, and the organization of filmic sense then owes to interpretive rules built of "linguistic rules for implication and inference" (1981: 183). Language thus leverages the analysis of non-fiction film, and in tying the sense of the image to implicative rules of language, Worth preserves in his way the venerable divide between the seen and the sensible worlds. Scenic sense becomes an operational outcome, and the achievement of an analytic structuralism. Presumably, the ethnographic cameraperson is one whose professional skills consist of just these operations, developed to a high level of fluency. At the same time, it can be readily appreciated that *seeing* is nowhere in sight of Worth's turn of phrase.

The Cine-Trance

In non-fiction film study, the work of field production – selecting, shooting, interviewing, etc. – tends to be treated as part of a larger discourse on formative but un-noticed arrangements of culture, history, narrative, and/or subjectivity (see Michaels, 1982 on bias; Heider, 1976, Nichols, 1994 and Sorenson and Jablonko, 1975 on prior commitment; Hastrup, 1992 and Nichols, 1991 on gender and gaze; and Caulfield, 1992, MacDougall, 1992, Ruby, 1982 and Taylor, 1994 on historical networks of ideology and convention).[18] The work of record-making is also treated for elements of style, and even signature (see Mermin, 1997 and de Brigard, 1975 on the distinctive records of Wiseman, the Maysles brothers, Robert Gardner and others). And by all accounts, ethnographic footage is marked by the contingencies of its practical circumstances:

> a pre-dominance of location shooting; a graininess due to the absence of studio light ... a wobbliness in spontaneous materials due to hand-holding of the camera and toleration in such material for temporary lapses of focus or framing .... (Vaughn, 1992[1979]: 103-104)

For Nichols (1991) these are the evidences of an "accidental gaze":

> The signs of "accidentalness" are the same signs that signify contingency and vulnerability for the documentary generally: chaotic framing, blurred focus, poor sound quality ... the sudden use of a zoom lens, jerky camera movements, the inability to foreshadow or pursue the most pivotal events ... (1991: 82)[19]

For filmmakers with cameras in hand, however, the situation becomes a practical, equipmentally mediated one, and sometimes we hear of the work of shooting in fairly unvarnished fashion, as the actual contingencies and good advice that follow from doing it, e.g.,

> (The filmmaker) should count heavily on the actual interactions and points of view of his subjects to tell him where to look next, or he must be prepared for many unexplained presences and absences of people and things in his record. Events have their own pace and content. (Marshall and de Brigard, 1975: 134)

> We shoot in long takes dealing with specific individuals rather than cultural patterns or analysis. We try to complete an action within a single shot, rather than fragmenting it. (David Hancock, cited in Young, 1975: 74)

> So much of it had to do with the level of anxiety you had about the situation that you were in. Is something going to happen? Is she going to do this, or isn't she? What *is* she going to do? Who's *she*? Have I got the right one? This little sort of stuff ... (Connolly, in Lutkehaus, 1994: 72)

The central insight of such accounts is of a scenic world already in possession of its affairs. To see one's way through affairs that are already and assuredly orderly, sensible, and accountable for those who are living them, organizes the cameraperson's task. The work of shooting is the work of looking for this order, and though known principally for his work in breaching the aesthetic of observational distance (or perhaps because of it), Rouch provides a rich gloss of what the work of the shot could be:

> For me, then, the only way to film is to walk about with the camera, taking it to where it is the most effective, and improvising a ballet in which the camera itself becomes just as much alive as the people it is filming ... I often compare this dynamic improvisation with that of the bullfighter before the bull. In both cases nothing is given in advance, and the smoothness of a *faena* (strategy of play) in bullfighting is analogous to the harmony of a traveling shot which is in perfect balance with the movements of the subjects ... It is this bizarre state of transformation in the filmmaker that I have called, by analogy with phenomena of possession, the "cine-trance." (1975: 93)

It is a distinctive kind of practical, embodied witnessing that Rouch is pointing to, one that has no use for formal, signed structures and finds a visibly ordered intertwining of balance and movement in their stead. The world promises a findable course, that once found can be followed and joined. Trances are familiar objects of formal analysis, and with the formulation, Rouch speaks of the shot-in-its-course as a militantly non-discursive practice. As trance, the work of the shot affiliates to those domains of practices-without-discourse that have historically furnished the objects of formal analysis, to be mapped and rendered articulate.[20] Now inserted into his analytic discourse, Rouch's trance marks a practice that is only seeably so.

II. A Visual Sociology

There are few resources in the literature of ethnographic film for bringing Rouch's trance into view. In large measure, this is because it posits a scenically sensible world – a world of visible order and meaning. To recover the work of the "trance" would require the study of scenic meaning, and this is a difficult program to find in the literature of film study.[21] Notwithstanding Worth's (1981) wisdom about what pictures can't say, *seeing* would seem to be the domain of social practice most kindred to the work of producing (and viewing) visual records, and I want to borrow on Jayyusi's (1988, 1991b) analyses of scenic intelligibility and Sudnow's (1972) treatment of interpersonal observing – the work and achievements of the glance – to sketch out how such a world might work, and how our seeing, and shooting, might be organized within it.

Jayyusi (1988) begins from Metz's formulation of the task for film study: "What must be understood is that films are understood" (Metz, 1974: 145). That they are is evident enough, and she begins with an argument for the fundamental continuities of "filmic texts" and the "cultural forms" of everyday life.

> We watch a film from within the natural attitude of everyday life, and we understand it much as we would understand the order and properties of the everyday social and natural world ... Our understanding of a film text trades off our knowledge of the structures of everyday activity and practical reasoning. (1988: 289)

We see through our cultural knowledge, and seeing is a cultural gesture in its every iteration. Filmic coherence trades on what we can call "viewer maxims" of everyday life, for example, that ordinary actions show an unrelieved temporal flow of developing detail, all of which need not (and cannot) be seen to make out their projectable horizons. Or, that persons and activities tend to be category-bound, and thus go together, or not, in recognizable ways. (See Eglin and Hester, and Hester and Fitzgerald in this volume.) Thus, teenagers do recognizably teen-age things, as do couples strolling in the park, or persons waiting on line. The coherence of the filmic is not then a formal analytic coherence, but rather an organization of practical objectivities, found in the scenic recognizability of things like courses of action, visible relationships, familiar routines, etc.

These recognitions are neither signed nor coded. They are not operations at all. Rather, we "recognize activities on sight," and the order, intelligibility and activity of our scenes are visually, reflexively available for the competent cultural witness (Jayyusi, 1988: 275).

Central to her argument is the visible order of social action. This is especially so of what Jayyusi speaks of as "activity-objects," meaning the affiliations of objects and activities. Certain things are done with cars, birthday cakes, pistols and pencils; each possesses an informal cultural logic of affiliating activities, "trajectories," and horizons of what can be sensibly, or surprisingly, found in its presence. Reflexively available in our accounts and descriptions, these trajectories are not the province of language structures. Rather, they are witnessable features of the everyday life-world, embedded in our ways of seeing social action, and thus part of the "scenic transparency" of the social world, and our images of it (1988: 273). This transparency is of course contingent and imperfect, and it is a world of bewilderment and puzzles as well. But we find puzzles and the rest *in* the recognizability of a world, evidently.

In subsequent work, Jayyusi (1991b) extends her analysis of the scenic intelligibility of images, and develops a strong critique of cine-semiotics, and especially formulations of the polyseme of the image, or the unrestrained plurality of its meaning. As a program, cine-semiotics misconstrues the relation of language and visual sense when it argues that "intelligibility overwhelmingly resides in language.. [while] the image remains inchoate to the viewer ..." (1991: 11). As she shows, action possesses its visual coherence, and there is no place in the world to find an image without a context for viewing it; images are never without their occasions. Thus, we can find on the street a photo of a birthday party, evidently, and find within its scenic organization a "proto-narrative" of who these people are and how this scene came to this, and how it came to us as well.[22]

Viewers find the scenic intelligibility of the filmic text, and ethnographic filmmakers find the unfolding ethnographic situation in the scenic intelligibilities of the ethnographic field. Jayyusi locates in our corpus of cultural knowledge and practices the organization of a world available for the seeing and for the filming. It is also a world available for inquiry and inspection, and Sudnow (1972) takes up a foundational practice for both organizing and interrogating this visible world, in the social organizations of the glance.

Glancing as Inquiry

For Sudnow (1972), the glance is a native order of observation and inquiry, and a constitutive activity. To "see at a glance" is to parse a field, and we can reasonably speak of our daily lookings as we drive, walk down the street, gaze at our surrounds, or our hands, as visual inquiries. However we might organize a scheme of seeings (looks, stares, noticings; see Coulter and Parsons (1990) on grammars of perception), the glance is a familiar practice for finding and deciding, and also producing, the sense of the affairs we find. Sudnow emphasizes the efficacy and seriousness of the glance, especially within settings and occasions for which only glances are possible or permitted. Routinely, we proceed with our findings-at-a-glance with confidence.

He develops his analysis of glancing's temporal parameters as the timing and co-production of the glance between persons. Glancers and those available at-a-glance produce within fine temporal durations fields of evident things, e.g., shoppers only browsing or in need of assistance, single persons or couples, or persons doing waiting, or conversation, where the sense of these things is overwhelmingly built of their recognizability as courses of action.[23] The glance is thus oriented to action's temporal organization and circumstantial detail, and trades upon the temporal parameters of meaningful social worlds.

Sudnow also analogizes the organization of interpersonal observation to the work of the photographic portrait session: Both entail collaborations within practical yet uncertain durations. Photographer and subject work to co-produce and record a 30th of a second that will stand, in subsequent viewings, as the state of affairs they intend to make observable – a countenance, gaze, engagement, etc. (cf. Barthes (1981: 33) on the "decisive instant."). What any actual portrait fixes is thus made of a local history of social productions and inquiries into the temporal course of those productions. These co-orientations are not peculiar to the studio. Winogrand's "American Legion Convention" (1964) lends material detail to Sudnow's elucidation of the glance. The image renders the visible-temporal order of a field, for the record.

In Winogrand's photo we see the timing of glances in their simultaneous productions. Simultaneously, persons on the street are gazing elsewhere, relative to the disabled man in their midst (who has found the single gaze that finds him). As the conventioneers are looking elsewhere (for some, it is also to the camera), it is not only an elsewhere from the man gesturing at the center, but from each other too. The production of each other's invisibility, itself an artful monitoring, is the activity that sustains the un-seen presence at the center of the frame, and does so as delicately concerted action. Their casual gazing is produced as a kind of activity that anyone can see, and Winogrand sees it, and what it achieves, well enough and timely enough to render visible a social-temporal organization of invisibility. Temporal parameters of action organize both the world and its rendering, and the photo fixes Winogrand's visual analysis of the scene. The first relevance of the glance for speaking of how the view-finder sees is thus a re-specification of what seeing could be – that it is fundamentally an exercise of inquiry and analysis. (For examples of the exercise, see Sacks (1972c) on how police see neighborhoods while passing in patrol cars, and Goodwin (1994) on "professional vision.") The work of non-fiction record making might then be understood as a radically situated, equipmentally mediated mode of inquiry, and an analytic practice from the outset.

"American Legion Convention" (1964)
by Garry Winogrand
© **the Estate of Garry Winogrand, courtesy Fraenkel Gallery, San Francisco**

Sudnow's analysis is highly recommended to students of visual sociology and representation. It provides for a world of ordered ensembles of action, built in and as fine scenic and meaningful durations, and available to inquiry. At the same time, as he points out, the work of the camera-person is not that of shoppers or bartenders. The view-finder sees differently, to different purposes, and from within a distinctive social-technical complex (see Lynch and Edgerton (1988) on technical complexes in science imaging). However, Sudnow provides us with a provisional specification of the practical work and circumstances of the continuous shot. On his authority, we can gloss the practical circumstance of the view-finder by revising Worth's (1981) locution: However it may be that pictures – and the scenic world – can't say "ain't," it is true really that "cameras can't glance." In the difference, the praxiology of seeing with a camera begins to come into view.

Cameras Can't Glance

In this phrase, our interests move from pictures, to the work of their production. I do not mean the phrase in any technical way, at least not as matters of imaging technology. I mean it rather for the thoroughly practical work of non-fiction filming – the work of seeing-and-shooting in the world, without thought of direction or rehearsal. That cameras cannot glance means that the world cannot be found in that unremarkably fluent way. The glance is swift and efficient, graceful and even covert. It is a measure of its efficacy that should a glance fail to find the sense of what it beholds, it can inquire again, and can do so within a temporal duration that effectively paces the affairs it witnesses.[24] By "effectively pace" I only mean that in the duration of one glance to a next, there is no sense of a field lost from view. To the contrary, fields are assembled, and we can say of the glance that its inquiry is masked by the fluency with which it finds a world. Working without the timeliness and grace of the glance, however, camera-looking reveals the achievements that the glance conceals. The records of non-fiction film and video offer us access to the work of assembling visible social fields, as practical courses of inquiry.[25] Cameras problematize the intertwining of inquiry and finding, and in these records, we can actually see cameras *looking* to find their way. Unable to glance, routinely they can only look, and sometimes stare.[26]

Finding a Fight

Unlike the competent glancer, cameras are vulnerable to what, indeed, we frequently find in non-fiction footage, viz., failed inquiries, or inquiries only – a looking that is evidently *still* looking, as evidenced by a continuing search. It is most familiar in novice footage, but not only there, and I want to develop grounds for a serious interest in such moments where the record fails-to-find whatever it could be looking for. In bringing them into view, we have a way of speaking of footage that may otherwise be unworthy of remark, and a first resource for recovering the work of the viewfinder's inquiry.

Said again, our native seeing-at-a-glance routinely shows a remarkably fluent course, indistinguishable from the affairs it finds, i.e., an evident world. For "camera inquiries," however, whether and how they become embedded in a found world may be problematic any next time, as seen below. The images in Set 2 are lifted from the remarkable ethnographic film *Ax Fight* produced by Tim Asch and Napoleon Chagnon (1975).[27] Part of my appreciation of the film is for their appreciation of the value of continuous footage. Through the first ten minutes or so, the program consists of long sequences collected on their second day in a large (200 persons) Yanomamo village. Following an introductory text laid over a map, and a strip of audio-only record to the effect of "Bring your camera over here; it's gonna start," the footage begins in the midst of a search: The camera is staring at an open-air longhouse, with sounds of crying, distress and loud talking. Some people are looking off to their left as the camera looks into the darkness of the compound and finds children clutching women

Image Set 2
Ax Fight **(1975)**
by permission of Napoleon Chagnon & Documentary Educational Resources

who are crying in their hammocks [frames 1 and 2]. There is evidently "something" going on, and not in the familiar sense that has it always so, but in the witnessable sense that Asch, as viewfinder, and we as viewers of his record, are in the midst of a motivated search, without knowing what could be promised for it, or where.

The evidence of his looking has nothing to do with knowing in advance what a "finding" could be. Rather, findings are enframed by the visibility of the search, and we could say of records that are still looking that the temporal, sequential development of the record is built of the looking, only. There is no trance here, only a record of things in-passing. What it means to "find" with a camera is tied to the course of the shot as a visual inquiry, and then not as a logic or strategy of inquiry, but as, for example, an inquiry into the directional properties of a gaze. Such that when we see a face in tears, we look for the object of the tearful gaze. Just *what* these faces point to is Asch's actual problem, and in no sense is it a theorist's question. It is rather practical, situated, and visual-analytic.

The viewfinder orients to the scenic, tendentious properties of the field, and as Asch moves between the women in distress, a torso crosses the frame, and the camera follows in a sudden and blinding pan [frames 3 and 4]. By and through sudden and even graceless camera movements, he discovers, frames, exposes, and produces a stable field of view [frames 5 and 6].[28] The work of his inquiry unfolds before our eyes, as he finds and frames a fight in progress. Image set 2 is lifted from this course.

As for what Asch finds, the argument I am making needs the evident character of a "fight." This fight could clearly be other things, e.g., dramatic play. Yet such an account, and any other sensible one, relies on the visibility of fights as fields of co-oriented action, and Asch's work of finding it is preserved, irrespective of what else we may then want to say about it.[29]

Asch finds the fight and frames a field of action. One of the combatants strikes a hard blow, and a standoff ensues, where the injured party is attended by kin folk who take up a verbal harangue on his behalf, all of which is stoically received by the first party. There is a social-moral ensemble here too, of hostility, injury, aid and restraint, organized between the parties and visible within the frame that Asch produces. The parties then separate, but the fight later resumes with axes rather than staffs, and we find it as Asch does. (See Image Set 3.) Holding a wide shot of the compound, Asch at first sees nothing remarkable as a man trots into view with an ax in his hands. The framing is unchanged [frame 1]. Other persons standing in view, however, begin to take notice, first turning, then walking, then running in the same direction [frames 2 and 3], and Asch finds in their developing orientations, not a trot across the round, but an onset, and joins them with a fast zoom [frames 4, 5, and 6]. It is not clear, literally, what he is pursuing. Looking into the shadows of the longhouse, intelligible scenes fade in and out of view. Softened by the lens, the lighting and the pace of action, the fight Asch (and we) can see is episodic; we see the flash of a blow landed or averted, and then lose our view of what happens next, or where. His looking is concentrated and sustained, alternatively finding and losing the scene as a continuous course of action. Not only the fight, but the work of his search is preserved in a record that shows his inquiry perhaps more clearly than the world it finds. As for what he finds, in the context of contemporary violence one could be taken

Image Set 3
Ax Fight **(1975)**
by permission of Napoleon & Documentary Educational Resources

by the restraint of a group of persons fighting with axes and machetes, and landing blows, that has no one mortally wounded. For all the "chaos" of the scene, the Yanomamo show a remarkable civility of restraint.

Though I am offering Asch's task and achievement as emblematic of the work of documentary record making, there are circumstances peculiar to it that also shape the record. Centrally, he could not hear the interactional organization of his scenes. He could not understand what was being said, and though there was still sense to hear, of conversational interaction there is none – no arguments, remonstrations or rejoinders.[30] Without complaint, we could say Asch's inquiry was deaf to its affairs, where the point of the remark is to suggest how else the field might have been found. The issue is not the adequacy of the record he has produced,

Image Set 4
The Village **(1967)**
UCLA Ethnographic Film Program

1 2

W: What are you up to this morning?
M: Eh?
W: What are ou up to this morning?
   (2.0)

5 6

W2: Chin, chin Doris.   W3: Ahha, we already finished ours.
   ((adjacent diners))   ((laughingly))

but how the inquiry might differently find its way and assemble the record from within a hearably sensible world. Asch may have seen different things had he been able to hear them. Setting aside the conjecture, in *The Village* (1967) it is sometimes an English speaking world, and that the camera person can hear its work does indeed organize the inquiry and the record.

Produced by Colin Young and filmed by Mark McCarty, *The Village* of Dunquin (1967) documents a traditional Irish community that is losing its ways under the pressures of poverty, tourists, and the flight of next generations to places elsewhere. (See McCarty, 1975 and MacDougall, 1985[1969] for discussions.) The production crew (including anthropologist Paul Hockings) film daily routines and weekend activities, including the arrivals of outsiders who come to experience and/or study a traditional subsistence community. The following scene takes place in the village inn. Apparently both tourists and locals frequent it, and McCarty records

 3   4

(W): What are you going to <u>do</u>
     this morning?
M: Uh, g' to take- ( ) get tha ( ) going
   to Tralee (wth old friends.) (1.5)

M: Look for ah 'hhive for tha place.
W: All tha way to Tralee?
M: Tralee, yeah.

 7   8

a brief sequence of breakfast. People are seated at common tables, some in parties, some not, weaving meals and conversations. Part of my interest in it is that unlike a church communion or fishermen launching their boats, here the view-finder is confronted with a desultory organization of persons and activity.

The breakfast scene reminds us of how, on any next occasion of entering the world with documentarians' purposes, we may only find the mereness of ordinary things. In its seamless familiarity, the world can become difficult to find for the record. There are things to see, and alternatively nothing at all, beyond the vulgar familiarity we already possess in and of such places (Garfinkel, 1988). To find an organization of guests at breakfast is a task whose course can only be discovered on actual occasions, and this is part of what McCarty's record records.

The shot runs for approximately 35 seconds. (See Image Set 4.) It opens on a table of four diners within a larger room. Though difficult to make out, there are various conversations underway. McCarty then pans away from this single table, down a long adjacent table, and comes to rest on the end pair of guests who are seated facing each other [frames 2, 3, and 4]. He does so as a conversational opening between them begins, and the two moves (the opening of the conversation and the settling of the frame) are themselves knitted together. The recipient of the opening is a villager who speaks well enough, but seems otherwise quite deaf. Thus, the conversational opening McCarty finds in the midst of other conversations already underway, begins with some near shouting. (See Appendix, p. 259, for information on Transcription Conventions.)

Having roughly pointed to how the shot begins and finds one among several conversations underway, we are positioned to look for how it continues. As the first conversation becomes hearable for closure, another begins – I'm told that "Chin, chin" is a kind of "cheers" or "bottoms-up" – and we see McCarty begin a slow move out of the two-person frame at the end of the table, and into a view of the next brace of guests [frames 5 and 6]. Simultaneously, a waitress is placing something between the two parties, and as the waitress begins to walk away, the camera begins moving too, doing so in a way that "catches" her pace, keeps it as she traverses the long table, and then comes to rest at the table that was first in view [frames 7 and 8]. The camera thus rides the passage of the waitress, doing its looking by attaching to her course of action. On finding the next field, it releases, and though we have no useful conjectures for why McCarty leaves one field to look for a next, we can see how his leaving and looking are synchronously done: He travels the room by finding lines of sight, conversation and activity. The shooter's inquiry is of native or endogenous coherences, finding in *their* course the continuous framing of the record.[31] This work of coming upon a world and viewfinding her way through its local organizations is identifying of the analytic competence of the non-fiction filmmaker.

The Coherence Made-Found

The organization of the scenic-social world is evidently of a kind that provides for inquiry – and findings – for which the coherence of social action is a foundational resource. There is a world, and because there is we recognize footage that fails to find what's going on there, by seeing, for example, that the viewfinder is still looking for it, or isn't looking at all (See Bateson's remarks (Brand, 1976) on how cameras locked on tripods cannot see).[32] Once pointed to, the notion that the camera finds its way has an evident character; we can see it in the footage, and our materials were selected to show it as the work of a visual inquiry. We can even suggest a descriptive measure of competently produced footage as the way in which the inquiry is embedded in the fields it finds. In such moments, we don't see the camera looking at all; instead we find an unfolding scene. Thus, McCarty's pan that moves with the waitress finds in her passage a course of action that finds still a next. The inquiry-and-what-it-finds become a single fluent course, assembling its record of the world this way.

We might call the organization of the continuous shot a kind of practical constructionism. It has a material-technical basis, and we don't need theory to provide for it; the record shows it to us. There are more theoretically based discourses on filmic constructivism too, especially those turning on a reflexive subjectivity: how the filmmaker as a social-historical actor unavoidably constructs the occasion of the record making, and thus the record.[33] In one iteration, Nichols (1991) formulates an "axiographics" of ethnographic film for addressing issues and ethics of representation:

> Axiographics is an attempt to explore the implantation of values in the configuration of space, in the constitution of a gaze, and in the relation of observer to observed. (p. 78)

This kind of "positional" reflexivity is to be found as matters of reasoned argument, wherein notions of "value" and "gaze" are deployed in the formal space of a theoretical discourse. Our alternative is to treat these objects (space, gazes and relations) as praxiologies themselves, available to analysis in and as their exercise on real occasions. We are thus proposing the primacy of ethnomethodologically reflexive practices for ethnographic film, whose records are perspicuous resources for the study of their own (reflexive) construction. (See Czyzewski, 1994 and Lynch, 1993 on these different orders of reflexivity.) And while the notion of inquiry has been my central way of speaking of filming's constructive work, still other formative intertwinings show up in the records. They are also made of the relations of the observer and the observed, but witnessably so, as in our next and last image set. (See Image Set 5.) It shows moments in which the camera is witnessing affairs to which it is already and unavoidably a party. We can say the sequence shows three consecutive moves of engagement that shape the field and how it is found for the record. Throughout, we see the view-finder working from within the local history

Image Set 5
Primary **(1960)**
by permission of Robert Drew, Drew Associates

1   2

Cr: There he iz now,
     whut do ya' say to 'em? (2.0)

5   6

H: I'll be 'ya, I'll be listening in...
F: [Ya' better get in (cause)
    I'm gonna see ya, by god...
H: So you come on down to tha

(H): white house, have a cup of
F: [Sure.
(H): coffee, huh?
F: [Sure.

and interactional organization of the scene to produce its documentary record. The sequence is the first scene of *Primary*. The film opens on a large man, a farmer in overalls and cap, standing on the porch of a modest wooden building. We can hear him, though not well, speaking to the production crew, and in lapses of speaking (we hear no rejoinders), he orients to them with his gaze. As he does, the door in the background opens, and Senator Humphrey emerges, walks down the stairs, and out of frame. The farmer (and others) orient to Humphrey's passing, and we see this because the cameraperson does not. Though we might imagine a shooting convention that says "follow the gaze," the cameraperson stays with the

3   4

F: Mr. Humphrey, I hope you got
    good luck. (0.7) ((loud))
H: Thank you so much my friend. =
F: [Yes sir,
    = Yes sir.

H: Thank you very, very much.
F: Sure.
H: You're very fine-
F: [See you tomorrow. Mm hm.
H: [You betcha.

7   8

F: ... (Add a little) schnops.   ((both laugh))

gazing instead, watching the farmer watching Humphrey's departure. He does so, it seems, because he has found a local warrant for his continuing shot more compelling than a convention. As Humphrey passes by, we hear a voice off-camera say, "There he is now, what do you say to him?" [frame 2] A couple of seconds later, the farmer hails, "Mr. Humphrey, I hope you got good luck." [frame 3] To this good wish, Humphrey rejoins, and returns to greet the man. To see how the continuous record is built is to see how in the crew's question, a field is cast.[34]

Of the farmer's early remarks to the camera, we can only hear that they are underway, and figure that in some way the record-making occasions them.[35] Of the crew's invitation to the farmer, it calls for a "kind" of thing to say – a typical, or recognizable thing to say on such an occasion (to a political candidate in passing), and thus calls for doing something ordinary (see Sacks, 1984 on "doing being ordinary"). Calling for a next action, the question organizes the interactional field and what might be found and recorded of it.

As we watch the farmer, we thus watch with an interest in where and how a response to the crew's invitation will be produced. It is a field framed *as* the waiting for what indeed the farmer will say, and in this way the crew's question shapes the framing of the record, and our instructions for viewing it. Our waiting for what the farmer does next then yields to the farmer's hailing and *its* interactional horizons, and in this fashion the continuing shot is oriented to the most local interactional field. If the prevailing question of non-fiction filming is something like "what next?," the first resource for answering lies within local interactional organizations. The crew's question thus yields a field of action, and the camera is finding its framing from within it.

In hailing Humphrey, we have a next engagement – an offer of good wishes – done as a rejoinder to the crew's question and calling for one too. The good wish then becomes an exchange and a handshake between the two men, as Humphrey returns to the farmer, and into the camera's view [frame 4]. Humphrey's return is of course open to interpretation. The play of the crew is not only in their question, but in their public work of looking with cameras and pointing with microphones. We can wonder in what measure the camera, rather than the farmer's good wishes, brings Humphrey back to the stranger. His greeting in return would then be understood as something of a mock-up, done for the record, just as the farmer's is. And indeed, Humphrey may have been oriented to the recording. No doubt he had still other ways with strangers, but these interests only suggest motives for the scene, and nothing of its material organization or the organization of its documentation. However it is that Humphrey returns to the farmer, Maysles records it from a position that has been waiting on a greeting in return. Thus, we *hear* Humphrey returning to the frame through his first remarks, as he walks into the microphone's range. This range is social-technical too, and also casts a field and organizes a location. That Humphrey is beginning from afar and develops his talk to fit and produce an interactional space – a meeting – is both the indispensable resource for the shooting, and also what it organizes and records. As the scene develops, both the farmer and Humphrey are in frame, though neither completely [frames 5 and 6]. We could say a *faena* begins as the camera moves in nuanced ways between the two, moving between their remarks and rejoinders, and showing an interactional organization in the organization of the frame. The farmer anchors the framing, interactionally and locationally, and that the film opens this way – with the candidate dwelling on the edges of the frame and the farmer's last words centered within it – could be made out as a device, or move by the producers, or an expression of their style or standpoint [frames 7 and 8]. The interpretation again suggests a motive for the record-making, and we certainly have motives. In addition, we have the practices of a motivated looking from within interactionally organized and technically produced fields, a kind of looking that seems to be of a piece with the disciplined practices of documentary filmmaking.

If so, we may have a beginning description of a body of practices that is shot-through with analyses of interactional sequence, space and duration, and have in them a glimpse of what Rouch (1975) may mean by the "trance." The record unfolds from within the territory of a question, that becomes a greeting, and then an exchange in return. To see for the record is to organize an inquiry from within the *social* orders of these spatio-temporal fields. If there is trance here, we find it within these densely local scenic-sociologies of action. The point is not to say that the record of their encounter is somehow the "right" one, but that it is cogent, methodic and available to description. Once seen this way, the work of producing the continuous record begins to come into view, and the record becomes accountable not to the play of theory, but to material fields of social organization and meaningful action, where both the inquiry and the world it finds are recorded as developing affairs in-their-course.

Conclusion

The work of the shot in non-fiction film and video is hugely exhibited in television news, ethnographic film, and amateur videotape. With the discovery of the entertainment value of home video, police arrests, and other calamities-in-real-time, the non-fiction shot has insinuated itself into the nearly universal venue of commercial television programming. As an object for analysis, the shot in non-fiction film and videography thus has the charm of a modesty coupled to a pervasive presence. When we see it, commercial or not, ethnographic or not, the shot shows the looking of a singular, local witness. In every case, we find in the shot both a record of the affairs witnessed, and a record of the witnessing too, where the work of looking itself is sometimes especially in view.

As viewers, our witnessing thus turns on a prior witnessing, and the filmic record becomes a record of its own production. Watching the camera find its way within affairs that are finding their way brings an alternative, material discourse to the analysis of the camera's "location."[36] As the practical task of finding the world, the work of the shot suggests a technical platform for specifying Schutz's (1962a) notion of analytic accounts as second order renderings of already cogent worlds. Documentaries show us events that already, formatively and endogenously possess order and coherence, and we get to see-hear of them in the record, as *its* produced order and coherence. As viewers, we have only the record, but also the promise of recovering a course of action, built of sustained, real-time interrogations of developing fields within and beyond the frame. In looking for the work of the shot, virtually nothing has been said of the more familiar topics of film study, e.g., standpoint, narrative, suture, and montage. Presumably, each possesses its own methods of production and study, as no less practical, social-technical organizations.

This discussion has borrowed heavily on the findings and programs of ethnomethodological studies. Of them, a virtual program has emerged without benefit of announcement, of studies of the fundamental visibilities of everyday life. In the visibilities of science laboratories and classrooms, mathematical proofs, Galilean physics, magic, maps, pictures, data complexes, lectures, police work, auto-tours, field guides, air traffic control, and elsewhere, a recurrent address is found to the evident character of achievedly familiar worlds, for the seeing (Anderson, Sharrock & Hughes, 1987; Bjelic, 1994; Bjelic and Lynch, 1992; Bogan, 1997; Coulter, 1994; Garfinkel and Burns, 1979; Garfinkel, Livingston & Lynch, 1981; Jayyusi, 1988; Law and Lynch, 1988, Livingston, 1987); Lynch, 1991a, 1985; Lynch and Edgerton, 1988; Macbeth, 1992; Psathas, 1979; Sacks, 1972c; Wieder, 1989, and the studies in this volume). In every case, seeing the world is reflexively implicated in building its evidences, and our interests in non-fiction filmmaking join a domain of kindred topics: studies of competent seeings from within social-technical complexes of order and practice. They are studies of order *as* practice, whose topics are therefore understood as methods first, and whose objects present themselves in and as the methodic life that sustains them.

To suggest that foundational kinds of unremarkable social organizations sustain filming's work is not to speak wryly of its achievements, e.g., of

Ax Fight, or *Primary.* Rather than a play of valorization/de-valorization, our analysis of what the viewfinder sees recovers a collection of topics. Via these topics of scenic-social order, we are positioned to expect, in principle, that in *every next shot* we might point to the sense or warrant of its course, and not in general but within the detail of developing fields, as the local analytic history of assembling the record. We may also come into possession of a useful way of speaking of this rendering and that one, for how they find their ways as practical analytic tasks and professional achievements. We might have words for their differences, finding our accounts in what the shot finds, understood now as inseparable from how it finds what it finds. Our analyses would then be understood as a set of instructions for building descriptions of these records as intertwining structures of practical action, in the world and through the view-finder.

Notes

1. This paper was first developed as a presentation to the 4th Annual Conference on Liberal Arts and the Education of Artists (1990), New York. I am indebted to Dušan Bjelić, Brian O'Connor and George Psathas for helpful readings of an earlier draft of the paper.

2. The interests and issues of this write up began several years ago in an extended collaboration with Richard Fauman. We were both then graduate students in social science, and fledgling videographers. Fauman developed his curriculum as an inquiry into the sociology of non-fiction film, detailing the production practices that yield accountably competent or professional programs. With time and divergent paths, I no longer know what development he has found for those topics, but the collaboration continues to be a resource to the interests developed here. Throughout their development, these topics have been instructed by Garfinkel's continuing studies in ethnomethodology (1967, *passim*).

3. See Feld and Williams (1976: 32) for a film-based research effort to "recenter analysis in experience, promoting a continuity of the existential and objective." See also Nichols' (1994: 63) critique of "discourses of sobriety [that] treat their relation to the real as non-problematic."

4. As for those watching the arrival of the train, Weinberger continues:

    > In another sense, the film is pure fiction: like Magritte's pipe the audience in their panic had intuitively grasped *That this is not a train.* (1994: 7)

    Alternatively, they were the first to learn that "this is a film," and their intuition may have been as peculiar as Lumière's circumstance. What Lumière and his audience encountered has long been extinguished, and what either can tell us about record-making and record-viewing is difficult to say.

5. My reviews of the history and literatures are brief and tendentious. Of the

technical history, the review takes up only a portion of it, in some of the first expressions of "observational cinema" (Young, 1975). Home movies, the camcorder and external flat screen viewfinders are some of the rest of it.

6. Rouch (1975: 87) points out that Vertov's "eye-in-motion" could "only move about in an open vehicle." Similarly, Flaherty found scenes of domestic life, but in diorama and re-enactment. He tells of Nanook's willingness to build and occupy an ice shelter with his family, and then dismantle half of it so that Flaherty might have sufficient light to record their "bedtime" routines. (Flaherty, 1924). ("COPS" is a syndicated television program produced with documentary footage of police responding to their calls.)

7. For Vaughn, the relevant transformations are essentially self-reflective:

> (T)he development of lightweight cameras and tape recorders, mobile and relatively inconspicuous, has brought documentary to a crisis which is largely one of confrontation with its own being. It is as if, having long watched itself approaching, it were now almost near enough to reach out and shake itself by the hand. Almost, but never quite. (1992: 99)

At least for its practitioners, we might expect that rather than a sense of crisis, they found new fields and settings for the development of their professional practices.

8. The work of *Primary* is substantially larger than my use of it here. At least as striking as its continuous sequences is the use of portraiture, juxtaposition, and montage, and one can see between the two campaigns a sea-change in representations of "the candidate." Rouch (1975) and Marshall and de Brigard (1975) attribute this sequence to the camera work of Richard Leacock, an attribution that Robert Drew and Richard Leacock have corrected (personal communication). Albert Maysles was the cameraperson for this scene, and for the second scene from *Primary* that will be discussed below.

9. My guess is that the camera was equipped with a very wide-angle lens. Shooting in wide angle maximizes the field in focus, and masks the movement of the hand-held camera at the edges of the frame. Such practices are becoming displaced by those of "steadycams" and the new image stabilizing software of the camcorder. Of the audio record, the impression is that the sound person was trailing the procession. What we can hear through the din seem to be *post hoc* remarks and appreciations made from one supporter to another as Kennedy passes by, e.g., "He shook my hand," or "Now I can't wash my hands."

10. The conventional ergonomics of the camera leave the left eye free to see the world beyond the frame, whereas what lies to the right of the camera's field is masked from view. A practical consequence is a tendency to shoot to the left, as it is there that the cameraperson can see the world before it enters the frame. We can see this tendency in Maysles' footage.

11. These are competing formulations, and respectful disagreements, in the literature. For Eco (1985) iconicity is itself a coded assemblage of the "perceptible elements actualized according to codes of transmission" (p. 596). For Barthes, this first place in the assemblage quickly yields to commutability,

and then polysemy, as the central post-structural extensions of image-semiotics (Silverman, 1983: 26-27).

12. Silverman (1983) traces the post-structural semiotic from Peirce, to Barthes, Benveneste, Derrida, Lacan, and their students. By her account the post-structural begins with the re-insertion of subjectivity(ies) into the relations of semiosis, and the aggressive study of signification's commutability, or reflexive regress. These topics are beyond my review. My sense, however, is that post-structural subjectivities also rely on a bright divide between visibility and sense, a divide the non-fiction filmmaker routinely crosses.

13. The characterization is most apt for the formative literature of the 1970s. More recent work informed by subaltern, critical and deconstructive programs is highly critical of the social scientism of much of the earlier literature. (See Asch and Conor, 1994; Devereaux, 1995; Hastrup, 1992; Loizos, 1992; MacDougall, 1995; Nichols, 1994, and Weinberger, 1994.) There too, however, social science shapes topics and disputes, though now oppositionally. And notwithstanding oppositions, there is virtually no dispute on the probity of theorizing, which is perhaps the first of science's cultural attachments. See Button (1991) on the continuities of the new analytic discourses to the scientism they would displace.

14. Here, I mean "documentary method" as developed by Garfinkel (1967) as a gloss for the sense-making practices of everyday life, lay and professional. On the competition between the documentary methods of social science and those of the folk world, see also Zimmerman and Pollner (1970) and Sharrock and Button (1991). See Coulter (1989) and Lynch (1992) for ethnomethodological and Wittgensteinian critiques of the skepticism that organizes formal analysis.

15. The question of touring isn't settled by the corpus of "members' films." (See Barnow, 1979; Bellman and Jules-Rosette, 1977; Chalfen, 1992; Feitosa, 1991; Michaels, 1982; Turner, 1991; Worth, 1981 for analyses of native films, and MacDougall, 1992, and Moore, 1994 for [different] critiques of how they are analytically deployed.) Member films are no less open to Weinberger's questions, though immune to the criticism: Natives aren't accountable to formal analytic (or "reflexive") discourses, and we look for their intelligibility on other, local-cultural grounds. In all cases, however, the master narrative embedded in Weinberger's questions remains unrealized. The play of "tourism" is not, then, on membership (professional or native), but on the work – whomsoever's work – of seeing for the record. The viewfinder is hopelessly touring, but not by asking questions of tour guides. Rather, she is looking for what can be recognizably seen. (See Bogen, 1997, on real tourists videotaping the real *Cheers* barfront from a tour bus, and the social organization of seeing that way.)

16. Though their highly original analyses of native non-fiction filmmaking are developed as structures of practice, Bellman and Jules-Rosette (1977) also anchor their analyses to a linguistic structuralism: The shot becomes fully accountable only from within the language metaphor.

In our analysis we essentially agree with Metz (1974: 151) that there are no phonemes in film. Individual shots are more comparable to simple declarative sentences because they are composed of a variety of camera movements ... (1977: 21)

17. (The) sign-event is used here to mean an organized group of signs – signs that are syntactically related and clearly delineated or framed in a way that sets them apart from other sign-events. (Ruby, 1982: 123 ff. 3)

Ruby's sign-event maps well onto Garfinkel's usage of "signed-objects," developed in remarks on the normal practices of formal analysis, whereby the lived world is made amenable to analysis by rendering its organization as a collection of signs, operating within fields of analytically constituted relations. Where formal analysis tends to find the order of signed objects, ethnomethodology finds the haeccities – and order and regularity – of local practice. (See Garfinkel, 1967; Garfinkel and Sacks, 1970; Heritage, 1984 and Lynch, 1993 on signed-objects.)

18. For example,

As an anthropomorphic extension of the human sensorium, the camera reveals not only the world but its operator's preoccupations, subjectivity, and values ... This notion is usually subsumed under the discussion of style. (Nichols, 1991: 79)

(T)he camera creates a photographic realism reflecting the culturally constructed reality of the picture-taker and is not a device that can somehow transcend the photographer's cultural limitations. (Ruby, 1982: 125)

The notion of "cultural limitations" is interesting, as though lenses constrained vision. These formulations offer covering statements about the work of the shot, generally. How the record is constructed practically, materially and in any actual case is our topic.

19. Though it is not clear how "pivotal events" in the life of the field are knowable in advance, Nichols returns to the primacy of subjectivity:

Long takes and minimal editing do not eliminate, though they may disguise, the psychodynamics that Malinowski reserved for his diary ... As long as human agency comes into play it will do so in relation to desire and the unconscious as well as reason and science. (1994: 62)

What is missing in his account of the unconscious, reason and science, is *practice*, or what could be methodic, or analytic, about producing a "long take."

20. de Certeau (1984) characterizes these practices as the natural resource of theory's essential operation:

Procedures without discourse are collected and located in an area organized by the past and giving them the role, a determining one for theory, of being constituted as wild "reserves" for enlightened knowledge. (1984: 65)

21. Bellman and Jules-Rosette (1977) are an instructive exception.

22. The argument is not of course that the transparencies of the image are

somehow thorough or "totalizing." It is rather that our cultural practices afford a world of "glance intelligible environments" (Jayyusi, 1991b: 6). We see well enough through our relevances and purposes a sensible array of persons, actions, objects in use, projectable histories, futures, etc. In Jayyusi's fine phrase: "It is not that the scene speaks for itself, but that it speaks itself ..." (1991b: 15)

23. As with every normative order of practice, the glance is then available to subversion, mis-direction, masking, etc.

24. We sometimes speak of those occasions as "double takes," and that they are deserving of special remark is itself a remark on the normal, fluent course we expect for each next inquiry-at-a-glance.

25. This opening is not to be confused with the development of "critter cams," those miniaturized wireless video cameras that are strapped onto dolphins, dogs, and baseball catchers. The promise of such records returns us to Lumière producing records as if the camera were not there. Though enjoyable, and even instructive, this is only surveillance, or a record-making relieved of inquiry.

26. MacDougall sketches a practical consequence of the difference between glancing and looking.

> (A)mong the Jie of Uganda I used a special brace which allowed me to keep the camera in the filming position for twelve or more hours a day over a period of many weeks ...(M)y subjects soon gave up trying to decide when I was filming and when I was not. As far as they were concerned I was always filming ... (1975: 113)

Glances can be furtive. Looking is not. Only as a simulation of surveillance was MacDougall's un-noticed looking achieved.

27. This work, and Asch's corpus more generally, has been criticized for its putative scientism, (citing, for example, the resort in *Ax Fight* to a lineage chart and a formal analysis of kinship for "explaining" the fight). Some of the criticism is agreeable. Other of it can leave us to wonder: By what (transcendental) means was the view-finder to know more of what he found, in the course of finding it? The following remarks cover the scene we are commenting on:

> The Asch/Chagnon films ... used formal tropes ... to gain a rhetorical advantage for science and explanation. Awash in constant havoc, foaming noses, screaming and crying women, their films allowed no recognizable expression or meaning to be generated out of the peoples' actions themselves. Instead, these films operated with a shrewd realist framing of apparent chaos. What comes to us from the synch sound and apparently candid images of people is, always, strange and chaotic. (Moore, 1994: 129)

Where Moore finds a "shrewd realist framing"; one could find instead the course of an actual framing, built in real time, as the best seeing Asch could do on this remarkable occasion. See also Weinberger (1994) for an account of our scene.

28. In no sense is any piece of this work graceless. I use the descriptor only to

convey what the local news, for example, prides itself on sparing us – the work of the inquiry and the history of the achievement of a stable framing.

29. After the fight sequences, the film furnishes the following commentary:

> First impressions can be mistaken. When the fight first started, one informant told us that it was about incest. However, subsequent work with other informants revealed that the fight stemmed from quite a different cause ...

It was later decided that the fight was animated by a fissure between lineages. For the ways in which Asch's footage is open to accounts, we're reminded of a life-world of sensible action, in addition to what may be said of it. The work of the shot is taken up with the evident life-world, first.

30. There is, for example, an engaging collection of sub-titled epithets cast by a single woman after the fight has ended. The film includes an edited version that moves this woman's "vituperative" remarks to the front of the sequence. As Weinberger (1994) notes, in the narrative version the scolding woman is cast as provocateur.

31. In fiction film this is a tracking shot. Here, however, it is the achievement of a sustained analysis of a field of action, rather than rehearsed direction.

32. There are of course *many* things going on within a scene, and at the same time not just anything. However the cameraperson organizes her inquiry, and whatever she finds, the record will show its order-productive course.

33. MacDougall (1992) extends the discussion, pointing to how certain cultures have proven more suited to ethnographic filmmaking than others (as evidenced by their over representation in the corpus), and how this may be tied to "European inventions and assumptions about behaviour and discourse" (1992: 91). The Maasai people, for example, are "superb explicators of events in their lives and their own social system," and thus fit well to a "Western realist tradition dependent upon a certain literalness of words and deeds and a focus upon events which (crystallise) deeper social issues" (1992: 93).

34. We could say that the crew only incites the natives, and, as in Clifford's critique of Geertz, does not "put its own subjectivity at risk" (Clifford, 1988: 41). The critique has its good sense. Yet once in hand, all interest is lost in what the crew's remarks become for the record-making, and how the field thereby assumes its documented shape and salience. How the crew's remark is implicated in shaping the record of what we see is lost to the criticism alone.

35. On how the camera's gaze may organize gestures in return, see Horwitz's (1979) study of "camera noticings," i.e., moments where the gaze of a camera is discovered by a native in some normal environment, e.g., a workplace, and gets an interactional rejoinder.

36. For post-structural discourses on the non-neutral, ascetic, psychodynamic, and ritual character of the camera's location in the world it records, see Asch and Conor, (1994); Burgin, (1982); Nichols (1991, 1994); MacDougall, (1975); and Tomas, (1988).

Chapter 7

Category, Predicate and Contrast: Some Organizational Features in a Radio Talk Show

Stephen Hester and Richard Fitzgerald

Introduction

In this chapter we examine some social organizational features of a radio phone-in show. Our approach draws primarily on membership categorization analysis (Hester and Eglin, 1997a; Sacks, 1992a), and to a lesser extent on (sequential) conversation analysis (Sacks, 1992a, 1992b).[1] Our focus is on the use of membership categories, category predicates and category contrasts. The show in question is the *Call Nick Ross* show which is produced by the BBC and is broadcast on Radio Four at 9:05a.m. on Tuesdays. Each show lasts fifty-five minutes and consists of callers "airing their views" and sometimes hearably "debating" with the host of the show, Nick Ross, on controversial topics typically "in the recent news." Also occasionally present in the studio is an "invited guest," typically one who belongs to a membership category which is, in some way, relevant to the topic of the show.

We begin by noticing the recognizability of the show as just that, it is produced as a *show*, and as such, as *entertainment*, designedly so, for its listening audience (there is no studio audience). The observable organizational "structure" or shapes of the show can be seen to constitute, at least in part, a solution to the problem of *how* to turn telephone calls into entertainment on the radio. Thus, the calls are not *just* telephone calls, they are organized in particular ways which are understandable in terms of what we take to be the predicates (interests) of media (radio) workers and the listening audience. Although there may, of course, be various ways of producing "entertainment" out of telephone calls, here, as the following analysis seeks to demonstrate, this is accomplished methodically in and as the ways in which the show's host *elicits* particular types of turns from callers, *relates* callers to the show's topic and *responds* to them in ways which promote discussion and debate. Callers do not speak directly to each other; rather, the show is one which is organized, mediated and managed by the host. Our analytic task, then, is to explicate how this is accomplished. Accordingly, this chapter is organized in terms of the following main sections: (i) trailing the show; (ii) introducing the guest; (iii) showing the callers; and (iv) generating debate.

Trailing the Show

The omnirelevant membership categorization device which is used to organize the show is "parties to a radio phone-in show." The standardized relational pair of membership categories comprising this device are: host and caller. For both of these categories, various activities, attributes, entitlements and obligations, etc. are predicated. These will be described subsequently. For now, our point is that they are projected in the trailers. That is to say, the trailers provide, in a general sense, for the kinds of activities in which the participants may engage and which they may exhibit *as* participants. On the day of broadcast there are two trailers for the show: at 8a.m. and at 9a.m. respectively. The 9a.m. trailer is followed by the "nine o'clock news" and the show is then broadcast at 9:05a.m. Its opening, or introduction, repeats elements of the 8a.m. and 9a.m. trailers. (See Appendix, p. 259, for information of Transcription Conventions.)

> *(1) 8a.m. Trailer NR[07:03:97](1)*
> P: In just over an hour Nick Ross will be taking your calls.
> N: Good morning, just about every morning from now until election day someone somewhere will publish an opinion poll. The headlines will tell you that Labor's lead is up or down or the same as before and we'll be invited to assume that we're being given a valuable clue about the results of the election itself, but are we? In 1992 most of the polls suggested that Neil Kinnock [the then leader of the Labor Party] would win, which of course he didn't, so might they get it wrong again. Do the polls influence how people vote are they a useful indicator of the public

mood or a dangerous interference in the democratic process? Have you been interviewed by the pollsters? Did you tell them the truth? Do you think how you vote on May 1st [date of the 1997 British General Election] might be influenced by what the opinion polls tell you today and tomorrow? I'd like to know what you think.

P: O one seven one five eight double four double four lines are open now and *Call Nick Ross* begins at five past nine.

(2) 9a.m. Second Trailer   NR[07:03:97](2)
P: Coming up at five past nine this morning *Call Nick Ross*.
     (0.5)
N: Good morning. If you believe what the opinion polls have been suggesting you probably believe that Tony Blair is likely to be the next Prime Minister, but if you believed them last time round you would have expected Neil Kinnock to have moved into Downing Street which of course he didn't do. Do the polls tell us something useful or are they, as the former minister Tristan Garald Jones has suggested, a kind of twentieth century witchcraft, pseudo-scientific horoscopes which pander to our desire to see into the future but which tell us nothing that we don't know already? Do you believe the polls? Do they influence what you think, perhaps even how you vote? Are they a useful measurement of the political pulse or a dangerous technique which can harm the election process? Do we take too much notice of them? If you have been a pollster or if you've been polled, if you use them in your work, I'd like to know what you think. Please call.
P: And the number to call is o one seven one five eight double four double four, o one seven one five eight double four double four. The lines are open now and *Call Nick Ross* begins at five past nine.

These trailers can be heard to project specific organizational features of the show. Thus, show trailers such as the above, and their partial repeats in the show openings (examined below), can be heard not only to *announce* the upcoming show, *inform* listeners what the *topic* of the show is, and *invite* listeners to call the show, they also *project* the organizing membership categorization device, membership categories and category predicates of the show's participants. In so doing, the trailers *identify* the kinds of activities in which listeners may engage should they choose and seek to become callers and participate in the show.

In extract (1), for example, listeners are informed that the topic is "opinion polls." The host lists contrasting positions on this topic and invites listeners to call and align with one position or the other. These contrasting positions are exhibited in terms of contrast classes: accurate or inaccurate, benign reflection or pernicious influence, truth or lies and influence or no influence. Lists such as these, as Sacks (1992b) suggests, can provide a:

> series of options to the co-participant[s], saying in effect, I'm giving you a bunch of what you and I know to be story sources; surely there's something out of this set of things that you can talk about more or less elaborately; tell me anything that you care to, under that range of possibilities. (p. 565)

The invitation consists in the host stating that he wishes to know what they (the listeners) think and, by implication, which side of these contrasts listeners/callers identify with. By inviting the callers to align with one of the contrasting positions on the topic and "say what they think," the host projects the kinds of activities which, for the show's duration, are locally operative predicates of callers. These activities are stating opinions, agreeing and disagreeing, justifying viewpoints, and so forth.

Likewise in extract (2) Ross deploys a similar list of contrast classes: the believable or non-believable, reliable or unreliable, the influence or non- influence and the beneficial or harmful character of opinion polls. Once again, then, the host projects the show's character by specifying and soliciting activities which are constitutive of it. Program openings repeat the use of these contrast classes and caller-predicate projections. Consider the following extract:

(3) 9:05a.m. Show Opening   NR[AP:16:97](4)*
    N: Sleaze. Eleven of John Major's ministers have had to quit be-
        cause of scandal. Should it be a dozen? Should Neil Hamilton
        resign? And now this morning new allegations with Michael
        Colvin in the frame and Michael Howard furiously denying
        insinuations against him. Are standards falling? Are politicians
        morally incontinent? Is it wrong to cling to office when your
        propriety is being questioned or is it quite outrageous that any-
        one should be hounded from their jobs because of minor indis-
        cretions years ago or unproven allegations in the press? Journal-
        ists after all enjoy the odd free lunch, the facility, the trip, the
        corporate hospitality. Should there be a public enquiry, as Tony
        Blair and Paddy Ashdown want? Should it look at who gets
        jobs on Quangos? [Quasi autonomous non-government
        organization]. How far should the moralizing go? Should
        former ministers be banned from taking jobs with companies
        dealt with while in government? When do gifts, holidays,
        business dinners, or even tea and biscuits stop being a normal
        part of public or private business life and become unethical?
        What would you give, what would you accept and what do you
        expect of others? Is virtue declining or are our moral

expectations rising? Do let me induce you to call in, o one seven one five eight oh double four double four.

Here, the topic of "sleaze" is announced and linked to a membership category namely "government minister." It is further indicated that some incumbents of this category have recently resigned from their position because of "sleaze." This is followed by a list of questions or positions which might be taken on the issue, and these are arranged contrastively. First on the hearably "negative" side, listeners are invited to agree or disagree on whether standards are falling, whether politicians are morally incontinent and whether it is wrong to cling to office if their propriety is questioned. Secondly, on the hearably "positive" (or supportive) side, callers are invited to align (or not) with positions such as "it is outrageous to hound people from their jobs" because of "indiscretion," that "people are innocent until proven guilty," and that it's "okay" to enjoy corporate hospitality and other "free lunches." Having set out these contrasting sides or positions which may be taken on the issue, the host then repeats his invitation to the listeners to call ("do let me induce you to call ..."). The host, then, can be heard to project in terms of these contrasts an orderliness with respect to what may be done by callers on the show. It is through the use of this projected orderliness, then, that the show's character as a set of categorial relations – "for" and "against" – is "set up."

Whilst it is a predicate of callers to "say what they think" and offer their "views" and "opinions," the particular topic locates and provides for the specifics of the content of these activities. That is, the callers not only engage in these activities which are relevant for the show in general, they also engage, as we shall demonstrate, in activities which are relevant for the task/topic at hand. What a "caller" *is*, what his or her predicates *are*, then, depends on, and in turn, reflexively constitutes the context and character of the task at hand. Indeed, not only are sequential features important in the organization of telephone conversations (cf. Sacks and Schegloff and Jefferson, 1974; Schegloff, 1979), so also are topical organizational features. The character of a call, that is its topic, will shape the type of turn (if not its sequential order). Answers are not just "answers" to "questions." They are answers to *just this* question and hence, with respect to their recognizable (and unique) adequacy, they will exhibit an orientation to the topic addressed in the question. For example, in the case of a "farewell" call, the caller may offer "best wishes," in the case of a death in the family, "sympathy" may be offered. In the context of this radio show, topics consist of debatable and discussable issues. Consequently, what is said is tied to each show's topic. So, what callers may do (what the predicates of "caller" are in this instance) depends in part on the kinds of sequential organizational features analyzed by Sacks, Schegloff and others, and also in part on the topical content of the call.

It is also observable that some trailers and show openings contain invitations to call to incumbents of particular membership categories which are recognizably relevant to the show's topic. One way to appreciate this is to recognize that there are specific and formal means whereby topics are made relevant for the parties to a conversation. As Sacks (1992b) points out:

> How do you make something topical? One way is to turn it into a "something for us." You can treat it as the most general content rule for conversation that people will talk overwhelmingly, not so much about *things* that *happened* to them, but about things *insofar as* they happened to *them*. Talking about whatever, it comes home to us. Which is to say, there are a variety of things happening in the world, like disasters. Their happening doesn't make them introducible into a conversation. What has to be done is to turn them into something for us. (p. 563)

In the radio phone-in this turning of the topic into "something for us" may be done by the callers to the show (a matter which we shall address below) or, as is the case in extracts (1) and (2) by the host. Thus, in extract (1) "persons interviewed by pollsters" are invited to call ("Have you been interviewed by the pollsters? Did you tell them the truth? Do you think how you vote on May 1st might be influenced by what the opinion polls tell you today and tomorrow? I'd like to know what you think."). Similarly, in extract (2) "pollsters" and persons "polled" are so invited ("If you have been a pollster or if you've been polled, if you use them in your work I'd like to know what you think."). Thus, the topic of the show is turned by the host into "something" for somebody, that is, particular callers.

On some shows, however, the categorial field of potential callers is not so limited; it is, rather, hearably "open," without pre-specified categories. This is evident in extract (3) above, where such category specification is observably absent. The host invites "you," which could be "anyone"; the invitation to call is open to "anyone" with an opinion on the matter at hand. One possible interpretation of this difference in "address" between "named categories" and "anyone," is that whereas for some topics there is a readily recognizable collection of categories which may be "topic carriers" (e.g. gay/straight with respect to the topic of homosexuality), for other topics the range of membership categories relevant to the issue may not be so circumscribed. Clearly, whilst "anyone" *can* have an opinion on the issue of homosexuality, it could be argued that there is a collection of persons whose opinion on the topic may be regarded as "informed" in that they stand in some readily available categorial relation to the topic.

Accordingly, it might be reasoned that there may be another class of topics, such as politics, the weather or work about which "anyone" can have an opinion. However, such a conclusion implies that there are connections between topics and categories which are specifiable in some decontextualized way, thereby reifying categories with respect to which topics are relevant. In contrast to this taxonomic approach is one which attends, in the specifics of the talk, to the ways in which categories are *made*, or are hearably, relevant. Thus, it is quite obvious that particular categories *can be made* specifically relevant to the topics of "politics," "weather" and "work": someone who is a "meteorologist" could be made relevant – in the sense that "talking about the weather" is a predicate of category "meteorologist," or at least knowing about it is; similarly, political scientists and politicians may be treated as having "special," ie. "insider" knowledge of "politics" and "social scientists" are conventionally categorized as having "expert" as opposed to general or personal knowledge about the world of work. The ties between topic and membership category for whom that topic has some "special," that is, predicated relevance, can then be used, but they need not be. This is a matter of local practice and variation; sometimes the host invites those who belong to particular categories which are hearably relevant, but at other times he does not. It is not that some topics exclude the possibility of selecting a category for it, since any topic can be made category relevant.

Introducing the Guest

If a guest has been invited to participate in the show, listeners will be informed of this in the trailers, and he/she will then be introduced in the show opening. Standardly, guests are introduced as incumbents of membership categories which are recognizably relevant to the topic of the show. Such "characters" appear "on cue" in that their presence is "unsurprising" in the sense described by Sacks (1992a: 182; 410). That is to say, there is an "unremarkable" categorial connection between the topic and the guest (and as we shall show below, between caller and topic also). Thus, in extract (4), where the topic is the explicit sexual content of teenage magazines, the guest is recognizably categorially connected: She is a member of an organization which gives advice to young people on sexual and relationship matters.

(4) NR[16:04:97](1)*
> N: ... o double four double four. Sitting opposite me in the studio is
> Alison Hudly from Brook Advisory, Hadly from the Brook

Advisory Centers which er give advice and contraception, incidentally, to young people. O one seven one five eight o double
four double four.

There is a similar discernible categorial symmetry between the topic for
debate and the categorial membership of the guest in extract (5). In this
case the topic is "road rage" and the guest's category membership is
"chartered psychologist" with a "research speciality" on the subject for the
RAC (Royal Automobile Club).

(5) NR[16:04:97](2)*
    N: ... call o one seven one five eight o double four double four. In
        our Glasgow studio is a chartered psychologist who has re-
        searched the subject for the RAC, he's Conrad King. O one
        seven one five eight o double four double four...

In the following extract (6), a "former cabinet minister" is named and
introduced. In this case the guest not only belongs to a membership category which is hearably relevant to the topic (political sleaze), he is also
recognizably excluded from co-membership of the list of allegedly sleazy
politicians who are mentioned. Thus, his being "above suspicion" is
achieved via his categorization as "unseduceable" and as "a man of com-
fortable independence." The guest, then, by implication, is positioned
within the terms of the debate as one who is not involved in sleaze.

(6) NR[AP:16:97] (4)*
    N: ... double four. With me is the outspoken former cabinet minis-
        ter and leader of the house, John Biffin. He has been described
        as unseduceable a man of comfortable independence o seven
        one five eight o double four double four. John Biffin, what does
        a man of comfortable independence think of your colleagues
        Tim Smith, Michael Colvin, Neil Hamilton and all the rest of
        them?
    J: Well I think its quite clear that er if they've received cash or
        received ...

Once the guest, if present, has been introduced, the host initiates the discussion. He does so in one of two ways. He either invites the guest to
state "what they think" about the topic or he invites first caller to do so.
Extract (6) contains an instance of the former (and relatively infrequent)
method. The induction of callers into the show is examined in the
following section.

Showing the Callers

In this section our concerns are threefold. Firstly, we consider some sequential features of caller induction; secondly, we examine host's first question, and thirdly, we analyze how callers are categorized and how such categorizations provide for the positioning of callers.

Caller Induction

Each show consists of a series of telephone calls. The number of calls varies from show to show, averaging twenty calls. When callers telephone the show, their call is answered by a receptionist who takes their name, location and the point they wish to make and then places them in a queue of callers which is visible to the host on a computer screen. Unlike queues which are visible to their members, a feature of telephone queues such as this is that the queuers do not know what their place in the queue is relative to the other queuers. Hence, unlike participants in queues which are visible to them, they do not have a sense of the unfolding and category flowing character of this social phenomenon; they do not have a sense of their changing category entitlements and obligations as the composition of the queue changes as people leave the queue and others "take their place" (cf. Lee and Watson, 1993). Like callers to "party lines" (Bogen, 1992), they are queuing in "interactional darkness." How they are brought from this void-like state to a state of participation in the show is accomplished via caller induction.

We do not have access to the talk between the receptionist and caller. What is clear, however, is that the host's induction of the caller on to the show and the caller's first on-air utterance comprise the latest in a coordinated sequence of utterances and actions involving the caller, the receptionist and the host. The host's first utterance to the caller is a "response" to the "call waiting" (a summons-on-hold, as it were); that is, even though the caller has had their call answered by the receptionist, they have not yet been put through to their final destination, namely the on-air show. The host's first utterance to caller, then, is a response to the caller's on-hold summons. As such, one of its features is that it "answers" the caller. However, whereas in other cases the answerer does not know the caller's name, in this case he does. So, when the host answers he does not have to initiate a greeting sequence to arrive at caller identification since this has already been accomplished for him by the receptionist. The immediate task at hand, then, is to indicate to the caller that they are now on-air, to introduce caller to the audience and to transform their call into something relevant for the show.

In the radio phone-in show under consideration here, callers are transformed into "show-relevant callers" via the use of several methods of caller induction. Drawing on the information on the computer screen, the host introduces callers to the listening audience in methodical ways which are exhibited in the following extracts. Five types of caller induction sequence are evident in our corpus of data. Type One inductions comprise two turns: (a) a host's turn in which caller is named, their location formulated and he/she is questioned for the first time; (b) a caller's turn in which caller answers the question. This is evident in the following extracts:

(7) NR[FE1594(3)]
> N: Francis -----[2] from from Birmingham what do you think?
> F: urhh I feel that the age of consent should stay at ...

(8) NR[JA2594(1)]
> N: John ----- from Staffordshire do you agree with that?
> (0.3)
> J: Er well huh in a way yes but I've got my own ...

(9) NR[FE1594(1)]
> N: Ray ----- from Thurrock in Essex do you think gays should uhh
>   pushed off from their sexuality until they're twenty one?
> R: Well no, I would go further than that I mean I'm ...

(10) NR[JA:10:95](2)
> N: Kathleen ----- from Tunbridge Wells in Kent do you have any
>   direct experience of this?
> P: I was in the prison service for over ten years .hhh and ...

It is observable that in each of these examples the host introduces the caller to the listening audience and inducts the caller on to the show by (a) stating the caller's name, (b) providing a location formulation for the caller and then (c) moving seamlessly to question the caller.[3]

Type Two induction sequences likewise consist of two turns, as in Type One, the difference being the absence of a question in the host's turn:

(11) NR[FE1594(4)]
> N: Naomi ----- from Wincham in Surrey.
> Na: Um I've got a number of gay friends I've I've in theater in the
>   literary world. I've got a number of gay friends and as far as I
>   can see ...

(12) NR[JA:12:96](3)*
> N: Julia ----- from Southport in Merseyside.
> J: Well I feel that um when you sort of give yourself to somebody
>   in a sexual relationship ...

The following extracts contain Type Three induction sequences. They involve two turns: (a) a host turn comprising a naming of the caller, their location formulation and a seamless first question, and (b) a caller's turn comprising an acknowledgment, a greeting and a seamlessly connected answer.

(13) NR[JA:10:95](5)
    N: Sarah ----- from Edinburgh what do you think?
    S: Yes good morning I'm I'm just an ordinary member of the ...

(14) NR[JA:12:96](2)*
    N: Pamela ----- from Teddington south of England what do=
                                        [   ]
    P: yes
    N: =you think?
    P: Oh good morning, yes I think that um when the engagement ...

(15) NR[FE1594(a)]
    N: Dave ----- from Normanton in Yorkshire what do you think?
                                         [   ]
    D: Hello
    D: Hello, yes I've got a couple of points I'd like to pick upon actually, I think Ian McKellan just a couple of ...

In these extracts, these introductions and first questions are treated by callers as "greetings substitutes" (Sacks, 1992a: 554), in that the callers, in each case, can be understood as having "returned" a greeting. Thus, in extracts (13) and (14) callers respond to the host's turn with "good morning" and in (15) the caller says "hello." Furthermore, it would appear that from the ways in which callers' turns are built that these return greetings are not produced as first pair parts of greeting sequences. This is because of the absence of a recognizable slot for a return (second pair part). Thus, the caller proceeds seamlessly from greeting to answer.

Callers occasionally do attempt to initiate a greeting sequence by pausing after their greeting, and such initiations occasion return greetings from the host. This is evident in Type Four induction sequences which consists of four turns: (a) a host's turn in which caller is named and their location formulated; (b) a caller's turn consisting of an acknowledgment and a greeting; (c) a return greeting from the host, followed by a question; (d) caller's answer. The following two extracts exemplify this type:

(16) NR[JA:10:95](3)
    N: Peter ur I've only got your first name I think it is Peter from
          Portland in Dorset
    P: Yes good morning Nick.

> N: Hello have you been a inside prison?
> P: Well, I'm a prison officer, and I've been a prison officer for 22
>   years ...

(17) NR[FE2597(1)]
> N: Eva ----- from York.
> E: Hello.
> N: H-hi what's your involvement or your interest in this?
> E: Er I have quite substantially er researched another miscarriage of
>   justice ...

It is noticeable in extract (16) that the host's first turn can be heard as eliciting the caller's surname. That is, the fact that the host "only" has caller's first name is something remarkable, a mentionable matter. Furthermore, unlike the preceding extracts, the host ceases to speak after having mentioned this, thereby providing a transition relevance point for the caller. Similarly in extract (17) the host ceases to speak after formulating the caller's location. One possible reason, therefore, for the occurrence of these "successful greeting" sequences is the noticeable absence of a question following the name and location in the host's first turn, and therefore its recognizable turn completion. Indeed, when the host recognizably stops talking, he provides therefore for possible turn transition relevance.

Finally, the following extract contains a Type Five induction sequence. It consists of (a) a host's turn comprising a naming and location formulation, (b) a caller's acknowledgment and greeting, (c) host return greeting, and (d) caller-initiated topic address.

(18) NR[NO2895](2)
> N: Richard ----- calling from Paris, in France
>   [   ]
> R: Yes good morning=
> N: =Hello=
> R: =But the comments ...

(19) NR[FE2597](3)
> N: Stan ----- from Penzance in Cornwall.
> S: Hello Nick.
> N: Hello.
> S: Er well we all know of the infamous Stoke Newington Police
>   Station ...

Following his introduction of the caller to the listening audience, the host proceeds (sometimes seamlessly, as we have shown) to his first question. It is to this occurrence that our discussion now turns.

First Question.

The host's first question is a "topic opener" (Sacks, 1992b: 565-566). As such, as Sacks indicates, although such topic openers provide for replies which are "an answer long," for example an agreement or a disagreement, in this context, as elsewhere, the opener is treated as an invitation to speak for *more* than "an answer long;" it provides for "extended" topical talk. As Sacks (1992b) suggests:

> ... one way of opening topics is specifically through the use of questions which are built such as to invite responses which are more than an answer long, but which admit at least answer-long response. So you're not violating the adjacency pair status when you refuse to take up the topical possibilities by doing merely an answer long response. That is to say, at the order of topical organization people can offer topical openers and people can reject them, and that's different then asking questions and people not answering them. You don't own the course of topical operation, but you can own next position and what's to be done in it. (p. 566)

There are two main types of first question: "open" and "closed." Open questions invite callers to say "what they think"; they do not specify a particular topic (though the topic-for-the-show remains omnirelevant). Closed questions invite the caller to state their opinion on what the previous caller had to say or the issue raised by the previous caller. Extracts (13), (14) and (15), examined above, contain examples of "open" questions: Callers are invited to say "what they think." The following extracts (20) and (21) contain examples of the second type of question, namely closed questions. In the first, caller is asked if they "agree with" what has been said previously.

(20) NR[JA2594(1)]
    N: John ----- from Staffordshire do you agree with that?
           (0.3)
    J: Er well huh in a way yes but I've got my own point to make if
           you don't mind.
    N: Yeh go on fire away.
    J: I'll be very brief um please hear me out (1.0) uh I've read the uh
           popular use ...

(21) NR[FE1594(1)]
    N: Ray ----- from Thurrock in Essex do you think gays should uhh
           pushed off from their sexuality until they're twenty one?
    R: Well no, I would go further than that I mean I'm virtually sixty
           years of age and I can remember uhh over those years ...

This second type of question has particular implications for the caller's response. Where the host asks a question which seeks only the caller's "thoughts," the caller may then proceed to their point. However, questions which ask directly for caller's opinion regarding the previous call delay such opportunity. That is, although a caller may have telephoned with a particular point they wish to make they must first attend to the host's question, which may or may not be on the issue for which they were prepared. As the following extract shows, however, callers do not always address the issue raised by previous caller when asked to do so:

(22) NR[JA:12:96](4)*
    N: John ----- from Cambridge d'you think that unfaithfulness
          generally backfires on one?
    J: .hh well I-I can't really say ur the way I was brought up was that
          one should aim for chastity before marriage and faithfulness
          afterwards, that's er a lifelong er exclusive relationship wi-with
          one's wife ...

In this case, after the question has received what otherwise could be heard as a reply and the adjacency pair is *now hearably complete*, the caller's turn does not revert back to the host. Rather, caller continues to talk and thereby produces a "more than an answer long' reply. Indeed, whilst it does not address the immediately preceding topic, it develops the *general* topic for the program. That the caller continues to hold the floor after the completion of the adjacency pair suggests an orientation to one of the category predicates of "caller": giving their opinion upon the topic at the first available opportunity. Furthermore, it is a predicate of caller that they produce *"more than an answer long"* turns. The first question, then, is treated as an invitation to speak at length.

Caller Categories

At the outset of this chapter we noted that the callers to the show are not *only* "callers." That is, the show does not consist of "ordinary telephone conversations." Rather, calls are organized as show-relevant calls and callers are transformed into "show-relevant callers." In this section our focus is on how this is accomplished. Whilst the caller remains an "on air caller" (rather than "caller waiting"), such omnirelevant category membership will routinely have other category memberships mapped on to it. Thus, once the call is under way new categories can be made relevant within its course. This may occur at any point in a call's duration. However, space precludes consideration of all such occurrences. Our discussion, therefore, is limited to how callers are categorized, and what the significance of such categorization is at the start of the call.

Caller categories may be proffered by the caller or presented by the host. At the outset of calls, callers are positioned topically in two ways. Firstly, the host may introduce the caller by name, place and a topic relevant category, whilst secondly, in the absence of the host's categorizations, the caller may categorize themselves in terms of a topic relevant category. An example of the former is the following:

(23) NR[FE1594(11)]
    N: I presume another Christian on the line but perhaps not so
          evangelical, Cannon Douglas ----- from Fontlow in West Sussex
          (0.3) what d'you what do you make of urm=
          [   ]
    D: I think
    N: =our last caller?
    D: I seem to be hearing an awful lot of rubbish. Sadly the ...

Thus, drawing on the caller's title ("Cannon"), the host categorizes the caller as "another Christian," thereby also invoking co-membership with the previous caller. Furthermore, it is observable that the host then deploys the category "Christian" as a membership categorization device whose constituent categories are types of Christians. The locally pertinent and variable category predicate which positions such Christians within the device is their degree of evangelism.

In the following three examples callers categorize themselves:

(24) NR[FE:1594(2)]
    N: Arthur ----- from from Shrewsbury in Shropshire.
    A: Hello.
    N: Hello what's your perspective ((on this))?
    A: Well, I'm a parent and a parent of both a boy and a girl. Urh
         they're both now well past the age of consent in fact er you
         know they're well on but the, I have had tremendous worries and
         concerns when and knowing I have a gay son, that he could be
         criminalized and put in jail at that time for something which the
         girl could not ...

(25) NR[FE1594(9)]
    N: Michael ----- from London what do you make of this?
    M: Um, well, Sir Ian has touched on the point that I wanted to
         make. I've been a gay journalist for twenty one years or more
         on *Gay News* and now more recently on *Capital Gay*, um so I've
         seen the act in operation ...

(26) NR[FE:1594(6)]
    N: Brenda ----- from Manchester, what do you think?
    B: Um, Brenda ----- from Manchester.
    N: I beg your pardon.
    B: I'm speaking on behalf of members of FLAG. We're family and
         friends of lesbian and gays ((sound of yapping dog)) um parents
         of lesbians and gays and we want justice and equality ...

The next extract contains a combination of the host categorization and caller self-categorization:

(27) NR[FE1594(8)]
    N: There's a doctor on the line. I don't know if it's a medical
         doctor. Doctor Elizabeth ----- from Peebles. Are you a medical
         doctor?
    E: Yes
    N: Are you er I take it you're not a specialist in AIDS by any
         chance are you?
    E: No I'm not a specialist in AIDS but I've been researching sexu-
         ally transmitted diseases which is a very much wider aspect then
         just AIDS which is a specific STD

These categorizations are significant in two senses. Firstly, they provide for, and reflexively elaborate, the sense of the caller's talk. That is, to begin with, they can be heard to *authorize* the caller's views and opinions. These "identities for a topic" serve to "position" the caller as being *able to speak* (in the sense of being heard as credible and plausible) on the topic. Thus, a predicate of "Cannon" (extract 23) may be presumed to be not only being knowledgeable about religion but also to have an opinion relevant to that expressed in the previous call. Similarly, in extract (27) the "doctor" can properly be expected to have insight, knowledge and relevant information about the topic of AIDS. Finally, it is observable that the caller in extract (25) grounds his remarks in his membership of the category "gay journalist," appealing to his longstanding experience of the topic at hand.

Secondly, these categorizations are significant in the sense that they can be heard to "appear on cue." Thus, it is not surprising, for the topic of the lowering of the age of consent for homosexual acts, that one caller would identify himself as the "parent of a gay son," a second caller as "a member of FLAG" (Family and Friends of Lesbians and Gays), a third as a gay journalist and a fourth as a doctor specializing in sexually transmitted diseases. That is to say, for *this* topic, these categories (characters) are un-remarkably relevant and appear on cue.

It may also be noted, further to our earlier discussion of the ways in which topics are made relevant for the parties to a conversation, that these self-categorizations by the callers exhibit the "general content rule for conversation that people will talk overwhelmingly, not so much about *things* that *happened* to them, but about things *insofar as* they happened to *them*" (Sacks, 1992b: 563). The topics of the show are here turned into topics *for the callers themselves* in that they mention their personal circumstances, experience, relatives, research and expertise in relation to the topic.

Generating Debate

A central feature of each show is debate. As we have indicated, the show trailers invite callers to align with one side or the other of various positions or opinions which may be taken or held on the topic in question. Callers are then asked to "say what they think" or to agree or disagree with last caller. However, since callers do not speak directly with each other, any debate is mediated and managed by the host. The debate consists in (a) the presentation or elicitation of a position for the caller and (b) counter-positioning by the host. The opinion/position offered by the caller is available to the host as a resource for adopting a contrary position, questioning or challenging the callers. Such interactional work by the host depends not only upon the position of the caller being apparent but also on the fact that whilst the caller's position for the topic is fixed, the host's is not. The opinions provided by the caller can be heard as belonging to them; the host, however, is not heard as giving his opinions but rather as representing *another side of the debate or argument, whatever that is*. Once the position is found, the host then takes a contrasting position. Now, clearly, the host cannot take up the opposite or contrasting position until he has established what the caller's position is, or what a position of the caller is. If the caller does not state his or her position, it must be *elicited*. In this section some methods deployed by the host in generating such debate are examined with reference to three examples.

Extract (28) contains an example of the host making use of the caller's position to generate debate via a request for a justification of the caller's opinion. Once given, the host adopts a counter position:

(28) NR[JA:12:96](4)*
    N: John ----- from Cambridge d'you think that unfaithfulness gener-
           ally backfires on one?
    J: .hh well I-I can't really say ur the way I was brought up was that
           one should aim for chastity before marriage and faithfulness

afterwards that's er a lifelong er exclusive relationship wi-with one's wife=

N: =Why should you have chastity before marriage?

J: Well, because I think er the physical sex really ought to be an expression of love and not-not that of which one aims primarily .hh um and I umm=

N: =Why if pe- if people enjoy it and both consenting adults and all that?

J: .hh well I think I think the problem is that the debate is being driven at the moment largely by men who would like to try out a number of relationships but ur want to marry a as the last speaker said ur want to marry a virgin and-and I think that the debate is actually being driven by people who want to have their cake and eat it .hh and I mean my marriage now thankfully has lasted for forty three years and and um that we didn't have sex until after we were married, and we've been faithful to each other since.

N: Is it driven by hypocritical men or is it driven by emancipated women or both?

J: Well, I think that's a very difficult one because uh ur .hhh I-I think perhaps before the introduction of the pill it was certainly driven by promiscuous men ...

In this extract, the caller states his position quite clearly, it does not have to be elicited. The position is a categorially ordered position: It involves a stipulation of the predicates of married couples. Firstly, sex should be a exclusive predicate of married couples; abstinence or chastity should be practiced by persons until they are married. Secondly, once married, couples should be faithful to each other. These stipulated category/predicate connections are then challenged by the host. His method of doing so is to offer an alternative category of which sex may be a predicate, namely men and women in search of pleasure or consenting adults. Like the caller's position, the host's counter position is one which is categorially ordered.

Caller's response to the host's counter position involves the use of the membership category "men who would like to try out a number of relationships but also want to marry virgins" (which is reformulated by the host as "hypocritical men"). Such men, caller argues, are responsible for the "debate" about sex before marriage. They afford the caller his contrasting category membership as one who did not have sex before marriage and who, by implication, is not hypocritical. The host's rejoinder involves another counter-position organized in categorial terms: Could not the "problem" of premarital sex also be explained in terms of the category "emancipated women" or, indeed, both emancipated women and hypocritical men.

In the following extract the caller states her position in category terms with respect to which the host produces a categorially ordered counter-alignment:

(29) NR[JA:12:96](3)*

N: Julia ----- from Southport in Merseyside.
J: Well I feel that um when you sort of give yourself to somebody in a sexual relationship at fir-especially the first time when you lose your virginity to somebody and you don't go on to marry them is er well in-in my personal experience it sort of has formed a spiritual bond twenty five years later I still think about that person every single day a::nd it is upsetting and I really feel that it are some very wise things in the bible about marriage and that staying together and staying with one partner.
N: D'you you use a very old fashioned term <u>giving</u> yourself.
J: Yes=
N: =Now, many people nowadays see sex as much as ur taking as giving.
J: Oh no I think um I think its giving hhh. I-I do think well perhaps people that is what's the matter people are too greedy people want too much th-they are hedonistic and their not prepared to give and to sacrifice some of their own life I-I mean I had to sacrifice a career for my marriage .hhh I did eventually marry quite a long time after my first sexual experience to obviously somebody else .hh and um I-I ha-I actually had to sacrifice my career and I stayed at home in fact in the end.
N: Why?
J: Why?
N: Mmm
J: Well, um I'd just finished a degree as a mature student and I became pregnant as-as I was about to onto post grad and I was going to do an M A either in theater-theater studies or theatre arts or a P-G-C-E I had lots of choices and er I, but my baby=
               [   ]
N: Um d'you can I
J: =was quite ill and I just felt as if I could not give, I had to stay=
               [   ]
N: yes
J: =with the baby, I had to be with my husband and my baby and to settle down

In this extract, the category which is introduced by the caller is that of "sexual partner." She points out that, for her, predicates of "first sexual partner" are "staying together" and having a "spiritual bond" which is not diminished by time. The host then takes up the caller's use of the predicate of "giving" and sets this within a contrast class –

"giving/taking." That is, Ross adopts a counter position in that he
indicates that another possible predicate of sexual partner is "taking"; he
"balances" the caller's view or position with this categorially organised
alternative. In return, the caller reaffirms her position and does so by
formulating a list of the predicates of "takers": they are greedy, hedonistic,
and not prepared to give or sacrifice. From this list, the caller then selects
"sacrifice" as something which *she*, as a "giver" and in contrast to
"takers," *has* been prepared to do. Thus, she sacrificed her career and her
chance of higher education, staying home with her baby and husband
instead.

Occasionally, the host finds the caller's opinion insufficient for counter-
alignment, thereby occasioning clarification of the caller's position. In the
following extract, such clarification is eventually accomplished when the
caller specifies in categorial terms his use of the predicate "appalling" to
describe homosexual behavior:

(30) NR[FE1594(1)]

N: Ray ----- from Thurrock in Essex do you think gays should uhh
   pushed off from their sexuality until they're twenty one?
R: Well no, I would go further than that I mean I'm virtually sixty
   years of age and I can remember uhh over those years I was
   appalled in fact when they made it, when removed it from being
   illegal urhhhm you know, it's what's heh-heh-heh.
N: Why does it worry you?
R: I was in I was in fact the person who said I believe in altering
   the age and as far as I was concerned it be altered to ninety
   providing they got the permission of both parents uh that's how
   strongly I feel about it.
N: Are you the leader of the conservative group on your council?
   I'm trying to place.
R: Yes, Thurrock Borough Council is down in Essex here.
N: Yup.
R: And I'm the leader of the conservative group.
N: Why does, why does homosexuality appal you so much?
R: Well, think of it, use one's imagination, you know, you perhaps
   unwittingly go into a pub or bar and you find out err to your err
   that it is habited by these people and they're appalling to watch.
   I'm I'm not a great, you know, I'm I'm not a member of the
   Roman Catholic err following but I do admire the Pope's
   description of homosexuality in that it is an abomination, it's
   absolutely dreadful, it corrupts the young, there's no doubt about
   it. When I was a young man you didn't see these hoards of
   people like you see today. It's really quite dreadful, and when
   you start talking=

N: =But I'm I'm not quite sure what you see when you go into
these pubs or clubs what it is you see that appals you?

R: Their general act, it, way you see=

N: =Showing affection for one another?

R: Uh, yes the way they carry on I mean.

N: But what do they carry on Ray, what's so upsetting?

R: Well, I don't mix with them, I mean I would actually steer clear
of them and this is perhaps one of the main reasons why I feel
like I do that, you know, you never used to see this sort of thing
when I was a young man.

N: But what is the sort of thing you see Ray?

R: Well, they act towards one another, I mean it
absolutely appals me, you see them=
[   ]

N: How do they act?

R: =putting an arm around one another and kissing and things like
that it is really quite dreadful=

N: =Ray, Ray forgive me, why is somebody kissing somebody else
dreadful? Isn't that isn't that an expression of love?

R: There is nothing dreadful about it in its true sense of the word,
there is uh um and uh um you know when one thinks of
comradeship as I remember it I mean I served in the British
forces twice, there ...

In this extract the caller positions himself firstly in terms of his age-category (he is 60) and as such he is in a position to "remember," as he says, when homosexuality was illegal. He then states that "he was appalled" when it was decriminalised and continues to be appalled by it. The host then makes several attempts to elicit what it is that "appals" this caller. Eventually, the caller identifies what he finds "appalling" by listing examples of behavior by homosexuals: They put their arms round each other; they kiss and do "things like that." The hearable position, then, is a categorial one: *These* behaviors (kissing etc.) belong in *this* device of appalling/dreadful things. Having finally elicited the caller's description of what specifically appals him, the host then proceeds to propose an alternate position. He does so by selecting one item from the caller's list – "kissing somebody" – and then offers an alternative device to which such an act may belong. Thus, he asks, "isn't that an expression of love."

It could, of course, have been different. Thus, it may be noted that the host could have responded to the caller's evaluation of homosexuality as "appalling" and "dreadful" by adopting the "contradictory" position, namely "not appalling" or "not dreadful." To have done so, however, would have invited a further contradictory responses, namely "yes, it is appalling," "no, it isn't" etc. Thus, contradiction occasions counter-contradiction of the kind displayed in the classic Monty Python sketch, "The

Argument Clinic." It may be suggested that whilst such an interactional event may "work" for a absurdist comedy show, it is hardly "informative" for listeners and does not "develop" the discussion, which is predicate of the show under consideration here.

In each of these three extended extracts the host generates the debate by eliciting the caller's position and by proposing a categorially organized alternative position. The precise categorial resources differ, however. Thus, in the first two of the extracts, the debate is organised in terms of the predicates of membership categories and, in particular, in terms of what those predicates *should be*. Thus, in extract (28) the caller argues *for* the predicates of chastity and fidelity in relation to the unmarried and married respectively. Similarly, in extract (29) the caller argues *for* the predicates of monogamy, sacrifice, and "staying at home" in relation to the category of married woman. In contrast, the categorial resources in terms of which the debate is organized in extract (30) consist of alternative membership categorization devices. Thus, the debatable point is whether the behavior of homosexual men belongs in one device or another. In all three cases, whether the debate is category/predicate based or device based, these resources are contrastively organized.

Concluding Remarks

We began this chapter by noticing the recognizability of the show as *entertainment*. We have sought to explicate how, in this case, "entertainment" is accomplished methodically by the host with telephone calls as his resource. In particular, we have described how the host *elicits* particular types of turns from callers, *relates* callers to the show's topic and *responds* to them in ways which promote discussion and debate. The host invites callers to state their opinions and air their views on particular topics. Callers relate themselves or are related to the topic of the show methodically via category-tied turns. The host generates discussion and debate by inviting callers to elaborate their positions and by aligning himself contrastively with them. The show is a product of the deployment of category, predicate and contrast.

Contrastive category work is, of course, not unique to this particular media event. Other programs, such as political interviews, news reports, plays, films, etc. make use of variants on the theme of category contrast. These continuities in method await further investigation, as does the question of why such category contrastive talk, even confrontation, is recognizably "entertaining" in the first place.

Notes

1. For a thoroughgoing sequential investigation, with subsidiary categorial focus, see Hutchby (1991). See also Hutchby (1996).
2. A series of hyphens indicates the caller's surname which is omitted from the transcript.
3. Space precludes discussion of "naming" and the use of location formulations. As Schegloff (1972) has indicated, the use of location formulations is a product of location *analysis* on the part of the speaker. It may well be, therefore, that the selection of location formulations by the host reflects also (following Schegloff, 1972: 90): "the need of mass media to formulate the location of events in terms recognizable to strangers" – hence the selection not of "local" location formulations but of "county" and "major city" locational formulations. At present time, however, such conclusions remain speculative.

Chapter 8

Moral Order and the Montreal Massacre: A Story of Membership Categorization Analysis[1]

Peter Eglin and Stephen Hester

Introduction

The crimes, horrors and tragedies of everyday life are endlessly topics of media attention and analysis. In this chapter we examine media coverage of the homicides which became known as the "Montreal Massacre" in which 13 female engineering students and a data processing worker at the Ecole Polytechnique in Montreal in December 1989 were shot and killed, and 12 others were wounded, by a gunman, Marc Lepine. In one class-room, witnesses reported, the gunman separated the men and women students, ordered the men to leave, then shot at the women, killing six of them. He was reported to have said just before opening fire, "You're all a bunch of feminists. I hate feminists." At the end of his "rampage" he shot himself dead. Our approach is an ethnomethodological one, specifically informed by membership categorization analysis (Hester and Eglin, 1997a, 1997b, 1997c; Sacks, 1992a). Accordingly, our analytic orientation is in line with ethnomethodology's study policy to treat recognizable features of social life as situated accomplishments of human activity, and hence as topics of inquiry (Button, 1991; Zimmerman and Pollner, 1971). Our interest, then, is in the Montreal massacre as a *members' phenome-*

non. We seek to examine media coverage of this phenomenon, how sense was made of it and how its significance was formulated. In particular, such coverage permits a respecification of sociological theorizations of the functions of crime and deviance, an argument which we address before analyzing our materials.

Respecifying the Functions of Crime and Deviance

Since at least Durkheim's famous third chapter in *The Rules of Sociological Method* (1982 [1895]) on rules for distinguishing the normal and the pathological, the argument that crime (deviance) is functional has become a standard feature of sociological theorizing of the functionalist kind. This is true in both the structural consensus and structural conflict traditions of functionalist theorizing (Box, 1981; Cuff, Francis and Sharrock, 1990; Hester and Eglin, 1992). Durkheim argued that crime is not only normal for a given type of society at a given stage of its development, but that it is also necessary for the functioning of any society (Sharrock, 1984). It serves to provide society with recurrent opportunities both to maintain the indispensable moral boundaries between right and wrong and to adapt them to changing environmental circumstances. It is clearly the *response* to crime that is critical to Durkheim's theorizing here. It is the opportunity to *criminalize* action and actor that is the crucial element. This theoretical step allows those conceptual approaches to crime and deviance for which criminalization is the central phenomenon to find Durkheim's argument congenial to their point of view. Thus it is that interactionist and constructionist textbooks in the sociology of crime and deviance commonly include Durkheim's argument (for example, Grusky and Pollner, 1981; Hester and Eglin, 1992).

The functionalist argument depends on the acts of denouncing the crime and the criminal being made visible to the population so that they may have their unintendedly integrative effects. The prevailing media of communication in a society then become the necessary vehicles for re-presenting the criminalizing acts carried out in courtrooms and other such criminalizing settings. That crime stories, it is often said, seem to occupy such a prominent place in media content, is then readily explained in terms of this theory. What is less attended is just how any particular crime report (or a series of them) accomplishes such a functional outcome.

Now it is true, at least since Spector and Kitsuse (1987 [1977]), that investigators have attended to the claims-making activities of moral, professional and program entrepreneurs for the ways in which putatively troublesome conditions come to be constructed as "social problems" such as "violent crime" or "violence against women." And interactionist studies have long attended to the organizational and interactional features of deviance attribution and processing by social control agents such as the police and court personnel through which particular actions and actors are assigned some deviant status or label (Rubington and Weinberg, 1987). In both constructionist and interactionist traditions this has included fairly close attention being given to the organizational and rhetorical features of media reporting of such conditions (Best, 1989; Fishman, 1980; Leyton, 1992; McCormick, 1995; etc).

The view that ethnomethodological studies can play some kind of re-medial role in the illumination of the topics of substantive sociological in-quiry derives from what may be called an *incorporationist* or *social con-structionist* view of ethnomethodology. From this point of view, ethno-methodological studies are regarded as providing the "minutiae" of social processes involved in, for example, the social construction of deviance, overlooked by other forms of sociological inquiry. Where sociologists have tended to produce "decontextualized" accounts of social action, ethnomethodology can supplement these "crude" depictions of social life by its close attention to the *in situ* specifics of social interaction. From this perspective, both sociologists and ethnomethodologists look through the same lens, so the difference between them is simply one of the sharpness of focus. Because of this continuity of vision, ethno-methodological studies can be *incorporated* into the sociological mainstream.[2]

Such a conception elides a key difference between sociological and eth-nomethodological accounts. Thus, in this incorporationist conception what the members of society do and say is viewed as constitutive of *sociologically defined* events and processes, including "the construction of social problems," the "exercise of power," the "social constitution of gender," "race relations," the "manufacture of crime," "social class," the "social construction of deviance," and so forth. This approach conceives of social action, including language use, as a resource for the solution of sociological problems. Thus, in relation to the functions of deviance, the media are cast into a role in a sociological drama rather than being approached as a site of locally ordered social action in their own right. The incorporation of ethnomethodology into sociological theories of crime and deviance contradicts ethnomethodology's indifference to the theoretical preoccupations of sociology. Thus, although for sociology the nature and functions of deviance are matters of theoretical debate, for ethnomethodology they are not issues about which any *theoretical stance* needs to be or should be taken. Rather, ethnomethodology seeks to examine the ways in which concerns with "deviance" inform members' locally ordered practical action and practical reasoning. In contrast to sociological theorizing, its concern is to describe the mundane practices in and through which persons are oriented to issues of what is deviant and what its significance may be in the course of such activities as reporting, describing, questioning, interpreting, deciding, explaining and formulating deviance. Accordingly, the problem is not to theorize the functions of deviance; rather, it is to examine what deviance is *for members*, and to do so by inspecting how that is made available in the detail of social interaction. In what follows, then, we examine how deviance is described, explained, understood and formulated, in short *ordered*, in a specific context, namely media coverage of the Montreal massacre. This permits the respecification of the functions of deviance because an integral feature of the media coverage of the *Montreal Massacre* concerned the question of its significance for "society."

The functions of crime and deviance are, then, here respecified not as phenomena to which the sociologist has "special" access, but as members' phenomena. Indeed, we would suggest that sociologists' particular claims in this regard are fundamentally no different from "ordinary" members' everyday methods of formulating the significance and consequences (both intended and unintended) of crime and deviance. Accordingly, for us, this means engaging in a form of ethnomethodological inquiry we have come to call, after Sacks (1992a, 1992b) "membership categorization analysis" (Eglin and Hester, 1992; Hester and Eglin, 1997a, 1997b, 1997c). The phrase describes both the analytic activity we carry out here as ethnomethodologists and that which is our subject matter, namely the membership categorization analysis performed by those members whose activities provide our research materials.

The event, which occurred on December 6, 1989, occasioned intense media coverage, including much commentary. We examined all articles on the subject published in *The Globe and Mail* (of Toronto) from Thursday, December 7 to Saturday, December 16, 1989, and selected articles in the *Kitchener-Waterloo Record* (our then "local" paper). (See Appendix at the end of this chapter.) This collection of materials proved sufficient for our purposes, as will become evident below. Coverage focused on the details of the killings as reported by witnesses (that the killer selected women as his target, what he said, etc.), the response of the police, ambulance service and coroner's office (what was in the suicide letter he left, a possible second suspect, etc.), the response of government officials (the Prime Minister, the Premier of Quebec, the Mayor of Montreal, etc.), the candlelight vigil and funeral/memorial services (who attended, what was said, the number of mourners, etc.), the character and life of the killer (who he was, whether he was insane, whether he was related to any of the victims, what his biography was, etc.), the response of university and polytechnic officials, engineers, academic experts, gun shop owners, relatives of the victims, survivors, students, women and representatives of women's organizations, and so on.

Given our pre-existing and abiding interest in membership categorization, we were soon struck by how the emergent phenomena constituting the "Montreal Massacre," notably the "problem of violence against women," were dependent on the categories and category predicates used by parties to the event to describe who was involved, what they were doing and why they were doing it. Mindful of the "Chinese-box" structure of successive accounts that can be seen in the case of "K" becoming "mentally ill" (Smith, 1978), we became taken up with members' own membership categorization analysis as performed in at least three sorts of accounts in our materials. These are (a) the newspaper's descriptions (referring to "gunman," "suspect," "students," "witnesses," "police," etc), (b) the killer's reported speech, "You're all a bunch of feminists," etc, and (c) the explicit descriptions and formulations employed in the commentaries ("women," "men," "male violence against women," etc). We will take up these analytic accounts in turn, examining the methods of membership categorization used by parties in constituting the accounts' various constituent phenomena.

The Newspaper Reporting as Embedded Commentary: Categories for Finding/Making News Stories

Now we'll say that for some pairs of activities, pairs of actions that are related by norms, that there's at least a rule of adequate description which says "character appears on cue," i.e., if the first takes place and it's an adequate grounds for the second taking place, then it's okay to describe the thing without having provided for how it is that that second person happened to come on the scene to do whatever it is they properly do, if one says the first occurs and the second occurs as well. (Sacks, 1992a: 254)

The *Globe and Mail's* first story was on the front page on Thursday December 7th, the morning after the massacre:

MAN IN MONTREAL KILLS 14 WITH RIFLE

A gunman went on a rampage at the University of Montreal last night, killing 14 people before shooting himself dead.

Police took away a second suspect in handcuffs an hour after the shootings began. Late last night, a heavily armed police tactical team was combing the six-story engineering building of the Ecole Polytechnique, which is affiliated with the university, for a possible third suspect.

Claude St. Laurent, a spokesman for the Montreal police, said the man taken away in handcuffs was being questioned. Some students said they recognized the man as a part-time physics teacher, but police would not confirm that or release his name.

Police also would not release the name of the gunman or any of the 14 other dead people.

Earlier, a spokesman for the Urgence-Sante, the Montreal ambulance service, said at least 12 people were injured.

Witnesses said two and perhaps three men – one of them carrying a hunting rifle – burst into a crowded computer class about 5:30 p.m., shouting anti-feminist slogans.

"He (the man with the gun) ordered the men and women to separate sides of the classroom," said Louis Hamel, 24, a second-year engineering student.

"We thought it was a joke, then the man fired a shot, and all hell broke loose."

Witnesses said the young gunman, who spoke French, roamed the halls and classrooms of the university's engineering building, shooting students on a least two floors.

The building, which can hold up to 5,000 students, was evacuated and sealed off by police shortly after the shooting began.

"I saw death close up and I shook," said Vantheona Ouy, 22, one of scores of horrified students who streamed out of the building.

"All I know is that a crazy guy came in here and began shooting at anything that moved," said Dominique Berube, 22. "It's our friends who have been killed."

There were reports that the gunman shot mainly women students, but police would not release a breakdown of victims by gender.

Francois Bordeleau, a student, ran from the first to the second floor and dragged people by the collar to keep them from going in the man's direction.

"It was a human hunt," he said. "We were the quarry."

He said he heard 20 to 30 shots and the man appeared to be aiming mainly at women. "I heard the gunman say: 'I want the women,'" Mr. Bordeleau said. That was confirmed by several other witnesses.

Witnesses said the gunman entered several rooms including the computer room and the building cafeteria.

In the computer room, he aimed at the wall and then ran out, said Lucien Justin, who was in the room. "Somebody locked the door, but he shot off the lock and then left a second time.

"I was terribly afraid, I ran like hell," Mr. Justin said.

At least 20 ambulances were on the scene, taking the wounded to four hospitals in the area.

The headline provides the news content of the story; it's a mass homicide. The event may be said to implicate an initial pair of categories for describing the parties, namely "offender" and "victim(s)." These may be said to constitute a standardized relational pair with respect to a potentially criminal act such as homicide (Hester and Eglin, 1992: Ch. 6; Watson, 1983). As such they provide for the relevance of others' actions and for their own transformation into other categories in the context of those others' actions. Sacks continues, in the passage quoted above:

> ... but if the first is, for example a violation, then you can provide that the second occurred. For example, "he was speeding and he got arrested." Perfectly okay ... What occurs is good grounds for the cop to do what he ought to do; he's on the scene and he does it. So he's introduced via the action he does, where the grounds for that action are laid out, though how he happens to be there need not be indicated. (1992a: 254, 183)

Thus the homicides reported in the headline and in the first sentence of the news story become the motive for the involvement of the police, and thereby the appearance of the police on cue, and without explanation, in the second sentence of the story.

Throughout this story and in subsequent news stories, the same means provide for transforming the offender ("gunman") into "[murder] suspect" and others present into "witnesses." This in turn makes relevant a search for other possible suspects, for the killer's motive and for other witnesses, and transforms what they and others (like neighborhood store owners and employees, the offender's neighbors, officials of the schools and colleges he attended and of the Canadian Forces in Montreal which rejected him, his landlord, family, friends, etc. (see, for example, Dec 9, (3))) know about the "offender" into "information potentially relevant to a homicide investigation." As traumatic medical events, they become the business of ambulance drivers and para-medics, of doctors, nurses and surgeons. As medico-legal events, they become part of the workload of coroners. And as major public events, they come under the purview of politicians – the mayor, the provincial premier, the relevant cabinet minister, the Prime Minister – and demand the presence of the news media.

As tragic personal events, homicides (like suicides and accidental deaths) invoke the relevance of "R," the collection of standardized relational pairs relevant to the search for help (Sacks, 1972a). Under the auspices of R the deaths of the victims become events in the lives of relatives and friends. They are entitled to be notified first, in accordance with the normative order for such notification. "Victims" become transformed into "daughters," "wives," "girlfriends," "friends," each category invoking its other pair-part, "parents (mother, father)," "husbands," "boyfriends (girlfriends)," "friends:" "'It's our friends who have been killed.'" The deaths become the occasion for grieving, mourning, remembrances, a candlelight vigil and funerals.

Furthermore, the killer's own categorizations of his victims, reported in *The Globe's* second-day coverage (and in that of other news sources) and examined in detail in the next section, provide further cues for further characters to appear. Thus, his description of them as "women," "engineers" and "feminists" makes relevant the responses of those who are co-incumbents of these categories. Such respondents and commentators become relevant not by virtue of the fact that they are related to or known to the victims, but because they are co-incumbents with the victims of such categories as "women," "engineers" and "feminists." Similarly, the setting – variously described as "Montreal," the "University of Montreal," "the six-story engineering building of the Ecole Polytechnique, which is affiliated with the university," "a crowded computer class," "the classroom," "the halls and classrooms of the university's engineering building," "the building," "two floors," "the first to the second floor," the "building cafeteria," "the computer room" (see Sacks, 1986) – provides for the relevance of commentary and response from "students," "professors," "deans," "presidents" and so on.

These categories and category pairs, together with their category-tied activities (Jayyusi, 1984: 37; Turner, 1971) and other predicates, provide, then, some of the procedural resources that news writer and news reader may use to produce and recognize, respectively, the relevance of the variety of actors and actions that appear in the text of the articles. Where the articles deal with "factual" topics, police, ambulance service personnel, doctors, the coroner, students and witnesses are quoted. Where the articles cite or refer to personal reactions of surprise, horror, fear and loss we are given "[t]errified students [who] describe shooting scene" (Dec 7 (2)), "[s]till in shock ... teary-eyed students and members of the faculty" (Dec 8, (2)), "[p]arents of some of the young women who died in the massacre [who] expressed shock and horror" (Dec 8, (9)), and "[w]eeping and holding one another for comfort, hundreds of women and men – most of them students, professors, politicians and community activists" (Dec 8, (7)). Where the articles engage in commentary on the scope, explanation and significance of the "problem" it is provided by persons referred to in terms of political, academic or other organizational (women's, engineering, etc.) categories.

Particular note is made of, and special treatment accorded to, persons who cross over categories, for this is one definition of "news."

> "December 6th will be among the blackest days in Montreal's history. The population is in a state of shock and the pain won't disappear in a couple of days," Montreal Mayor Jean Dore said ... Mr. Dore, wiping tears away, said one of the victims was the daughter of a friend and had been his own daughter's babysitter. (Dec 8, (2))

> Maryse Leclair, 23-year-old daughter of the director of public relations for the Montreal police, was stabbed with a hunting knife found on the floor beside her body, Andre Tessier, head of the force's organized crime squad, confirmed yesterday. Pierre Leclair discovered his daughter lying dead on

the floor when he entered the building after answering reporters' questions outside. (Dec 11, (1); see also Dec 8, (9))

That is, in the first extract, Jean Dore is both the "Montreal Mayor" and as such an official commentator on the massacre; at the same time he is the friend of the father of one of the victims who was herself babysitter to his own daughter. In the second extract, the "director of public relations of the Montreal police," at the scene in his occupational capacity, is also "Pierre Leclair," the "devastated" (Dec 8, (9)) father of one of the victims (see also KWR Dec 7 (2)).

In this way, then, these categories and predicates provide for the coherence of juxtaposed and sequentially organized discrete items of information as they turn up in the story. They provide, that is, for the "story" itself, in two senses of "news story" – the sense in which the expression may be used to refer to a particular bounded textual item, a particular news report, and that in which it may be used to refer to the "ongoing story" being told in such reports and in associated commentary. For with these resources the newspaper may produce an elaborate skein of actual stories, each one touched off by some predicated tie to, or transform of, the initial set of categories. There may be a "big story" and a variety of little stories, and these of course can change their status over time. What we wish to bring out here is how the category-generated stories that make the "Montreal Massacre" news embody embedded commentary *about* these events. Whereas in the next two sections of the chapter we examine the *explicit formulations* of the significance of the events contained in the commentary about them, here we are concerned with those assessments of the events' significance that are embedded in the very means by which the stories themselves are generated. In no particular order, then, here are the "stories" we take it are being told in the news reportage itself, and the commentary they implicitly contain.

(a) The Horror Story

What we get is a horror story (see Johnson, 1989) as "Scores of horrified students ... streamed out of the building" (Dec 7, (1)), and "Terrified students describe shooting scene" (Dec 7, (2)). The horror turns on the disjuncture between the membership categories made relevant by the setting and those made relevant by the event *when a character appears who is definitely NOT on cue.* The killing of fourteen members of the "enemy" during wartime may be describable as a "routine ambush" or "skirmish" or, indeed, "massacre" if the circumstances warrant (as in My Lai). On a university or college campus where the institutionalized identities are "student," "teacher," "member of staff" and so on (Sharrock and Button, 1991: 159), the transformation of category identities to "offender," "victim," "witness" and so on invoked by the killing of four-teen "students" occasions florid reportage in terms of a horrific scene. In *The Globe and Mail*, the event is referred to as follows: a "rampage" (Dec 7, (1); Dec 8 (9); Dec 11, (1)), "shooting rampage" (Dec 8, (1); Dec 9, (3); Dec 12, (3)), "killing rampage" (Dec 8, (1)), "massacre" (Dec 8, (2), (7), (9); Dec 9, (1), (2), (6); Dec 11, (1), (4); Dec 12, (1), (2), (3), (4), (5); Dec 13, (1); Dec 16, (1)), "The Massacre in Montreal" (Dec 8, (4); Dec 12, (2)), "the Montreal massacre" (Dec 8, (3), (10); Dec 16, (1)), "massacre at the University of Montreal" (Dec 13, (2)), "slaughter" (Dec 12, (2), (3)), "wanton slaughter" (Dec 8, (4)), "systematic slaughter" (Dec 8, (6)), "mass slaughter" (Dec 9, (6)), "mass murder(s)" (Dec 8, (6), (8), (10); Dec 11, (1), (3), (4); Dec 12, (1)), "mass shootings" (Dec 8, (11)), "horrifying executions" (Dec 8, (3)), "slaying" (Dec 13, (1), (3)), "brutal slaying" (Dec 11, (1)), "bloodbath" (Dec 8, (9)), "carnage" (Dec 9, (1)), the "violence in Montreal" (Dec 9, (5), (6)), the "University of Montreal murders" (Dec 12, (6)), "the bloodiest crime in Quebec's modern history" (Dec 16, (1)).

Many of the reported reactions of witnesses turn on the disjuncture be-tween setting-related and event-based categories and their conventional predicates. "'I was doing a presentation in front of the class and suddenly a guy came in with what I think was a semi-automatic rifle ... We thought it was joke'" (Dec 7, (2)) until "'the man fired a shot, and all hell broke loose.'" One witness reported that "'I saw death close up and I shook.'" Another said it "'was a human hunt ... We were the quarry'" (Dec 7, (1)). Another said:

> "I went to the bathroom and when I came back people were running out, screaming, 'There's a crazy guy in there. He's shot people.' I went to get my things and saw there was blood in front of the photocopy machine. Someone told me the first person he shot when he came out of the classroom was a girl in front of the photocopy machine." (Dec 7, (2))

As we noted above, Pierre Leclair, director of public relations for the Montreal Police, "arrived at the scene of the bloodbath to find his daughter lying dead on the floor ... in a pool of blood" (Dec 8, (9)). What is horrific, then, is: someone shooting a gun, not at a target range, but in a classroom during a class; taking part in a class then seeing a classmate killed before your eyes; being a human being but feeling like a hunted animal; going to the bathroom then being told someone is shooting people; passing the photocopying machine but seeing blood in front of it; going to a place to do your job, but finding your daughter there dead in a pool of blood (see Hester, 1987). What is horrific is the desecration involved when the routine settinged activities and objects of a college campus are turned into the scene of bloody murder. The reporting, that is, expresses revulsion at this breach of the bodily and social integrity of everyday life incarnate in the categorial organization made available in the institutionalized setting of a mundane place.

(b) The Story of Tragedy

A second thing we get is the story of a tragedy, a term used routinely throughout the coverage to describe the event. What is tragic is the victims' loss of their future lives, and the consequent losses entailed for their relatives and friends. The tragedy, that is, is formally located in the organization of two membership categorization devices, namely the stage-of-life device (Atkinson, 1980; Sacks, 1974) and "R," the collection of standardized relational pairs introduced earlier. In terms of the stage-of-life device the victims are describable as "young people," and, as such, may expect the conventional future predicated of the category "young person." Moreover, that anticipated future is shaped by the expectations of "success" conventionally associated with the particular category of young person called "student." The tragedy is founded in the affront to the value expressed in the right to life and security of the person when students get death instead of degrees, when "'[f]ourteen young women [are] brutally mowed down in the beauty of their youth when everything seemed to assure them of a brilliant future, useful to society'" (Dec 12, (1)). It is located in the disjuncture between the predicated and actual futures of these murdered young people, these dead students.

The tragedy is further based in the interruption of family and collective biographies. "They came to mourn and they came to say a final, tearful goodbye to their daughters, their sisters, their friends" (Dec 12, (1)). The categories are made relevant by R, in which they are tied to their respective pair-parts: parents, brothers/sisters, friends. The deaths become events in the lives of those referred to in terms of the categories naming their respective pair parts (Drew, 1978: 15). Those deaths become tragic when they are unexpected, since, in part, R organizes relationships specifically for the purpose of engaging in "the search for help" (Sacks, 1967, 1972a). When death comes suddenly in the family, when your best friend is killed, incumbents of the related pair-parts are denied the opportunity to provide the very sort of life-saving help their category position makes available to them, and obligates them, to give. The disjuncture is particularly acute in the case of the police officer who is, as it were, especially obligated to come to the assistance of those in trouble, but arrives at a scene in which there is nothing he can do to bring help to his own dead daughter. The category-predicate disjunctures are what make the tragedy, as the tragedy makes the news, and does so recognizably

(Anderson and Sharrock, 1979: 380-81; Hester and Eglin, 1997c: 42, 45; Johnson, 1989: 9-10).

Insofar, then, as the categorial organization of the stage-of-life device and R guide the selection of events to which reporters are assigned, and the selection of interviews and other speech they report, then embedded in the reporting of the event is a commentary on it. Losses are to be mourned, tragedies lamented. The newspaper gives brief obituaries based on interviews with family members recounting the lives of the victims (Dec 11, (5)), family members' heartfelt reactions are quoted (Dec 8, (9)), and reporters follow the categories to the funerals to quote the eulogies that reflexively warrant their stories (Dec 11, (1); Dec 12, (1); Dec 13, (2)).

(c) The Crime Story

What we get, too, is a crime story. It's a mass killing that quickly becomes a "mass murder." For a few days it's a detective story (trying to identify the killer, searching for "a possible third suspect," locating a motive, etc.) (Dec 7, (1); Dec 8, (1), (9); Dec 9, (3); Dec 11, (1); Dec 12, (3); Dec 13, (1)). But as big crime stories go, this one is short-lived since its projected career through the criminal justice system – each stage providing an opportunity for further reporting – is foreclosed by the killer killing himself. There will be no "search for the killer," arrest, charging, bail hearing, preliminary hearing, jury selection, trial, sentencing and so on. Moreover, the killer announces his motive and leaves a letter identifying himself and explaining his actions. Nevertheless, this theme frames the early reporting as the reporters follow the categories to the police station and the police news conferences. The very obviousness of this step conceals the evaluation of the event that the step entails. What the killer wanted to be seen as a political act, presumably transcending or suspending its possible status as a crime, is treated in the reporting *as* crime (cf. Hester and Eglin, 1992: Ch.6; see also Ch. 8). And as a particular kind of crime, namely mass murder, it is taken up in commentary (in which, among other things, it is compared to other mass murders). See the section on The Professional Commentator's Task below.

(d) The Gun Control Story

What we get, further, is a political story about gun control. The killer is a "gunman" from the start, who killed "with a rifle." But since "gun control" is a public policy issue, this is a theme with political ramifications. It provides one sense in which the story is political. Reporters are assigned, the issue reviewed, interviews held with relevant politicians

(Dec 8, (8); Dec 9, (4); Dec 11, (6)). Again, the structure and content of the reporting implies an evaluation and commentary on the significance of the event. This is a matter of political responsibility. Indeed, part of the tragedy, implies the story, is that the deaths may have been preventable had the proposed legislation been passed that would have banned the type of weapon used in the killings.

(e) The Story about the Killer
What we get, also, is a story about a killer (Dec 8, (1); Dec 9, (3); Dec 11, (1), (3); Dec 12, (3); Dec 13, (1)). The conceptual grammar that embraces criminal act, motive and biography-and-social-background guide the reporting to the standard sources, the police, the coroner (the disposal of the body? (Dec 13, (1))), the neighbors, the neighborhood stores, the landlord, the family, the mother's divorce records, the friends, the school, the college, the army recruitment office. That is, since the act is taken to be deviant its agent must be deviant, and that demands explanation. As we detail below in the following section, the newspaper's orientation to the relevance of insanity is revealed in some of its reporters' own descriptions, in some of the witnesses' reactions deemed fit to record, and in the noting of the absence of a record of psychiatric treatment received by the killer. At the same time it is revealed that he had a plan, including a "hit list," his target was "feminists," his motive was "political," he had recently bought the gun, and so on. Much of this appears in the reports of police news conferences, notably on the second day (Dec 8, (1)) when a paraphrase of part of a three-page suicide letter left by the killer is provided by the police. As he reports in subsequent stories (notably Dec 13, (1)), the reporter (Victor Malarek) tried to get the letter released, but to no avail.

Nevertheless, the newspaper does not pursue the "political angle" in its reporting. Though a tiny article reports that a "Violent film on terrorists preceded tragedy" (Dec 9, (2)), the killer is not called a terrorist, nor is he compared to other terrorists (though a list is provided of previous "mass murders" (Dec 8, (11)), which is quite a different frame of interpretation). His political goals are not elaborated, the question of the efficacy of his methods not raised. The structure and content of the reporting, based in the categories of description employed, exhibits a preference for viewing him as an instance of social pathology rather than as the "rational erudite" he sought to be. "He was not a very politically astute man, but he was, as terrorists are, more political than the people who try to understand him socially or psychologically" (McCormack, 1990: 32). This, then, is a story about a killer, but not, except in briefest part, the "killer's story." This, too, then is an embedded commentary.

(f) The Story about the Killing of Women

What we get, finally, is a story about the killing of women. This story runs through the following articles: Dec 7, (1), (2); Dec 8 (1), (2), (7), (12); Dec 9 (1); Dec 11, (1), (4), (5); Dec 12, (1), (3), (4), (5); Dec 13, (1), (2), (3)). We say "runs through" rather than, say, "is told in" because, although the victims are identified as women in all the reports, the articles, with one exception, are not in any strong sense *about* women or, indeed, the killing of *women*. That is, outside of the commentaries (see The Professional Commentator's Task below) and one news report, that the killer killed "women" is not consistently a topic of the reporting. This stands in contrast with the other stories outlined above. "Horror," "tragedy," "crime" (the crime of murder), "the killer" and "gun control" are all explicitly referred-to and oriented-to topics of reporting. Despite the killer's reported announcements in speech and writing about who he was killing – women/feminists (see next section) – *this* story is not one that clearly emerges. That this is so is, fairly obviously, a category-based phenomenon.

Thus, in the first day's articles witnesses report "'two and perhaps three men ... shouting anti-feminist slogans,'" that "'[h]e ... ordered the men and women to separate sides of the classroom,'" that "the gunman shot mainly women students," that "the man appeared to be aiming mainly at women," and that "'I heard the gunman say: "I want the women,"'" which last "was confirmed by several other witnesses" (Dec 7, (1); see also Dec 7, (2)). But these observations are reported alongside others in which the gender of the victims is not topicalized: "'All I know is that a crazy guy came in here and began shooting at anything that moved ... It's our friends who have been killed'"; "'[i]t was a human hunt ... We were the quarry'" (Dec 7, (1)). Furthermore, one of the accounts of the separating of the women and men in the classroom is accompanied by the witness's assessment that "'[i]t doesn't make sense'" (Dec 7, (2)).

The lead story on the second day specifically notes that the victims were not only women but that the "[k]iller's letter blames feminists" and "contains apparent hit list of 15 women" (headline, Dec 8, (1)) and "a vicious diatribe against women." The article refers to "his vendetta against women." It contains, too, a report of a "reconstruction of the killing rampage" by the police which makes plain that the intended targets were women (but not that the killer formulated them as "feminists"). Nevertheless, the article contains many other details about the inquiry gathered from the police news conference which is the chief source of the story. These refer to the discovery of the killer's identity, how he obtained the weapon, and so on.

The second front-page story on the second day qualifies "a man's ... killing of 14 young women" with the adjective "senseless" both in the cited phrase and in the headline, "Quebec mourns senseless deaths" (Dec 8, (2)). The article compiles a variety of activities under this title including flags flying at half-staff and the removal of Christmas decorations from the engineering school. Of those specifically referring to people, the first is the tragedy story of "teary-eyed students and ... faculty ... mourning their friends." The second describes the "lone gunman, Marc Lepine" as one "who apparently hated women." The third refers to "university officials" and "parents of the victims." The fourth is a "candlelight vigil to mourn the loss of students and friends." The rest of the article does contain a number of explicit acknowledgments that the victims were women; it also includes the claim that "'[i]t was a lunatic who went on a rampage with the reinforcement of a lot of misogynist social values'" (Ms. Nero, "a spokesman for the Committee de Defence des Femmes"). In short, that women were the killer's intended victims is problematic for witnesses, respondents and reporter alike. It's a story hedged with qualifications. It's a story that "competes," as it were, with the stories of tragedy and horror:

> Everywhere on the streets, in restaurants and on open-line radio shows, Montrealers were discussing the tragedy, wondering what had triggered this man's vendetta against innocent women and questioning how this could have happened on the staid University of Montreal campus. (Dec 8,(2))

A single news report does report the event as one about "women." It is headlined, "Hundreds in Toronto mourn killing of 14 women" (Dec 8, (7)). The article begins as follows:

> Weeping and holding one another for comfort, hundreds of women and men – most of them students, professors, politicians and community activists – met yesterday before a statue of a crucified woman on the University of Toronto campus to mourn the 14 women who were murdered in Montreal on Wednesday night. For many, the massacre was the brutal culmination of a season of escalating violence and hatred directed at women, especially toward those who are trying to make their way in professions – such as engineering – which have traditionally not welcomed women. They were horrified when Alice de Wolff, a Toronto organizer for the National Action Committee on the Status of Women, told them that among all the calls the organization's Ottawa office received yesterday from women across Canada, there was a threatening one from an angry man who told them "that Marc is not alone." (The women were murdered by a young man named Marc Lepine.)

It is noticeable that the actors in the story are referred to in terms of the gender device (women, men). That is, to be perfectly obvious, the women are not only referred to as "women," but the men are referred to as "men."

That this is a category election, not simply a selection, is made visible through the provision of alternative descriptors ("students, professors, politicians and community activists") as, effectively, sub-categories of "women" and "men."

The rest of the article (a) quotes the gathering's speaker saying, "'Remember the women who were killed because they were women ...,'" (b) introduces the segments of women's reported speech that follow by saying, "again and again, whether they were speaking during the brief service or just talking among themselves, the women described the hostile society around them," and (c) presents the segments themselves in which reference is made, for example, to "a continuum of violence," "the issue of violence against women," and the "fear women live with every day." We consider these formulations, and others like them, in The Professional Commentator's Task below. We mention them here to note that in keeping with the categorization of its subjects as "women," the article formulates the "14 women who were murdered" in terms of (a problem called) "violence against women." While the focus on "women" clearly distinguishes the story it tells as a story about the killing of women (and not one about horror, tragedy, etc), it still misses the story told by the killer himself, what a later commentator calls "Marc Lepine's political killing of women" (Dec 12, (2)). We take this up in the next section.

Finally on this topic, let us note one interesting piece of categorial work that marks this report (Dec 8,(7)) as itself hearably "feminist." It occurs in the opening two phrases where activities predicated of R-based categories are attached to the gender categories of "women" and "men." That is, while we have indicated above how the story of tragedy is located in part in terms of the organization of relationship pairs relevant to the search for help, here the writer associates R-tied predicates, namely "weeping" and "holding one another for comfort," with membership categories not conventionally members of R, namely "women" and "men." The construction invites the reader, as it were, to see the "tragedy" as a matter relevant to the "relationship" between woman and woman, man and man and, presumably, woman and man. As Sacks argued for "hotrodder," revolutionary social change is (at least) a matter of changing the categories of everyday life: "there's an order of revolution which is an attempt to change how it is that persons see reality" (Sacks, 1979; 1992a: 398). Stevie Cameron, the reporter, takes her cue from Marc Lepine, the counter-revolutionary, who treats a category ("women") as a group.

The Killer as Commentator: What will I be seen to have done?

The newspaper stories report witnesses saying that while advancing down the second-floor corridor of l'Ecole Polytechnique the killer said, "I want the women" (Dec 7, (1), (2)). He is then reported to have entered a second-floor classroom and, before killing six women, to have said, "You're all a bunch of feminists. I hate feminists" (Dec 8, (5), (6), (9)). He is also reported to have said, "I am here to fight against feminism, that is why I am here" (Dec 9, (1)). He is also reported to have said, "You're women. You're going to be engineers. You're all a bunch of feminists. I hate feminists" (KWR Dec 7 (1)). Furthermore, as we noted above, it was reported that at a police news conference held on Dec 7 a selective paraphrase was provided of a "three-page suicide letter" found on the dead gunman: "'First, he mentioned he was doing this for political reasons. He said feminists have always ruined his life ...'" (Dec 8, (1)).

Why might a person announce what it is he or she is doing in the course of doing it? After all, it is a commonplace of conversation analysis to point out that a characteristic of much spoken interaction is that inter-locutors do *not* standardly formulate what actions their utterances are performing as a running accompaniment to those utterances. Rather they rely on the resource provided by "next turn" for other speaker to do an understanding check if required. Formulating the gist of the conversation *is* done by parties to the talk at particular points for particular purposes (Heritage and Watson, 1979), but not because there is some general deficiency carried by all talk's utterances that requires they be supplemented by a running explicatory commentary. "Ordinary language is its own metalanguage" (Habermas, 1972: 168; see also Sacks, 1963; cf. Wittgenstein, 1958). This brief excursus into conversation analysis, however, gives a clue to the killer's "problem." The next action implicated by his announcement is the implied event contained in the announcement, namely some expression of his hatred, here shooting women dead. The implied next action is not conversation. Furthermore, his evident third action is suicide. These actions of his can be seen as attempts to remove the relevance of, and in part the opportunity for, others doing understanding checks where they can test any doubts they might have about what it is he is doing (see Cuff, 1994: 37ff.). Thus, we have one basis for the accountability of his announcement.

But why might he suppose that others *might* mistake the meaning of his action without the accompanying description? If it is not that actions necessarily require "repair" to be intelligible, what "determinate alternative possible account" (Cuff, 1994: 42) of the meaning of his action might the killer suppose he had specifically to counter? He tells us in his suicide letter, leaked to the press almost a year later (*La Presse*, Nov 24, 1990) and subsequently included in the English language edition of *The Montreal Massacre* (Malette and Chalouh, 1991): "Even if the Mad Killer epithet will be attributed to me by the media, I consider myself a rational erudite ..." He anticipated, quite correctly as it turned out, that he might be perceived as being mad for having killed fourteen strangers and then himself (see Jayyusi, 1984: Chp 8, esp. p. 187). The relevance of an orientation to insanity on the part of reporters, respondents and commentators is revealed in the frequent description of him or his actions in such terms as "crazy" (Dec 7, (1)), "a lunatic" (Dec 8, (2)), "insane," "insane people," "insanity," "sick minds" (Dec 8, (8)), "crazed gunman" (Dec 12, (1)), "crazed man" (Dec 12, (4)), and in the later report that "a majority of [polled] Canadians" see the murders as a "random violent act ... by an insane person" (KWR Dec 29). It is present, too, in the admonition not to see them in this way: "It would be a great mistake, I think, to see this incident as some kind of freak accident, the act of a madman that has nothing to do with the society in which we live" (Dec 8, (5)); "[m]ental illness is a familiar excuse" (Dec 12, (2)). It is most striking, however, in the following passage:

> Throughout the day, homicide detectives and journalists worked feverishly, trying to piece together more personal information on the man who systematically and calmly slaughtered 14 young women. Oddly, police could not turn up any evidence that Mr. Lepine had ever received psychiatric treatment. Mr Lepine was born .... (Dec 9, (3))

The danger of the insanity ascription for the would-be rational actor is that it removes the agency from a person's acts; the acts become symptoms of the disease he is suffering from, and not the intended outcome of his motivated agency. And so he speaks, showing his sanity by giving a reason: "You're all a bunch of feminists. I hate feminists." As Watson (1983, 1990) has shown for "nigger" and "fag" and "tramp" (see also Wowk, 1984) in his study of police interrogations of murder suspects, members may treat giving a category as a sufficient answer to a question asking for a reason for murder.

But there's a further side to his "problem." Could he not, after all, simply let his other actions speak for themselves? His act of separating the women from the men is self-explicating; he wants the women, not the men. He makes gender relevant by partitioning the classroom population on this ground. The problem is, this doesn't make the "feminists" visible. Feminist identity is not available to visual inspection. He solves the problem by naming out loud his victims as feminists. As it happens, according to one reported witness, he does get conversation in response to his announcement (Dec 9, (1)):

Ms Provost said that when Mr. Lepine burst into her classroom, ordering the male students to leave and the women to remain, she tried to talk to him. "When we were alone with him in the room ... he said, 'I am here to fight against feminism, that is why I am here.' Maybe I was still not realizing fully what was happening, but I told him: 'Look, we are just women studying engineering, not necessarily feminists ready to march on the streets to shout we are against men, just students intent on leading a normal life.'"

He apparently takes no notice, and starts shooting, which raises the question: Who is he speaking to, that he takes no notice of this reply? It is politics he wants to be seen as engaged in, not random slaughter by a crazed gunman, and not action for personal gain. He writes in the suicide letter: "Would you note that if I commit suicide today 89-12-06 it is not for economic reasons ... but for political reasons. Because I have decided to send the feminists, who have always ruined my life, to their maker ..." The letter is unaddressed. If politics defines his action, then presumably citizens are his audience, mediated by the police, the coroner and "the media." As a counter-revolutionary terrorist he is not content for the functional significance of his crime to be the unintended outcome of the response to it, or for the wrong significance to be attached to it by whomever. He is his own political sociologist, and provides the right reading for all to see. Although he intends not to be available for the news interview he knows that his act will make news and so he can address himself to "Anon," the citizenry, the public, the people who read the news. And they can find that he is talking to them (see Hester and Eglin, 1997c: 35-38).

The categorial logic of his reported speech is concise (if chilling). He categorizes his intended victims as "women," making their gender relevant. He then attaches a predicate to that category, "You're going to be engineers," which names a second category, "engineers." This category is, however, one conventionally hearable as being at odds with the gender category he has just used, being properly associated with the other category of the gender collection, "men." However, the disjuncture is resolved with the provision of a third category, "feminists," which is hearable as meaning "those women who would do men's jobs." Since these women are going to be engineers, and engineering is a man's job, and only feminist women would take men's jobs, then these women must be feminists. This is what is unacceptable to him, and is at once the basis of his hatred and the subject of his hate. This conclusion gives him a political problem which he chooses to address by killing these "women," "who are going to be engineers," who are thereby the hated "feminists." Just how he may have come to solve his political problem in this particular way is a question we take up in a further paper (Eglin and Hester, 1998).

A significant warrant for our analysis of the killer's analysis is that it is reproduced in that of Ms Provost as she attempts to talk him out of his apparent project. She does so by dissociating the category "women" and the activity "engineering" from the category "feminists." She supplies a replacement predicate for "feminists," namely "ready to march on the streets to shout we are against men." And she re-categorizes the women present as "students" who are "studying engineering" and are "intent on living a normal life," where that would, by inference, exclude "marching on the streets ..." If the would-be killer is after feminists, she is saying, he is in the wrong place.

The Professional Commentator's Task: Making Sense of Murder

In section three of this chapter, we considered the embedded commentary pertaining to the Montreal massacre, and in section four we examined Lepine's explicit formulations of his act. We now turn to the explicit formulations of the murders contained in the "professional commentary." In the period of coverage under scrutiny here, such commentary came in the form of editorials, op-eds, columns and interviews reported as news stories, as follows: an op-ed by Emil Sher, "a Montreal writer," entitled "The massacre in Montreal: Speaking about the unspeakable" (Dec 8, (3)); an editorial entitled "Why were women in the gunsight?" (Dec 8, (4)); an op-ed by Diana Bronson, "a Montreal journalist who wrote the following commentary for CBC's Morningside program," entitled "A time for grief and pain" (Dec 8, (5)); a column by Michael Valpy entitled "Systematic slaughter is without precedent" (Dec 8, (6)); interviews with Elliot Leyton, "an anthropologist at Memorial University in Newfoundland," and James Fox, "a criminologist at Northeastern University in Boston," entitled "Mass murders not increasing, Canadian anthropologist says" (Dec 8, (10)); a column by Stevie Cameron entitled "OUR DAUGHTERS, OURSELVES," featured on the front page of the "Focus" section of the Saturday paper (Dec 9, (5)); a column by John Allemang entitled "Violence and anger" (Dec 9, (6)); a second column by Michael Valpy entitled "Litany of social ills created Marc Lepine" (Dec 11, (3)); a second interview with Elliot Leyton, additionally described as "[A] Canadian expert on mass murders" and "author of Hunting Humans, a study of serial killers and mass murderers," entitled "Slayings deal blow to gender relations, murder expert says;" an op-ed by Melanie Randall, "a doctoral student in political science at York University and a researcher-activist in the field of women and violence," entitled "'Men cannot know the feelings of fear'" (Dec 12, (2)); a third column by Michael Valpy entitled "Risk of murder linked to non-domestic roles" (Dec 12, (6)); a column by Lise Bissonnette entitled "The self-centered hype of Montreal massacre" (Dec 16, (1)); and an editorial entitled "Grieving together" (KWR Dec 12 (2)).

There's more brief comment from a variety of sources included in news stories about particular events, or in one or two of the columns already cited; such sources include an anthropologist, three psychologists, five sociologists, a criminologist, a political scientist, spokespersons for women's organizations, spokespersons for pro-feminist men's organizations, two deans of engineering, representatives of engineering associations, a woman Rabbi, Anglican ministers, a university chaplain, government and university officials responsible for women's issues, a lawyer, well-known feminists, politicians, counselors, newspaper editors, university presidents and other administrators, students and student organization representatives.

We have already noted the category-relevance of the array of commentators and the category-tied character of their comments and quotes. The selection of commentators is organized in categorial terms, conducted in terms of category relevance, where for features of the murders a collection of relevant categories of commentators is a touched off matter. In general terms, and in the sense explicated in Sacks's (1992a) discussion of "character appears on cue" (discussed in section three above), those who comment are an unsurprising collection whose commentary does not have to be explicitly provided for. Yet the very unremarkability of those who comment and of the comments they make belies formal organizational considerations pertaining to the selection of *these* resources for telling the news. Thus, if the event is an X, then select Y (but not Z) as a commentator for quotation; similarly, if the victim is an X, then Y (but not Z) as a comment. These formal considerations can be said to "organize" the story of the Montreal massacre. Thus, in so far as the murders constitute "crime" then categories of commentator for whom commenting about crime is a recognizable predicate can be expected to, and indeed unremarkably do, appear on cue: sociologists, criminologists, anthropologists, psychologists, persons who have written books about mass murderers, murder experts and other characters with a "special interest" and skill on issues such as criminal motivation and the causes of crime are used to address topics "touched off" by the "crime." More particularly, for our purposes here it is unsurprising that the report that Lepine murdered not only (young) women (who were students) but also addressed his victims as "feminists" should make relevant and therefore provide for the appearance of co-incumbents of these categories as commentators. That is, they become relevant by virtue not of the fact that they are "known" to or are related to them (for example, as family) but because there are categorial connections between the victims as occupants of the categories "women" or "feminist" (so-called) and the commentators as co-incumbents of these categories or as spokespersons for the incumbents of them. Accordingly, as can be seen from the list above, in addition to professional journalists and columnists, commentators and those quoted were drawn from categories such as "feminist writer," "spokespersons for women's organizations," "researcher-activist in the field of women and violence," "spokesperson for pro-feminist men's organizations," "university officials responsible for women's issues" and so forth.

Space precludes analysis of the entirety of this corpus of commentary. Instead, we will concentrate on the major story carried in and as the commentaries. Thus, earlier we identified the "stories" contained in the "embedded commentaries" in the newspaper reports. One of those stories was that of the "killing of women." In the commentaries which followed, and in some cases which were coincident with, the reportage, the overarching story was that of "male violence against women" and, by extension, a story of "men and women" and "male-female relations." That is, the story in the commentaries was fundamentally not only a story about Lepine and his victims but about what the murders "represent." We consider this "story" contained and carried in and as the commentaries' explicit formulations with respect to: (a) showing/finding the *collection* to which the killings belonged – what kind of killing it was; (b) *explaining/accounting for* the occurrence of the killings; and (c) the *consequences* of the killing.

(a) Collecting the Action

If Lepine speaks directly and categorially to his victims and indirectly to the public, media commentators respond indirectly to him and categorially on behalf of his victims. These responses not only condemn the massacre itself, they also condemn what Lepine, his action and his avowed motivation *represented*. The commentaries are ordered in categorial terms. Indeed, it is unsurprising that this should be so since Lepine himself makes relevant such a categorial response both by his selection of "women" and "engineering students" as his victims but also by his transformation of them into "feminists." If Lepine provides an account for, and thereby one way of making sense of, his killings, then a major preoccupation of the commentaries which followed is with providing an account which not only makes sense of his murderous acts but also of the account which he provides for them.

The murders are not treated as murders *tout court*; rather, the murders are *generalized*; they are transformed from a collection of murders into an instance of a "bigger problem," namely "violence against women." In the manner of a "Chinese-Box," the murders are treated as an instance of what they *represent*, namely "violence against women." This, in turn, is encapsulated by some commentators within "wider" collections, such as "misogyny" and "male chauvinism." This is evident in Dec 8 (6) where it is said by a criminologist that it is not just a case of "mass murder": "we haven't had this happen before, where a mass murderer chose 'the Auschwitz ramp' .... for half the human race...;" rather, according to a "sociologist," it represents "the historical continuity of violence against women." Likewise, Bob Wadden (Toronto Men's Forum), in Dec 11 (4), indicates that "This sort of thing happens every day ... women are abused every day." In Dec 8 (5) by Diana Bronson (a Montreal journalist), the collecting work is done in terms of a formulation of "what he represents." Thus, she writes:

> It does not matter that the man who decided to kill 14 women – and he clearly did decide to do that – killed himself afterward; it is not of him I am afraid. I am afraid of what he represents, of all the unspoken hatred, the pent-up anger that he expressed. Hatred and anger that is shared by every husband who beats his wife, every man who rapes his date, every father who abuses his child, and by many more who would not dare.

Similarly, Melody McLoughlin Marratto (Chaplain at St. Jerome's College), in KWR Dec 14, is quoted as follows: "for the incest survivor, the battered women, the rape victim, what happened in Montreal can only be understood as a symbol of the larger problem of men's violence against them."

As in the last two quoted extracts, a number of commentators list the co-members of this collection. For example, in Dec 12 (2), the following rhetorical question is posed: "But how different is Marc Lepine's violence from that of the many husbands who batter and sometimes kill their wives, or from that of rapists who stalk women on the street or break into their homes?" The answer quoted is that it is only different in its "scale": "the only difference between his crime and less visible ones is the scale of the violence." A further example is contained in KWR Dec 18, where Richard Clarke (Guelph-Wellington Counseling Center) remarks that "Marc Lepine, in his *extreme* behavior is at the *extreme* end of what a lot of men do with their lives, which is they get isolated, and contain their pain and their fear, to the point where it comes out explosively and aggressively" (emphasis added). Similarly, in Dec 8 (4), Emil Sher, a Montreal writer, states: "the wanton slaughter of 14 women at the University of Montreal has taken male violence against women to unimaginable lengths ... We discuss the weather or last night's game with fluid ease, but when it comes to rape, assault and battery, we stall." The collection's constituent categories are, then, arranged positionally, higher and lower, relative to each other, in terms of the dimension of the degree of violence perpetrated against women.

Furthermore, the collection "male violence against women" includes what are recognizable as various "myths" about male-female relations, and in particular, a collection of "mythical" predicates of women and a collection of predicates of "male chauvinistic men." Thus, in a parody of "male chauvinist man" Sher continues:

> Do men have nothing to say about violence against women? We do. "Assaulted women like being beaten," a police officer said in a study prepared by the New Brunswick Council on the Status of Women, perpetuating a dangerous myth before launching another. "I tell them, 'You like it since you stay with him.'" He continues: "And I tell the guy to hit harder. If they go to court, these men have no chance. There is no justice. Feminists and Stalinists have influence on the judges." Clearly, at least one Manitoba judge has yet to be swayed by these "feminists and Stalinists," or by any other women branded with the labels we reach for when feeling defensive. He condoned the behavior of a man who had pleaded guilty to hitting his wife. "How does a person admonish his wife," he asked, "if she goes out on the town with other people ... when she should have been home looking after the children or cooking, or whatever else she is expected to do?" What we expect them to do is to talk about violence against women as though it were "their" problem and theirs alone, as though men have nothing to contribute to the issue other than a well-placed fist. And we expect women to keep things in perspective, to be reasonable. To point fingers is unladylike. When we hear words such as "misogyny" we counter with "hysterical," dismissing women's concerns as the shrill protests of feminists and castrating lesbians. Or maybe "it's just that time of month." WORSE we try to defuse anger with misguided humor. Why talk seriously about violence against women when we can joke about it? When the Canadian Federation of Students launched an anti-date-rape campaign with the slogan "No means no," students at Queen's University were swift to respond with versions of their own, all in the spirit of a "good joke" – "No means tie me up," "No means kick her in the teeth."

These myths, then, are themselves part of the collection, part of the problem of "male violence against women." Continuity with other acts of male violence is also accomplished by referring to the collection "weapons which are used in violence against women." Thus, in Dec 8 (3), it is said that "the author of the Montreal massacre used a semi-automatic rifle, but that is only one deadly part of the arsenal turned daily against women. Fists are still the preferred weapons in domestic disputes – marginally less violent than firearms, but as ugly and sometimes fatal." Besides these "physical" weapons, the commentator points out that there is also "a wide range of psychological artillery," including laughing and joking at stories of women's suffering and treating with contempt the campaign against date-rape. Such psychological weaponry was observably deployed, it is said, "in the House of Commons where, in 1982, Margaret Mitchell, a New Democratic Party MP, was greeted with jokes and laughter when she raised the subject of wife-beating." Similarly, "more recently, we were given a discouraging glimpse of contemporary campus attitudes at Queen's University in Kingston, Ont. When female students launched a 'No means no' campaign against date-rapes, male students responded with a contemptuous 'No means more beer' placard."

As indicated earlier, for some commentators, the killings themselves and the problem of male violence against women which they represent, are subsumable under a wider collection, namely "male chauvinism." For example, Elliot Leyton, who is identified as an "anthropologist," is quoted in Dec 11 (4) to the effect that, "the killings demonstrate how male chauvinism threatens women's lives." Similarly, others collect the killings as an expression of "misogyny." Gordon Cleveland (Dec 11, (4)), a member of an organization called "Men for Women's Choice," for example, states that "the killing had lifted the veil on one society's collective secrets – widespread misogyny." Stuart Summerhayes, an Anglican priest, uses the same collection when he says, in KWR Dec 11 (1), that "I know this incident was evidence of a pervasive feeling in society among men that can only be described as misogyny." Several commentators categorize the killings as an expression of "hatred of women." For example, in KWR Dec 14, John Vellinga, President of the University of Waterloo's engineering society, is quoted as follows: "The same hatred and ignorance which drove Marc Lepine to his despicable act is alive and well in many sane men, men who should realize that they are no better than the murderer, that their sanity is the only thing preventing their hatred from springing out in gruesome display." Relatedly, others described the killings as "expressions of resistance" (against women).

(b) Accounting for the murders

A second theme of explicit media commentary on the murders is their *explanation*, and these accounts comprise further category analysis. One class of this involves the use of *personal* membership categories (Hester and Eglin, 1997b) whilst others deploy "categories of social configurations" (Coulter, 1982; Hester and Eglin, 1997b, 1997d: 157). We shall consider some examples of each.

One variety of the use of personal membership categories in explaining the murders involves the gender-category of the victims. This is evident in Dec 8 (5) where it is said that "fourteen women are dead for one reason: they are women. Their male classmates are still alive for one reason: they are men." This account implies Lepine's own category analysis: his deliberate selection of his victims because they are women, and more specifically in his eyes, feminists. A second variety of the explanatory use of personal membership categories involves the imputation of predicates to the category incumbent such that the act in question "follows from" his or her category membership. Some commentaries made use of the membership category "lunatic" (or "madman"). For example, in Dec 8 (2) it is said that the murders were committed by a "madman" and a "lunatic," and they are therefore "senseless" and "irrational." Other commentaries make use of the membership category "man," attributing "violence against women" to incumbents of this category. The use of "man" in this way is evident in Dec 11 (4). Thus, it is reported that Sasha McInnes of the Northern Women's Center, in an open letter to men and in an ironic reflection of the kind of gender-category analysis done by Lepine himself, blames the killings on their gender. As she puts it, "this is a men's issue, this is men's violence; this terrorism and these deaths are your creations and your shame." Similarly, in KWR Dec 9, it is reported that the deaths are an "expression of resistance to expressions of the equal worth of women and men" and that

> both the roles of women in our society and the relationships between men and women have changed. We must not deny that this reprehensible act is a manifestation of deep resistance to expressions of the equal worth of women and men.

Some commentaries make use of category-predicate combinations in transformations of "men" in "anti-women" and "anti-feminist" ways. In Dec 8 (4), for example, the writer proposes that when "women pursue careers in male bastions" and when "women grow financially independent," then "men feel threatened" and that such men then "retaliate."[3] Similarly, in Dec 8 (3), the predicate which is combined with "many men" is "deep-seated fear and resentment" which results in a violent "rearguard action" against women:

> if the arrogance of male dominance is to be found, naked and unashamed, at the heart of our democratic system and in centers of higher learning, it is evident that a deep-seated fear and resentment is at work among many men in the larger society. The passing of the old order, just and reasonable as the changes are, has proved indigestible to some, and they have chosen to launch their own forms of *rearguard action* – raging perhaps at the "Ms" designation which removes marital status as a major identifier of womankind in print, or deploring the erosion of the traditional family in which mother does not own a briefcase. (emphasis added)

"Sociological" categorial accounts stress the "wider" categories of social configuration (Coulter, 1982; Hester and Eglin, 1997d) in terms of which male violence against women in general and this murder in particular are understandable. For example, in Dec 8 (3) the editorial writer opines, "It would be rash to build too elaborate a structure of cause and effect on the fragile base of one demented mind, but the horrifying executions at the University of Montreal do emerge from a social context and cannot be disowned." In Dec 11 (4) an anthropologist is quoted as saying, "I think we have to understand how virulent and malevolent sexist feelings can be ... Whenever a social group rejects its subservience, as women everywhere have been doing, it threatens those in power ... No catastrophe is unrelated to major changes in society." In Dec 8 (5) the writer states, "It would be a great mistake ... to see this incident as some kind of freak accident, the act of a madman that has nothing to do with the society in which we live. The killer was angry at women, at feminism, at his own loss of power. He yelled: 'You're all a bunch of feminists' on his way to killing fourteen women."

In a number of articles, personal and sociological category analyses are combined. For example, in Dec 8 (2) it is reported that "... a spokesman for the Committee de Defence des Femmes," said that, "[t]he event did not happen in a vacuum .. [i]t was a lunatic who went on a rampage with the reinforcement of a lot of misogynist social values and a message that violence against women is okay.'" Similarly, in KWR Dec 9, Rev. Dorothy Barker, chaplain for the University of Guelph's ecumenical campus ministry, is quoted as saying in an interview that: "people are recognizing that it's the work of a madman who has been fed by social attitudes on the gender issue." Similarly, in Dec 8 (3) the editorial writer says:

> Crazed as he may well have been, the killer who carefully separates males from females before the shooting began absorbed his attitudes from the society around him. Collectively, unconsciously and sometimes overtly, we have provided him with all the context (albeit wildly distorted) he needed. This is a society that still moves with reluctance, and sometimes with bitter resistance toward acceptance of the idea that women are entitled to equality in areas formerly dominated by men. Despite the changes that have been made – or possibly because of them – there is fertile ground for the misogynist or male chauvinist ... it would be rash to build too elaborate a structure of cause and effect on the fragile base of one demented mind, but the horrifying executions at the University of Montreal do emerge from a social context and cannot be disowned.[4]

c) Formulating the Consequences of the Montreal Massacre
Sociological functionalism makes a distinction between manifest and latent functions. Either way, these are consequences of the act/event in question. As such, sociological accounts trade off a common, everyday practice, namely formulating the consequences of acts/events. With respect to the Montreal massacre, a variety of such consequences are formulated.

According to "people attending a memorial service," the murders emphasize "male attitudes toward women" (KWR Dec 13 (1)); according to Sharon Severinski, a graduate student in social work, "It *made* [*women*] *realize* how vulnerable we are," and "it *had an impact* on some men, (especially those who were already trying to improve gender relationships) (KWR Dec 13 (1), emphasis added); according to the Prime Minister, it is said to have "*raised questions* about violence in our society and about violence against women"(Dec 8 (2), emphasis added). Similarly, in Dec 8 (5), it is said that the murders serve as a *reminder* "of how deep misogyny still runs in our society," and in KWR Dec 18 the residents of a women's shelter are quoted as saying that the massacre "*affirms* that many of their spouses could have, and still could, kill them" (emphasis added). Furthermore, Lepine's "rampage," according to Paula Caplan, a "Toronto psychologist and ... leading feminist," "*echoed the experience* of many women in Canada" (emphasis added). In KWR Dec 11 (2), the murders are again "a *reminder* of the violence women face every day," and serve to make women "*realize* that as women, we live in bondage in the common fear that we have" (emphasis added). Furthermore, the massacre is said to promote feelings of *social solidarity*. Thus, in the previously quoted article it is said that women can "see their own personal experience with male violence and can relate it to other struggles in our society – blacks, homosexuals, Jews and communists." Likewise, in Dec 11 (4), the killings not only caused the kind of damage mentioned in the headline but according to Elliot Leyton (anthropologist at Memorial University in Newfoundland), they "*demonstrate* how male chauvinism threatens women's lives" (emphasis added) and *point out* "that the underlying biases and prejudices still exist in society that discriminate and target women."

Beyond reminders, affirmations, demonstrations, damage and other such functions, several commentaries stress how the massacre served to raise consciousness and change practices. In KWR Dec 13 (2), an executive managing editor of the Montreal Gazette is quoted as saying that "there's a lot more awareness out there now among the male reporters of the feminist case in this terrible shooting..." Indeed, as a result "the Montreal News tabloid temporarily suspended publication of its daily Sunshine Girl and Saturday Weather Boy." Similarly, in KWR Dec 18 it is reported that "men" are "suddenly searching for positive steps to take" and instances are cited of a sociology professor who "has decided to include domestic violence in a new course .. on the sociology of human rights," and of the Men Against Violence Against Women who have drawn up a statement which "deplores violence against women and urges campus administrators to develop educational programs that will improve relations between the sexes." In the same piece it is reported that "growing numbers of men have abruptly had their consciousness raised in the wake of the massacre." One example of this, perhaps, is the report in Dec 12 (4) that "Pierre Belanger, dean of engineering at McGill University, said the killings ... raise concerns about the profession's image" and that "sexist publications put out by engineering students at many universities across the country may no longer be acceptable in this new environment ... the massacre puts them in a very different light."

Besides formulations of the consequences, writers also pointed out what *should be done* as a result of the murders, and in the light of the "misogyny" they represent. Thus, in Dec 8 (3) it is said that "the tragedy should persuade us to look intensely at the ground in which hatred takes root. It is time for men to talk with men about their continuing oppression of women. Sadly, it is still a time when women have reason to be afraid." Similarly, in Dec 8 (4) it is said that "[w]omen have always spoken out against the violence they encounter at home, at school, at work, on the street. Every year they hold rallies and candlelight vigils to demand their right to Take Back The Night. It's time men began to talk about how we can give back the night, and return what was never ours to begin with." Finally, a number of commentators stressed that "the massacre proves need for ban on automatic guns."[5]

Commenting on the Commentators: The Organization of Categorial Dispute

Just as the explicit formulations constituting the "story" of "male violence against women" and more generally "male chauvinism" and "misogyny" appear on cue, so also does an "alternative" story. Thus, the story of male violence against women is categorized as the "feminist" story, thereby occasioning the relevance of a non-feminist counterpart. The dispute between these two "versions" of the murders is then carried in the commentaries as a further "story" which is organized in terms of the contrast class: feminist/non-feminist. It is the dispute about the "correct" formulation of the murders which then becomes the story carried in and as further commentary.

The non-feminist view is contained, for example, in reports that "some men" are unable to see the continuity between the murders and other forms of male violence, misogyny and male chauvinism. For example, in KWR Dec 13 (1) it is reported that:

a graduate student in social work ... Severinski said many men on campus still can't see a connection between the panty raids, attitudes toward women in society, and the shooting in Montreal. The shooting has had an impact on some men, especially those who were already trying to improve gender relationships ... but for other men, it hasn't changed anything. Many still don't connect this with what we saw the panty raids to be, a form of violence against women. They still see it as good clean fun, just a bunch of people having a good time.

Likewise, in KWR Dec 29 it is reported that "a majority of Canadians see no connection between the Montreal massacre of 14 women and violence against women in general." The evidence for this is a poll conducted for Southam News. And in KWR Dec 12 (1), it is reported that:

across the country a debate is raging over the implications of the gunman's act, and it is causing growing divisions between women who call themselves feminists and those who do not, between men and women, and even among men. Two main opinions have polarized the issue. For some the shooting is viewed as an isolated act of a madman. For others, particularly feminists, it is an extreme example of the often violent male treatment of women woven into the fabric of Canadian life.

Instances of the contrast or rift between "feminist" and "non-feminist" versions are collected and cited. These include the female engineering students who protest to a feminist instructor that the death has been "made into a feminist issue," the "drowning out" by boos from male and female students of a female instructor who "generalized about men's hatred for women," and the reports that both men and women objected when "men" were prevented from attending a (women only) vigil for the victims, and were not permitted to address a crowd gathered in commemoration.

In the non-feminist version, what the murders are *said* to represent is itself organized in categorial terms, and is analyzed as such by its proponents. Thus, the *representation* of the killings as "male violence against women," "male chauvinism" and "misogyny," the *explanation* of the killings as a product of a "mad male chauvinist" in a social context of widespread misogyny and the *formulation of the consequences* of the murders as "reminding," "affirming" and "demonstrating" the pervasive "problem of male violence against women" are treated as *predicated* of a particular membership category, namely "feminists." Opponents of the feminist formulations accuse the feminists of having "hijacked" the murders for their own political purposes. They take issue with these explicit formulations of the feminists. The alternative view is offered in the following piece from KWR Dec 12 (2):

The national outpouring of grief has been interrupted by those who would have all men accept blame for the murderous actions of one crazed man. Men have been excluded from vigils and rallies on a presumption that they have no business there. Counter-productive feminism ignores that the victims had fathers, brothers and boyfriends who suffered terrible loss, too. It ignores the reality that all grieve when 14 lives are extinguished in wanton violence, whether the victims are women, children - or men. Inverted chauvinism deflects attention from the terror that erupted. Turning horror into a bandwagon will not help the cause of women or end the real violence too many suffer. With 14 now laid to rest, those who have usurped the high ground of mourning should bury prejudice. For the sake of shared humanity, let us join to ensure such tragedy does not occur again.

Several organizational features of this (and other commentary) may be noted. Firstly, there is dispute with regard to the collection to which the murders belong. Thus, it is not "just" an instance of male violence against women; rather it is an instance of violence *per se*. Likewise, in KWR Dec 12 (1), a spokesperson for REAL Women of Canada is quoted as saying that the murders are "one incident from a violence ridden society, in which men brutalize men and children beat up other children." Secondly, the non-feminist view accuses its feminist counterpart of *overgeneralization*. That is, feminists are accused of treating violence, chauvinism and misogyny as predicates of "all" men rather than as predicated of a limited sub-section of the category. Thirdly, feminists are accused of *obscuring and ignoring* significant dimensions of the phenomenon. Thus, as we observed earlier, the recognizably "feminist" character of reports and comments about the murders involves in part the attachment of R-based predicates to the gender category of "women," such that women, in co-category incumbency with the victims, can recognizably and properly "grieve," "weep," "mourn" and so forth, activities routinely predicated of "family members" and other "intimates." In the above commentary, this version and the entitlements it provides for are set in competition with two other collections which, according to the writer, are ignored by feminists: R, on the one hand, and "humanity" or "all," on the other, both of whose relevance, according to the writer, is "ignored" by feminists. Their having "usurped" the tragedy is evident in this "claimed" entitlement to, and apparent exclusive "ownership" of, the predicates of members of R. In this sense, then, the commentary can be heard as "counter-revolutionary" in so far as it can be heard to challenge the feminist version of the murders, what may be done and by whom in response.

The story of dispute is carried not only in reports and commentary containing the non-feminist alternative; it is carried also in feminist responses to their critics. Thus, the "backlash" itself becomes "news" and a topic of commentary. A major example is a piece in Dec 12 (2) by Melanie Randall, "a doctoral student in political science ... and a researcher-activist in the field of women and violence." She "counters" the re-collecting work of the non-feminists and reasserts the applicability of the "male violence against women" collection on the grounds, firstly, that the victims were, after all, *women*, and, secondly, that all "females" share co-membership of the category "victims." As she puts it, the non- or anti-feminist view "challenged women's right to grieve, to rage at the vulnerability and terror we feel as a condition of being female."

In the feminist response it is not only the murders which are to be included in the collection of "male violence against women;" so also is the "backlash" itself. Thus, it is categorized as "explicit hostility toward women, especially feminists." As such, it is then co-collected with graffiti calling on people (men?) to "kill feminist bitches," Queen's University students' responses to the "no means no" campaign, and the reported incident after the massacre when male students pointed fingers at female students and pretended to pull imaginary triggers. The commentator asks how to make sense of this and then does so with the following formulation: "it is a chilling display of threatening and hateful behavior." Again, it is claimed that some men "need to assert their own power through invoking utter panic and terror in women." She goes on to argue for pervasiveness of "violence against women," listing the following as categories of acts which "assert men's power": police officers who blame victims for being sexually assaulted, judges who accuse sexually abused 3 year old girls of being "sexually aggressive," the "outspoken misogyny" of so-called "father's rights" activists who challenge women in court for child custody, the resistance to non-sexist language and to feminists' insistence that it be used, terrorist acts against women's services, the violence committed against abortion clinics and the embarrassment of the women who attempt to enter them. As the author says, "what happened in Montreal cannot be understood as anything other than a deliberate and brutal expression of the larger problem of men's violence against them."

The dispute – the contestable character of the murders, of responses to it and of commentaries on it – is, in its turn, subjected to explicit formulation of its consequences. Thus, in KWR Dec 12 (1) a "sociologist" is quoted as saying that "reactions to the shooting" will in turn have two different kinds of consequence: firstly, they "will cause some women to disavow feminism," while secondly, others will be propelled "into the feminist fold to try to improve women's lives in society." Further, "[a]nd I think there will be other women who will be greatly strengthened by this, who will be more sure that we must continue to work at this." In other words, these reactions will have the functions of "modifying," "maintaining" and "clarifying" (the activities defining) the moral boundaries of male-female relations (cf. Box, 1981).

Concluding Remarks

In this chapter we have sought to respecify the functions of deviance as a members' phenomenon. Such respecification led us to consider the formulative work evident in the commentary embedded in the newspaper reportage, in the murderer's formulation of his act, and in the explicit formulations of the significance of the murders contained in media commentaries. In so doing, we came to discover the "formal" categorial resources used in these various sites of formulation. These resources comprise, as it were, the "apparatus" or the "machinery" which is deployed in telling the story of the Montreal massacre (and its constituent stories). It is, indeed, a story of membership categorization analysis, through and through.

Notes

1. *Acknowledgments:* The authors are grateful to Debbie Chapman, Dorthy Madden and Anna Toth for their help in compiling and preparing the data used in this paper. Thanks are also due to the Wilfrid Laurier University Research Office and to John McCallum, WLU Library, for their assistance.
2. For an enlightening discussion of the problems attending any attempt to investigate ethnomethodologically the "intuitively available" topics of social structures in mainstream sociology, see Schegloff (1991).
3. As Sacks (1992a) says in *Everyone has to lie* with respect to "everyone" such a category does not literally mean "all the people in the world." Rather, it is categorially limited to a particular group or collection of persons. In the descriptions under consideration here, "men" also is recognizably limited categorially, namely to those who are chauvinist or anti-feminist and as such, men for whom "feeling threatened" and "retaliation" are category predicates. As Sacks (1992a: 550-1) puts it:

   > Now, "everyone" might seem in the first place to be a "summative" term. But let's leave it open as a possibility that it's a "categorial" term, and governed in the way those are. It might be, for example, that terms like "everyone" and "no one" stand in juxtaposition to one another. If you come home from a party, for example, and someone asks you who was there and you say, "No one," then, that there were 12 people there doesn't matter for the correctness of "no one." "No one" means "under some formulation of who should have been there, no one was there." Likewise, it might be the case that when asked, "Who was there?" somebody says "Everyone," then there are formulations of "everyone" which provide for the fact that "everyone was there" indeed, though millions of people weren't.

4. Other commentators sought to spread the causal net (and the collection to which the murders belonged) far wider. Space considerations preclude their analysis here. They are examined in Eglin and Hester (forthcoming).

5.   See Eglin and Hester (forthcoming) for a full discussion of the gun control issue/story.

Appendix

In the text of the chapter we identify each article by its date of publication together with a number. In the case of the *Kitchener-Waterloo Record* we add the prefix *"KWR"* to distinguish its articles from those in *The Globe and Mail*. The numbers simply distinguish the different articles published on our topic on that day. The order of the numbers generally reflects the order of appearance of the articles in the paper; that is, for example, "(2)" appears either on the same page as, or on a later page than, "(1)." Some of the *KWR* citations have no number as we referred to one article only from the paper for that day. The following lists give, for each paper, in chronological order, the title, by-line and page number of each article according to its "date and number" in the text. Where an article appeared on the front page we indicate whether or not it was the lead article. In a page number like, for example, "A7," the "A" refers to the main news section of the paper; a "B" refers to the front page of the "Local" section of the *KWR*; a "D" refers to the "Focus" section of the Saturday paper containing major feature articles and editorials. Bold face indicates that the original headline was either in particularly large type or particularly bold face or both. Underlining indicates underlining in the original, while italics indicate a slanted type face in the original.

The Globe and Mail

Dec 7, (1)	"**Man in Montreal kills 14 with rifle**," Canadian Press and Staff, Montreal, front page (lead article)
Dec 7, (2)	"Terrified students describe shooting scene," Canadian Press, Montreal, page A5
Dec 8, (1)	"**Killer's letter blames feminists** / *Suicide note contains apparent hit list of 15 women*," by Victor Malarek, The Globe and Mail, Montreal, front page (lead article)
Dec 8, (2)	"Quebec mourns senseless deaths," by Patricia Poirier and Barrie McKenna, The Globe and Mail, Montreal, front page
Dec 8, (3)	"Why were women in the gunsight?" Editorial, page A6
Dec 8, (4)	"<u>The massacre in Montreal</u> / **Speaking about the unspeakable**," by Emil Sher, Mr. Sher is a Montreal writer, Montreal, page A7
Dec 8, (5)	"A time for grief and pain," by Diana Bronson, Ms Bronson is a Montreal journalist who wrote the following commentary for CBC Radio's Morningside program, Montreal, page A7
Dec 8, (6)	"Systematic slaughter is without precedent," MICHAEL VALPY, page A8
Dec 8, (7)	"Hundreds in Toronto mourn killing of 14 women," by Stevie Cameron, The Globe and Mail, page A13
Dec 8, (8)	"Opposition MPs demand long-promised gun control," by Richard Cleroux and Craig McInnes, The Globe and Mail, Ottawa, page A13

Dec 8, (9)   "Police suspected more than 1 sniper was loose in school," by Benoit Aubin, The Globe and Mail with Canadian Press, Montreal, page A13

Dec 8, (10)   "Mass murders not increasing, Canadian anthropologist says," by Robert MacLeod, The Globe and Mail, page A13

Dec 8, (11)   *"Canada's past includes other mass shootings,"* Canadian Press, page A13

Dec 8, (12)   "14 dead women identified," Canadian Press, Montreal, page A13

Dec 9, (1)   *"Don't have feelings of guilt, woman hurt in massacre urges her fellow students,"* by Benoit Aubin, The Globe and Mail, Montreal, front page

Dec 9, (2)   *"Violent film on terrorists preceded tragedy,"* Canadian Press, Montreal, page A6

Dec 9, (3)   *"Killer fraternized with men in army fatigues,"* by Victor Malarek, The Globe and Mail, Montreal, page A6

Dec 9, (4)   "Lewis will not commit to tough 1978 gun law that wasn't proclaimed," by Graham Fraser, The Globe and Mail, Ottawa, page A6

Dec 9, (5)   **"OUR DAUGHTERS, OURSELVES,"** by Stevie Cameron, The Globe and Mail, page D1

Dec 9, (6)   "Violence and anger," WORD PLAY by John Allemang, page D6

Dec 11, (1)   "Thousands of mourners wait in silence to pay final respects to slain women," Staff and Canadian Press, Montreal, front page

Dec 11, (2)   "Aware of symbolism," letter to the editor, page A6

Dec 11, (3)   "Litany of social ills created Marc Lepine," MICHAEL VALPY, page A8

Dec 11, (4)   "Slayings deal blow to gender relations, murder expert says," Staff and Canadian Press, page A9

Dec 11, (5)   *"Families, friends remember victims' lives,"* Canadian Press, Montreal, page A9

Dec 11, (6)   "Ease of getting gun in Canada 'unacceptable,' Mulroney says," The Globe and Mail, Meech Lake, Que., page A9

Dec 12, (1)   "3,500 friends, relatives bid a tearful farewell to murdered students," by Victor Malarek, The Globe and Mail, Montreal, front page

Dec 12, (2)   **"'Men cannot know the feelings of fear'** / Yet an anti-feminist backlash has been intensified by the massacre in Montreal," by Melanie Randall, Ms Randall is a doctoral student in political science at York University and a researcher-activist in the field of women and violence, page A7

Dec 12, (3)   "More massacre details to be released by police, but an inquiry ruled out," by Victor Malarek, The Globe and Mail with Canadian Press, Montreal, page A14

Dec 12, (4)   "Quebec engineers observe day of mourning," by Barrie McKenna, The Globe and Mail, Montreal, page A14

Dec 12, (5)   "Tension grows at Queen's over sexism controversy," by Stevie Cameron and Orland French, The Globe and Mail, page A14

Dec 12, (6)   "Risk of murder linked to non-domestic roles," MICHAEL VALPY, A8

Dec 13, (1)   "Police refusal to answer questions leaves lots of loose ends in killings," by Victor Malarek, The Globe and Mail, Montreal, page A18

Dec 13, (2)   "*1,000 fill church in Montreal to mourn victim of massacre*," by Patricia Poirier, The Globe and Mail, Montreal, page A18

Dec 13, (3)   "Students' newspaper warned to end sexism," by Orland French, The Globe and Mail, page A18

Dec 16, (1)   "The self-centred hype of Montreal massacre," LISE BISSONNETTE, page D2

Kitchener-Waterloo Record (KWR)

Dec 7, (1)   "**Killer hated women/**14 dead in rampage at college," by Penny MacRae, The Canadian Press, Montreal (lead article).

Dec 7, (2)   "Policeman finds body of daughter," Montreal (CP), page A5.

Dec 9   "300 at Guelph ceremony mourn death of students," by Margaret Mironowicz, Record staff, Guelph, front page.

Dec 11, (1)   "Priest confesses shame over 14 slain," by Margaret Mironowicz, Record staff, Cambridge, page B1.

Dec 11, (2)   "100 attend Speaker's Corners vigil for 14 women slain in Montreal", by Monica Gutschi, Record staff, page B3.

Dec 12, (1)   "Mourners see better world/Massacre debated as 14 buried," Montreal (CP), front page.

Dec 12, (2)   "Grieving together," Editorial, page A6.

Dec 13, (1)   "Killings re-kindle panty-raid debate," by Rose Simone, Record staff, page B1.

Dec 13, (2)   "Girl photos bumped to back pages by shooting," by Chisholm Macdonald, The Canadian Press, page A12.

Dec 14   "Universities honor 14 dead/Hatred continues, UW service told," by Margaret Mironowicz, Record staff, page B1.

Dec 18   "Montreal massacre shocks men into action," by Margaret Mironowicz, Record staff, page B1.

Dec 29   "Montreal slayings seen as random violent acts," Toronto (CP), front page.

Chapter 9

"Frenching" the "Real" and Praxeological Therapy: An Ethnomethodological Clarification of the New French Theory of Media[1]

Dušan I. Bjelić

The New French Theory of media, associated with Jean Baudrillard and Paul Virilio[2], announced the "disappearance" of the master referent (the "real"), the end of the "tyranny of reason,"[3] and "reality-cide." A tone of euphoria, rather than nostalgia, prevails, a tone equivalent only to the be-heading of the King in the streets of Paris. Their argument goes that the "real" is understood as a simulacrum, meaning that fiction operates as reality, where reality is constituted by the relation between the sign (that which represents) and its referent[4] (that which is represented). Because the "real," according to Baudrillard, is only a relational invention, the "real" has always a fragile and only temporal stability. The power of reason, meaning and order are being severely destabilized by the media's ability to reprocess the "real" by simulating it. The "real" disappears through the vertigo of media simulations and representations, creating only appearances without corresponding reality. The sense of the "real" is sustained solely by our belief that something is being represented in the circulation of signs and images and thus, they conclude, reality is identical with the media operations of the production of appearances. The abduction of the "real" is not a malfunction of the system but is, rather, its universal code, its DNA.

In this study I will respond to what I call a *representational fixation* on the part of The New French Theory offering as therapy the ethnomethodological prescription that "meaning is practice." Following ethnomethodology's prescription, I will treat meaning as a practico-descriptive category; hence, I will offer an alternative interpretation of understanding meaning in media, one which serves as an alternative to the theory of code as a *cultural axiom*. My aim is not to counter the obvious seduction of the French prose with a puritan denouncement of this "sin," but rather to explore if there is still or any remaining seduction left in this analytical argument.

"Frenching" the "Real" by Means of Code

According to Jean Baudrillard (1985, 1988b) there are three grand versions of the relationship between the media and the "real": the "optimistic," the "pessimistic" and the "ironico-antagonistic." The "optimistic" version was promoted by Marshal McLuhan (1964) and is based on the hope that the new electronic media will turn the heterogeneous communities of industrial societies into a homogeneous global tribe transparent to and in agreement with itself.[5] Although McLuhan's analysis of mass media is anthropologically profound, his analysis of the media's hyperoptimistic consequences on social reality remains, for some, disproportionally naive. Hans Magnus Erzensberger (1970), for example, a progressive German publicist and poet, takes a more cautious and "pessimistic" view of the media. The media as a technology of mass consciousness constitute, for him, a contradictory category; they are in the hands of private owners and oppress the masses' awareness of the real conditions of their existence.[6] Seen from this dialectical view, the mass media, Erzensberger (1970: 26-27) concludes, are a source of oppression but, when placed in the hands of the suppressed masses, also a source of potential emancipation.

The first two grand versions of the media, Baudrillard argues, are not as antithetical to each other as they might initially appear. They both presuppose the giveness of the "real." In contrast to McLuhan and Erzensberger, Baudrillard casts in relief his notion of anti-reality, an "ironic" view of the "real," in which the mass media are "simulative devices"[7] of the "real" shrewdly employed by the masses to "escape as reality"[8] from the tasks of the social. Simulated models of the "real" lead to the collapse of structural regimes of meaning by blurring what was always a clear distinction between reality and signification, the latter of which was providing a stable sense of the "real" (See Genosko, 1994: 1-6). Much like McLuhan, Baudrillard sees the media as a process and transient anti-environment, as an artificial reality which re-processes the "real" into its simulated model. But he departs from the scheme of McLuhan by denying any evolutionary role of the media. The media, for Baudrillard, conceal a conspiracy, a subversive alliance between the media and their "fatal strategy" to objectivize and the "evil strategies" of the masses to liquidate themselves as meaningful and real subjects by being objectivized.[9]

Baudrillard's co-conspirator against the "real," Paul Virilio (1995), has a somewhat different theory of the disappearance of reality. Unlike Baudrillard, who sees the cancellation of the "real" primarily as a semiotic issue, Virilio (1995:141) maintains it is a result of a techno war against our human senses, a media development of visual anti-phenomenology. Practices of disillusion, according to Virilio, are incorporated into various techniques of media representation which, as a result, lead to a certain defeat of perceptual faith in the process of creation of what Merleau-Ponty called the "Great Object."[10]   Much like Baudrillard, Virilio (1995) perceives mass media not as a technology of the representation of the "real," but rather as a "terminal art" (p. 65) of spreading blindness by means of wiping out the world from our vision. "Synthetic vision" of the "terminal" and the "industrialization of the non-gaze" are products of the new technology of the "optoelectronic" environment in which reality is slick, fast, and invisible, much like a *Stealth* plane, the F117, whose image is being destroyed before it appears on the screen, a synthetic object that anticipates the disappearance of its own image, a destruction of its own representation (Virilio, 1995: 64-65). The military and the media complex adopt such practical magic for various deceptional/representational reasons and this magic, this synthetic perception, takes the world away from our eyes. The new apperceptual techniques cover what, in his view, "was invisible to the naked eye with the mask of the visible" (p. 65). As more techniques of representations develop, Virilio concludes, these "cancellations of reality" spread (p. 68).

The French theorists unanimously agree that the irony of the "real," the product of the same subversive alliance between the masses and the media, operates through some kind of code. The meaning of the word "code" itself, however, is a source of dispute. In the broadest sense, according to Eco (1984), code usually refers to "... having a linguistic competence, a language, a system of rules, world knowledge or encyclopedic competence, a set of pragmatic norms, and so on ..." (p. 164). More specifically, a code is a "system of rules for the combination of stable sets of terms into messages" (Genosko, 1984: 36), or "the most economic way of sending a message" (Eco, 1984: 169) without creating ambiguity. For some, as for Barthes, a code is a fixed rule within the storehouse of culture, that "which is already known and already organized by a culture" (Eco, 1984: 187). For others – say, Jacobson – a code transforms: It is " a mechanism which allows transformations between two systems" (Eco, 1984: 187), or "a code is not only a rule which *closes* but also a rule which *opens*" (p. 187). For the social sciences, a code is embedded in the matrix of a social regime and is a part of its sui-generic reproduction. Levi-Strauss, for instance, promoted the view that collective interaction in a society is not spontaneous but is governed by the same code as social structure (Eco, 1984: 167). Gilles Deleuze and Felix Guattari (1983: 262) argue that the code operates according to the given axiomatics of the regime's representation and production, and forces this structural order upon the flow of the prestructured desire. The code co-ordinates and regulates the flow, deterritorializes its origin, and reterritorializes its placement in the machine of the "socius." Hence, the code is a despotic regime which, in modern capitalism, permeates and crushes desire.

Baudrillard, like Deleuze and Guattari, gives a despotic feature to the code, but for him, the code has aesthetic and seductive features, ironic plans and evil strategies. "The code *terrorizes* the process of communication by fixing the two poles of sender and receiver and by privileging the sender" (Genosko, 1984: 36). In order to ensure its reproduction, the code reduces communication to "munication," ensures non-ambivalence by excluding ambivalence. Baudrillard focuses on "... the obligation (which replaces the code understood as a cold, remote and digital structure) to give and receive *between* persons in the absence of their abstract separation and togetherness ...." (Genosko, 1984: 36). Although his code is a controlling scheme of communication, it is open to instrumental influences. In the age of electronic media, the code's *basic operation* is a media event; it simulates the real in media, but this simulation is a strategy, by which the code produces a disappearance as a "code-like togetherness" of the masses separated by the abstractness of social life. One might think of Baudrillard's and Virilio's notion of media as a "heaven's gate technology," based on the social contract of disappearance.

The following part of my analysis consists of a kind of "forensic investigation" into the conditions of the media's "reality-cide" which will take us to the scene of a crime. I will consider two cases of the simulation of the "real" by the media in order to show what Baudrillard and Virilio mean when they say that the "real" disappears through the operation of the media. In addition to explaining their positions, I will offer an alternative way of understanding the question of the "real" in the media.

The Image of the "Sniper": Who is being shot?

Stable reality puts certain constraints on what something can or cannot be. For example, a single object cannot be a member of two mutually exclusive categories; a thing cannot simultaneously be in and out, round and square. One finds similar constraints in the discourse on the Bosnian war. A single person cannot be an Orthodox Christian shooting Muslims and a Muslim shooting Orthodox Christians. Ignoring the common mixed-ethnic and religious background of the people of Bosnia, the media discourse has drawn the war along antagonistic religious and ethnic divisions. These assumed and habituated positions are referents for the war identities.

But the visual grammar of image representation – a montage – can invent its own rules of meaning independent from the rules of the grammar of ordinary life, as early film theorists pointed out.[11] By this they meant that through the practice of montage an image as a sign receives an invented referent.[12] For example, the video tape of the beating of Rodney King as it was edited for a TV audience conveyed an opposite meaning from the one edited for a white jury (Goodwin, 1994). To be sure, as a representational technology, mass media are not excluded from the art of representation and the shifting of meanings. The following two examples will illustrate this point.

During the early days of the War in Bosnia, ABC dedicated various special prime-time programs to educating its audience on the cultural and political background of the war. I will analyze two segments from two different programs that use the same shot of a sniper as a concluding image, but are organized in such a way as to provide different, and mutually exclusive, ethnic identities for the sniper in the otherwise identical shot. The first example, "The Land of the Dragon" with Peter Jennings, introduces the audience to the starting conditions of the conflict in Bosnia, specifically discussing events in Sarajevo during the Spring of 1993. The second example, *Prime Time Live* with Diana Sawyer, offers a point of contrast.

Peter Jennings' narration and the sequence of images, including that of the sniper, were edited in the order displayed in Image Set 1. From this organization of shots and narrative, the impression is created that the ethnic identity of the sniper in frame 5 is Serbian. The shooting is an example of Serbs not accepting the Bosnian separation from Yugoslavia. Since the Serbs are opposing the cessation, it follows that this shooting must have been done by a Serb.

Image Set 1

The Serbian

offensive spread through Bosnia
and Hercegovina in March 1992.

The Serbs were convinced that
the Muslims and the Croats

who lived there would vote for
Bosnian independence from
Yugoslavia,

which the Serbs found unacceptable.
((shooting))

Compare the meaning of the same image with that in the next edited sequence narrated by Diane Sawyer of "Prime Time Live." (See Image Set
2).   In this segment the same sniper reappears, but now as a Muslim, a
young Muslim student who, in his words, doesn't want to be a sniper but
is forced into this position because Serb Christians are terrorizing his
neighborhood.   In the reality of editing, the same image *can* be what in
pre-represented life is impossible: In a single moment, it can be both a
Serb and Muslim.   Did not the entire war revolve around the ethnic
differentiation among the identities formed by a long history, cemented in
religious dominations, rituals, and communal patterns of life?[13]   But all of
this history, the phenomenal referent, is liquidated by means of editing, in
order to talk about the reality of the history.   The irony is that the "real"
was simulated by the model of anti-reality.   Cases such as this "fact-cide"
facilitate Baudrillard and Virilio's ironic stance on media representation.

Image Set 2

...so now already an estimate that
10,000 people have been killed,
many of them killed by snipers who
seemed to care nothing about the
target: children and civilians. The
prime minister, Milan Panic, claims
that recently, snipers have been offered $500 for killing a journalist.
What you are about to see is an excerpt from a French documentary
on snipers narrated by John
Kinonas, a highly unusual glimpse
of these anonymous assassins.

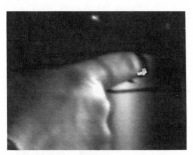

They lay in wait, stalking the
next victim

through the gaping windows of the
abandoned high-rise,

Bosnian Muslims who work
a 24 hour shift

shooting at human targets

throughout the streets of

"I was born here."

His name is Predrag. He is a 26
year old university student turned
urban guerilla. "Four months I am
a soldier ((sigh)) I don't want to
be a soldier..."

But he joined the struggle
because he says the Serbian
Christians are terrorizing his
his neighborhood. ((shooting))
"we must go, go, go"

In his controversial essay, "The Gulf War Did Not Take Place," Baudrillard (1995a) proposed something that shocked many social realists, namely, that the war in Gulf couldn't happen. He did not mean to deny that there were military activities in the region, but, rather, to claim that whatever happened over there was not a war as we know it. He takes the reciprocity of meaning between the actual event and representational practices as the criteria for the mutual legitimation or the mutual cancellation of meaning. By this he means that the reality of an event – let's say a war – is given by the order of its representational practices, by the news; and that the reality of news, by the rule of the reciprocity of meaning, is given by the reality of the event: If one of the poles is fake, the other cannot be real. If the war is not a war then its representation is not a representation either; if the war is a referent and the news a sign, then the war is a referent of edited signs. Baudrillard (1993) illuminates his thesis with reference to Brecht's characters:

> "This beer isn't a beer, but that is compensated for by the fact that this cigar isn't a cigar either." If the beer hadn't been beer and the cigar really had been a cigar, then there would have been a problem. That's rather like my book about the war, that the war wasn't a war, but that is compensated for by the fact that the news wasn't news either. If the first had been a war, but the second not news, there would have been a disequilibrium. And then there's the other quotation, later, when Kalle says: "Where nothing is in its place, there's disorder. Where everything is in its place there's nothing there, and that's order." And the war is just like that. (p. 180)

The media simulated the reality of the Gulf war as a way of representing it and, as an unavoidable consequence, canceled the meaning of the war by canceling the meaning of the news. The media produced a coherency of the war – its chronology, strategy, casualties, aims, etc. – even when there was only an "electrocution" of Iraq. When they reported on a bombing campaign that consisted only of shooting Iraq's hardware decoys, the media were still "covering" the war. The "war" was war, Baudrillard insists, only by virtue of the operations of the media. The media, as Baudrillard sees them, are unique and potentially, if not actually, subversive in any epistemic, meaningful regime. In short, media operations decompose the representational mechanisms essential to any meaning-regime and replace them with simulated models of the regime. It follows that actual world events, which supposedly are referents for the media representations, are progressively going "referent- anorexic" in the face of the produced simulational models. The "disappearance" of the meaning of war as we know it, Baudrillard concludes, is reciprocated by the disappearance of the meaning of news as we know it. This symmetry of disappearance is still in balance: In the same way that the world, by means of the media news, is no longer a world but only its simulational model, so too is news, which is supposed to cover the real world, no longer news. There is no news if there is not a reality of the world and no world if it is not represented as real. What remains, according to Baudrillard, after the symmetry of a progressive elimination of meaning, are only media operations, the circulation of images.

To apply this argument briefly to the image of the "sniper," the simulated ethnic identity is a fake referent. Taking up the simulated identity as if it were an actual identity and then editing the narration around it, according to Baudrillard's argument, implicitly devalues the status of the news as news. The boundaries between the referent (the actual person) and its representations (the edited image) are collapsing by virtue of editing practices. The remaining relation is that the edited image is the sign and the referent at the same time, and the news (about the war) is not anymore about the real event but about a self-referential sign which produces a "terminal art" of "spreading blindness" by bringing the war closer to spectators. "Who is shooting and who is being shot?" Obviously, nobody in a real space and time; this crime is happening in a simulated space and time and the media spectators are the inside pedestrians who should look for cover.

Should ethnomethodologists be disturbed by Baudrillard's announced "suicide" of social reality?[14] The "disappearance" of the "real" through media simulation is not, for ethnomethodologists, a call for alarm. Ethnomethodologists have never lived off of or for the concept of social reality, although they have always found it an interesting topic for inquiry and clarification. Ethnomethodologists would ask: Is our understanding of the "disappearance" through the simulation of the "real" secured by reference to cultural code and beyond the conditions of the simulational actions themselves? In approaching this question I will offer an account of my own participation in media simulation.

The Event and the "News"

During the war in Bosnia there were numerous initiatives by various non-profit organizations in the United States to help war victims. One such mission was lead by the Veterans for Peace, a nation-wide organization with its headquarters in Portland, Maine. Knowledge of the Serbo-Croatian language became, during the war, a valued expertise. Because I am a native of the Former Yugoslavia, a rare ethnic group in Portland at that time, I was promptly identified by the Veterans for Peace and asked to help them as a translator during the reception of the arriving victims. Although my initial task was just to translate, due to various circumstances, it rapidly expanded, and soon I was cast into the position of a cultural interpreter for the hosts and for the guests. I was a therapist, a guardian, and a lecturer. One of the most attractive aspects of this task was appearing in the media.

Portland is, by any criteria, a small and, in many respects, a provincial town. Although the state of Maine has prominent Senators on the Senate Foreign Relations Committee, foreign delegations rarely come to Portland; no summits have been held here, and no peace treaties were ever negotiated or signed in Portland. When, then, a local humanitarian organization got a piece of the action in the highly publicized war in Bosnia, it naturally became very pertinent news for the entire region. The sense presented in the media was that even though Maine is a remote state, it can still be part of important global affairs. When children from Bosnia started to arrive in Maine the media made it into a prominent news story. Local newspapers ran articles about the children of the war; photos of their serious and exhausted faces covered the front pages; stories of their individual injuries were told, not without revealing the horrors of the war; local radio stations set up a series of interviews with various local scholars, who were asked to give an in-depth analysis of the historical background of the war; all four local TV stations (affiliates of NBC, ABC, CBS and Fox) covered these events with short but prominently positioned stories on their six o'clock news programs. I followed the scope and the nature of the coverage from the sidelines until one day I became a participant.

Given my ability to translate between Serbo-Croatian and English, Veterans for Peace asked me to serve as an interpreter for a family about to arrive from Bosnia. At Andrews Air Force Base in Washington D.C., I met a wounded teenage boy, his mother, and younger brother, all of whom I was suppose to accompany from Washington to Lewiston, Maine, where the teenager was scheduled for hospitalization. On my way to Washington, I was told that at the end of the trip there would probably be a news conference with the mother. It would be dishonest to deny that I was thrilled about this; as an ethnomethodologist who was sometimes interested in media practices, I looked forward to the opportunity to get an inside glimpse of the production of the media's representation of world events. I regarded it as a rare and optimal situation for my analysis of the media.[15] What I didn't know, however, when I slipped comfortably into my seat on the way to Washington, was what my role in making the news would be. My "script," I thought naively, would simply be to translate questions and answers, to leisurely observe the media's production of the news. It never dawned on me that my "translation" would be, to inject Baudrillard's rhetoric, a part of the great "conspiracy" against the "real."

By the time I boarded the military plane at the Andrews Air Base, I had learned the story of the Bosnian family's tragedy. Arnel Martinovic, a Muslim, was hit in the head by shrapnel when Croatian artillery shelled his village near the city of Mostar. He had been cared for at an inadequately equipped local hospital and remained paralyzed. He was rescued by U.N. personnel and admitted into the US military hospital in Split, Croatia, from where his journey to the U.S. via Germany began. Zineta, his mother, a simple village woman with little or no cosmopolitan sensibility, told me with visible anxiety that she did not know where they were going, except that in a general sense she believed that her son would be helped. Unlike many immigrant mothers who have plenty of time to reflect in advance about the New World, Zineta had time neither to prepare nor to fantasize. She arrived with the help of the Pentagon and entered into the New World quickly, where she was instantly offered her "fifteen minutes of fame." While listening and observing her intense anxieties, I found myself offering her not only linguistic but also emotional and cultural support.

When we landed at the Lewiston military base, a welcoming delegation of locally prominent figures came into the plane to escort the mother and me, while medical personnel transported the boy from the plane into the first emergency car. The welcome was extended, flowers handed over, and the information conveyed that the mother would have a news conference in front of the plane. While TV crews were documenting the passage of the boy from the plane into the emergency car, the rest of us were descending the steps to the tarmac. Standing behind a line of cameras, the reporters called to us. We approached the microphones and the first question was addressed to the mother: "What do you have to say about the trip?" I turned to her. She was hiding behind my back. I translated the question. She looked at me confused and in an unpleasant voice said,"I don't have anything to say," as though she were insulted by being in the spotlight. "Well, you have to say something," I insisted, "It will be very humiliating if you don't say anything." I was explaining to her not only the content of the question but, above all, the *context*. Cornered by my insistence, she finally made a concession. "Well," she said, "you say what ever you want." I turned around without anything to say and a license to say anything I wanted. That evening, the local 6 o'clock news[16] carried my "translation": "She says thank you very much, she said as a mother there are no words a.. a.. a.. That can express her gratitude for the help that her son is receiving from you she is overhelmed (overwhelmed) with the good reception and the help from all sides ...."

The transcript of what was aired that evening is provided in Image Set 3 . The audio and visual data are synchronized as they were aired. The report begins with a brief history of Arnel's trip, establishing his identity and the reason he was brought to the U.S. The story is told in overlap with images of Arnel leaving the plane and being transferred into the first emergency car. He appears puzzled with the attention that he is receiving from the journalists, as well as from the medical personnel, who are quickly and skillfully preparing him for his journey in the ambulance. He, however, is monitoring the coverage of himself (image # 2) and orients himself to the production of the coverage by looking at the cameras and

Image Set 3

Reporter: It was a long journay for
Arnel Martinovic

all the way from his hometown Mostar
to Germany, to Washington, to Maine.
But in spite of what he went through

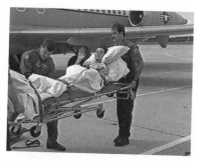

he still can manage a friendly wave.
That he has even that much energy is
nothing short of amazing. After being
caught in an artillery attack,

Arnel spent three days in a coma, the
victim of a head injury. A British nurse
found him and got him in an American
MASH unit

and a group, Veterans for Peace, got
him here. Unlike many of his friends,

he was lucky to still have a mother to
come with him.
Me: She says thank you very much.
She said, as a mother, there are no
words a.. a.. a.. that can express her
gratitude for the kind of help that her
son is receiving from you. She is
overwhelmed with the good reception
and the help from all sides.

Reporter: That help comes from
many sources: the Pentagon
donated the plane, the Central
Main Medical Center donated
medical care....

waving to them (#3). The boy's productive orientation to his own coverage is acknowledged by the reporter and commented upon: "... he can
still manage a friendly wave ... that he has even that much energy is nothing short of amazing ..." He is loaded in the ambulance and the story
shifts to his mother. The mother and the translator are not named but the
reporter's voice overlaps with the image (image # 6), ("unlike many of his
friends he was lucky to still have a mother to come with him...") suggesting that the mute woman with flowers is the mother, and the man with an
accent standing next to her is a translator. The mother's answers were
translated, and from the translation one hears that she is speaking as a
mother of this child, "as a mother...," therefore, to the American people,
and that she is very thankful for the help that she is receiving from her
generous hosts. By cutting her "translated" utterance at "... help from all

sides ...," the report topicalizes the "help": That which is relevant for us, the American viewers, is our input in her son's recovery. The report builds upon this message of "help" coming from "all sides," from various identifiable institutional centers, both military and medical, delegated by the American people (#7). Significantly, in constructing this account, the report assumes the *accuracy* of the translation.

I would like to retreat back to the transcript of the event in order to provide an alternative to the code-analysis. My object of analysis is the double feature of my production, what I produced for the public record and what passed unrecorded by the public. Specifically, my object of analysis here is a paired object consisting of two asymmetrically significational parts: what the mother actually said – "I have nothing to say" – and what I translated – "... and as a mother..." The entire problematic of the signification and its analysis, whether theoretical or ethnographic, is located in this detail. "I have nothing to say" is not a detail available in the transcript of the video tape, while ".. as a mother," is. The meaning of the second utterance, which I will call the "data detail," is embedded in a transcript of a tape, and is therefore a part of the logic of a "viewer's maxim of seeing."[17] Such detail, however, is unavoidably altered by the presence of "productional detail," a detail embedded in the structure of the event itself ("I have nothing to say"). There are two parallel rules of signification interlacing here, set by the two different contexts: one of the *viewer* and the other of the *producer*. Let me distinguish between them more carefully.

In the first context, the "viewer's maxim of seeing" rests on exhibited categories regulated by the event itself; it is in this event that I, a native of the Former Yugoslavia and also a father, was selected to be translator for the occasion and, by the same rule of the event's selection, that she was a mother of the wounded child. She, according to this rule, receives the reporters' questions and I translate the questions and the mother's answers. Within the context of two different "category-bound activities" (Sacks, 1974:221), answering/translating, the working assumption is that the mother is answering the question and that the translation is accurately rendered. The assumption about the accuracy of my translation, furthermore, presupposes the adequacy of meaning, not structural or ontological, but by reference to what I said the mother said. The criteria for *accurate* translation is established only as a relational criteria within the assumed categorizational division of labor between the mother and translator. That which was said *before* and for the translation is the "actual," the "real," by virtue of being contextually first, relevant to be translated for the occasion, and in the mother's native language. The English translation, which is immediately *after*, is by virtue of its temporal placement, categorized as a representational operation and as such has an element of accuracy.

There are two criteria in this case for establishing the *accuracy* of my translation, one the ethnographic/spectator's, the other the praxeologic/producer's. The praxeological criteria is the one which requires an actual *production* of hearing and the *skills* for understanding what the mother told me; ethnographic "accuracy" is an interpretatively assumed category. In the assumed temporal division of labor of speaking and with the competent comparison of the two contextual categories of speaking, the mother's and my own, the status of the translation is established as a representation of the *actual* or *simulated* answer, but this criterion is a *privilege* of the competent producer, while the non-competent and only presumably accurate translation is given via the logic through which the tape is edited. The question of the "real" and the representational would have been raised *as an issue* only if some discrepancy between the "real" and the representational, thus between the accurate and simulational, could be established. But this would require from analysts the ability to identify competing contexts as competing schemes of interpretations. The question of what is "real," therefore, is not answered by reference to the cultural axiom of the code, but by reference to the question: for whom and for what purposes? For the TV audience, my translation was real. For the reporters, who actually could have seen the discrepancy in time between the brevity of the mother's answer and my lengthy translation, and thus have some suspicion aroused, it was real enough. For the mother, my translation was "real" so long as she could hide behind me, pretending that her answer was being translated, dodging the responsibilities of the news conference. And, for me, my talking was not a real translation but it was appropriate for the occasion. From this analysis, the "real" appears not to be a fixed referent but a moving target, which discloses the mobile constellation of various perspectives on the event that afternoon in a front of the plane.

The Instructional Field of the News Conference as a Method for Producing the "Real"

In the immediate aftermath of the above event, a couple of interesting questions arose. When the media attention forced me to deliver the mother's answer, I knew that I could not literally translate "I have nothing to say" or "Say what ever you want." I could not have done it because I felt in the moment that it would be too embarrassing for me to give an "accurate" translation of her answers and too impolite for her to have said them. Expectations were built as to what type of answer was appropriate and I was the party in the entire order of the event responsible for fulfilling those expectations. I knew that "Sorry folks, she has nothing to say," was not an option, that the "actual" was not "good enough" news. These interesting contextual contingencies of the order of the event emerged on this occasion.

The reporters didn't have control over her answers or her choice of words, but they constructed the civic event, the news conference, composing its humanitarian character in which every participant – the Pentagon, Veterans for Peace, Maine's hospitals, and, of course myself – donated a piece of good will, went the extra mile in order to help the victims. This event also was a situational "draft" which put constraints on its various participants. I understood her saying "I have nothing to say" as dodging the "draft" and I was "drafted" into producing the event, which was to help manage its humanitarian character with and for those who invented it, the media complex itself. Placed into this media context, I started to "fulfill" what the native "failed" to deliver. When the spotlight shifted to me, the humanitarian character of the occasion brought out the "best" in me and I was ready to deliver the required work according to my understanding of the logic of the occasion. My position as a translator in the production of the news conference, allowed, as does any translation, for a contextual adjustment to the ruling spirit of the moment. What adjustment of my translation was to be made was guided by my orientation to the context of the media event. Baudrillard might claim that my "translation" was done for the media and for that reason my "translation" was not translation at all. But his would be a claim based on a dogmatic sense of translation.

A dogmatic sense of translation is a term used in theology and hermeneutics referring to the principles of faithful transition of meaning from one language into the other, "a meaning which proceeds from the relation to the truth of what is being said" (Gadamer, 1975: 162).[18] Translation, as a problematic form of communication for Gadamer, reveals the constitutive principles of the *Verstehen*. He writes:

> Thus the linguistic process by means of which a conversation in two different languages is made possible through translation is especially informative. Here the translator must translate the meaning to be understood into the context in which the other speaker lives. This does not, of course, mean that he is at liberty to falsify the meaning of what the other person says. Rather, the meaning must be preserved, but since it must be understood within a new linguistic world, it must be expressed within it in a new way. Thus the translation is at the same time an interpretation. We can even say that it is the completion of the interpretation that the translator has made of the words given him. (p. 346)

Gadamer acknowledges the gap between the authentic meaning and its translation, which can be narrowed down but never closed by the interpretation of the authentic word. It is within this gap that translation as interpretation meanders between the falsification and the preservation of the authentic meaning. Jurgen Habermas (1984: 134) refers to Gadamer's principle of translation as a hermeneutic utopia of universal validity based on the dogmatic notion of "truth" as that which is right, sincere and authentic. Translation, for Habermas, is one form of understanding which is a component of a communicative process. Translation, just like any other form of the *Verstehen*, is responsible not to the transcendental rules of accuracy but to the rules of rationality of the communicative process. Habermas emphasizes the pragmatic reason of communication rather than "faith to the spoken word." A translator, in this view, is a "virtual participant" in the production of meaning. Translation involves some pre-understanding of the original context, as Gadamer asserts, but not, Habermas insists, a pure intuitive interpretation of the original context. Habermas hoped to defeat the orthodoxy of the translation's validity by relocating its judgement and competency from a sacred referent to a pragmatics of communicative context (1984: 135-136), to the rational structure of contemporaneous communication. Wittgenstein's position clarifies Habermas' insistence on the context. Wittgenstein's (1968) referent for a competent translation is not a sacred meaning but "a point of time and a way of using the word" (p. 175) which grasps and, at the same time, allows for the translation of something alien into our customary form of expression.

To return to the issue of dogmatism: Baudrillard's code of communication, we learned earlier, involves a one-directional circulation of signification ("munication"), much like Gadamer's model of the *Verstehen*. Admittedly, their understandings of the referent are diametrically opposed. While for Gadamer the referent is always authentic, for Baudrillard it is always fake; nonetheless, their forms are both dogmatic. An alternative to Baudrillard's "municational" referent is offered by Habermas' and Wittgenstein's contextual reference. If translation is bound to the "point in time and the way of using the word" as Wittgenstein insists, than its reference is in the rationale of the occasion, or in the game that is being played. To apply this notion to my own translation: My translation followed the rules I acknowledged at the moment of inventing the answer, and thus had no reference to the sacred word. The validity, judgement and the competency of a translation is not given by codifying meaning, but through a further specification of the context in which the words are being spoken.

This brings me to my final point: "How did I know what to say?"

There is a passage in Exodus (Chapter 4.) which may clarify this question. Moses found himself of "a slow tongue" when asked by the Lord to speak his words to his people.

10. And Moses said unto the Lord, O my Lord, I *am* not eloquent, neither heretofore, nor since thou hast spoken unto thy servant: but I *am* slow of speech, and of slow tongue.

11. And the Lord said unto him, who hath made man's mouth? Or who maketh the dumb, or deaf, or the seeing, or the blind? Have not I the Lord?

12. Now therefore go, and I will be with thy mouth, and teach thee what thou shalt say.

13. And he said, O my Lord, send, I pray thee, by the hand *of him whom* thou wilt send.

14. And the anger of the Lord was kindled against Moses, and he said, Is not Aaron on the Levite thy brother? I know that he can speak well. And also, behold, he cometh forth to meet thee: and when he seethe thee, he will be glad in his heart.

15. And thou shalt speak unto him, and put words in his mouth: and I will be with thy mouth, and with his mouth, and will teach you what ye shall do.

16. And he shall be thy spokesman unto the people: and he shall be, *even* he shall be to thee instead of a mouth, and thou shalt be to him instead of God.

Obviously the mother was of "a slow tongue" when confronted by the cameras, but there is always an eloquent brother who is of "a fast tongue." I put words in her mouth ("She said, as a mother I have no words to express ...") not as an idiosyncratic deed but as a deed that has deep structural roots in the situation of public spectacle. If the Lord is the ruling "spirit" and the "spirit" occupies the same position as the context of the occasion, it follows that the "essential reference" faced by Moses or by the mother will be articulated by someone. In the movie *Network*, the mad anchorman was selected by the "spirit" of the network to be a new prophet. When he naively asked "why me?" (instead of "what truth to speak?") the "voice" responded, "because you are on television dummy!"; television, the "voice" continued, is not about truth but about a public spectacle. Although my "translation" was not completely an *ad hoc* invention, I knew, more or less, that I would be in a media situation in which the mother would be asked to extend some gratitude. When confronted by cameras, I was not a "dummy." I discovered that, when the omnipresent eye of the "Great Object" opened in front of me, I spoke in "tongue." This "spirit" was not a sacred word, but my own understanding of and work for the occasion. Nor am I alone. I later saw an interview with a father of a boy who tragically became paralyzed by playing hockey and who became an object of public charity. When the father, reiterating in his TV interview my "translation," said something like "I have no words to express my gratitude for the help ...," I understood the degree to which the media organized a *method* for the proper production of the event for and by the media situation. Orientation to the media situation was the condition of the news conference, and its order is to meet the established typical mode of the "proper" answer, i.e. the "same" kind of proper answer on and for the screen. The media complex, the "Great Object," organized my intervention into the "real" by instructing me with a camera to orient myself towards what, from my position, was supposed to be the "real" of the screen; what appears as "real" is the screen's methodic rendition of its typical surface. The self-regulating surface provides methodic self-instructive guidance, not as an pregiven code of action, but as the "premise" and the "outcome" of my own practical response to the worksite of the news conference.

The Method

My involvement in producing the news was not governed by an ethnographic research design, even though on first glance it might appear as though I was a participant observer. The fact that I was in the "field" where the situation was unfolding in front of my eyes does not make me an ethnographer. The ethnographer's primary task is to analyze the social order of others on the basis of the ethnographer's observational code.[19] I, on the other hand, was observing my own production of the situation. Ethnography always rests on a certain dosage of guesses as to what the actors are up to, which allows for and is compensated for by creative interpretations on the part of the ethnographer's experience. My situation, in contrast was, first, that I was in my own context and, second, that my own context was subversive to any ethnographic gaze because it was one of simulation, except to my own self-referential gaze. In the same way that Garfinkel's (1984[1967]) "Agnes" treats "practical circumstances as a texture of relevance" (p. 175) which allows her to pass as a legitimate female (or, for that matter, in the same way that an F 117 passes unnoticed by destroying its representational image), so I passed the immediate observers as a legitimate "translator" by virtue of "spreading the blindness" quickly and unnoticed, while at the same time preserving the privilege only for myself to know about my own production.

Neither is my analysis a type of an ethnomethodological and conversation analytical work, which analyzes the naturally occurring phenomenon by virtue of analysis of a video tape. A video tape as "data" about this event is an insufficient resource, because the tape of the event is of simulated practices which passed the camera unnoticed.

It should be obvious by now that having analytical access into the context of the production of the tape complicates the question of signification. The discrepancy between what was "actually" said by the mother and what was translated by me becomes, I have argued, an issue only when the context of production is offered and, by virtue of this contrast, the "simulational" and "real" can be identified and speculatively contrasted – raised, perhaps, as a semiotically "catastrophic" issue, but a catastrophe which, I have insisted, is always the "premise" and the "outcome" of the particular practical context. We have seen that signification shifts with redescription of the context, and the detail which shifts the meaning is precisely the one *not* available in the analysis of an "egalitarian" distribution of a video tape. Rather it is a *privileged* detail available only through my self-referential analysis as a *detail-producer* of the very conditions of the event. Analytical transcription evaporates from the surface of the white paper (See Bogen, 1992), or the tape, because the data is "inscribed" in the body of the analyst.

What complicates generalizing about the production of meaning by means of crude simplification and makes, indeed, conditions worse for understanding it, are totalizing accounts of signification by the theories of code. The challenge for ethnomethodology, in light of the theory of code, should be whether or not it can recover the "missing part" which is especially challenging in the age of ironic and, for Baudrillard, "evil" strategies of simulation in which the "missing" is the *simulating*. The demon is in the detail, and the uniquely adequate strategy for the ironic conditions of media representation is, in this case, to unchain the demon dwelling in the constitutive detail of the simulation to counter the demon *universalis* dwelling in the code.

In my self-referential analysis, the "missing part" from the tape redefines the meaning of the tape analysis, but because this detail is praxeologically invisible (a demon's practical joke), neither theoretical nor ethnographic analysis has privileged access into the conditions of the production of meaning.

In comparison with my description of the news event it becomes clear that Baudrillard's "catastrophe" of the "disappearance" of the "real" makes its appearance only if one is able to compare the mother's answer to my translation. This is not a theoretically-available criterion but it is productionally discoverable. The theory of code solely on the view of the consumer, a "viewer's maxim of seeing," namely, on the ethnographic gaze. The tape is *edited* in such way that the mother's talking is *cut out* and is not available for the viewers. Second, even if it were available on the tape, one must have bilingual skills to detect the discrepancies. These skills are not the property of the tape, but of people who have acquired them. Only having these skills makes analysis of the originating conditions of the simulation possible. Similarly, the theory of code emphasizes the representational (edited) meaning of the event, not the productional meaning of the event. If the recorded event on the tape is a simulated event, then it is so only by virtue of somebody's discovery. The code analysis can cover the already accomplished and discovered operation of a simulation, but it has no methodological capability to discover the production of simulation: *simulating*. To understand *simulating* news requires a different set of rules, namely, rules of the production of the event and not the rules of interpreting what it means once it is accomplished. To put it simply, while ethnomethodology describes simulating production, the theory of code speculates about the cultural signification of that which is assumed to be *simulation*.

Finally, because my "translation" simulated the "real," and the "real" event "disappeared" at the moment of its representation, it could have been a case of the "catastrophe" of signification as Baudrillard might have claimed. An alternative explanation could be offered as well. Not only did the mother's "actual" answer, in which she was true to her own feelings, offer a form of resistance and a competing context for the reporter's event, but her response is not easily interpreted in relation to a code. She might have been dodging the "draft" because she was tired, embarrassed, shy, or simply ignorant of the media context. My "translation," on the other hand, could be interpreted as a move in the game of chaperoning, correcting, or acting for her, in terms of the "spirit" of the event. Just as luggage is cleared of prohibited belongings for proper entry into our world, and a stamp pressed on an alien passport, so the mother was cleared in my "translation" from her own context in order to enter our world "properly." That this routine was followed was the real news of the day.

Notes

1. I would like to thank David Bogen, Lucinda Cole and Doug Macbeth all of whom in various ways helped me to produce this paper.
2. My primary focus is the work of Jean Baudrillard (1983a, 1983b, 1985, 1987, 1988a, 1988b, 1990, 1993, 1994, 1995a, 1995b, 1996a, 1996b, 1997) and Paul Virilio (1995).
3. Although Michel Foucault did not condone Baudrillard's and Virilio's ironic and anti-rational views on the media, he nonetheless was among the first to initiate an attack on the rationality and Enlightenment in his own early work. In his "Introduction" to George Cangulhem's *On the normal and the pathological*, Foucault (1991) introduced the notion of the end of reason. He writes: "A reason whose structural autonomy carried with it the history of dogmatism and despotism – a reason that, as a result, produces emancipation only on the condition that it succeeds in freeing itself from itself" (p. 12).
4. Theories of the referent (semiotics and semiosis) contain one of the most debated theoretical issues, that of the relationship between the sign and the referent as real (Genosko, 1994: 34). There are competing and mutually ex-

cluding theories of referentiality. C.S. Peirce, who introduced the semiotic diagram of sign/referent, and Ferdinand de Saussure's structural linguistics differ in designating different referents to the sign: The latter excludes real objects as referents, since they are non-linguistic and not referential, while the former considers real objects as referents only in the cases of "icons" and "indices" (Eco, 1976: 68). Similar disagreement on the question of the referent can be found between Umberto Eco and Baudrillard. Eco, for example, excludes the referent from the theory of code because it would contaminate the theory of code (Genosko, 1994: 35). For Baudrillard, Eco's theory makes a metaphysics of the referent and the referent must be included in the theory of code because it is invented by it. Influenced by Louise Hjelmslev's work in glossematics (Genosko, 1994: 63-68), Felix Guattari and Gilles Deleuze contrast their polysemiosis of meaning with the homogeneity of Peirce's diagram of semiotics; they reject any structural scheme of theorizing about meaning because language has no unified, autonomous domain of its own.

Baudrillard acknowledges, as do Deleuze and Guattari, a fictive character of the dichotomy of the sign and the referent, but he intends to preserve this relation as a fiction in order to release his theory from any referential constraints (theory as a science fiction) and implode the rules of structural linguistics; the referent is only a phenomenological halo of the sign, a sign's alibi (Genosko, 1994: 39-40). The type of simulacrum which is constituted only by the self-referential sign, now free from any structural constraints, is no longer a site of crisis but of significational "catastrophe," a collapse of meaning, power and order (Baudrillard, 1987; see Kellner, 1989: 84-89).

5. Although McLuhan (1964) doesn't topicalize the concept of the real, he nevertheless implicitly articulates the concept when he theorizes about the evolutionary role of the mass media. In outlining the specific character of the media environment for humans, McLuhan distinguishes technological from natural reality in one important sense. The technologically real is an artifact, an anti-environment in contrast to the Natural environment, and, unlike the latter, artificial reality is neither passive nor external to humans but active and constantly reshaping itself (p. vii). Mass media, like all technology, are an extension of human nature which have a distinct function: The medium "controls ... human association and action" (p. 9) and, just as TV reprocesses film, the mass media reprocess the fragmented society of the industrial age into a globally unified media tribe. Media technology, produced in the artificial anti-environment of fragmentized industrial societies, is processing the very same originated environment into a unified global village. McLuhan gave the mass media a prominent role among the other technologies: Mass media technology is self-referential. Mass media are their own context. Media are in this respect unlike other technologies.

6. Unlike Orwellians or Marxists who singlehandedly ignore the media because they see them as means of manipulation, Erzensberger is willing to explore the egalitarian and emancipatory potentials of the new media. He agrees that the media are technologies of manipulations – after all, every media representation presumes editing, cutting, dubbing, etc., – but much like Benjamin and Brecht, he does not shy from what technological progress has to offer for

the subversive action of the masses. He asserts that "a revolutionary plan should not require the manipulators to disappear; on the contrary, it must make everyone a manipulator" (Erzensberger, 1970: 20), by which he means that the media may be democratized and the masses may participate in representing their social reality. Those who create history should document it with all possible instrumental means and operations (cameras, video cameras, tape-recorders, transistors etc.), *there* and *then*, when it is created. If media operations (the arts of manipulation) are not democratized, decentralized, and used in the form of a direct action, the prospects for the masses' emancipation are pessimistic. For him civil violence in Bosnia and Los Angeles offers examples of the negative consequence of a non-democratized media. He observes:

> The media trance in which they find themselves is not a matter of imitation, but the direct feedback between image and reality. There are countless criminals who feel that they are not really involved in their actions. They convince themselves that they didn't actually beat other people to death, that it was all 'television.' Theories of simulation are born out in the most absurd way by some people's inability to distinguish between reality and film. (Erzensberger, 1994: 54)

Erzensberger insists that privatized media control the production of images, that "feedback" between the real and its image creates the conditions of simulation which, as a consequence, "magnify the person who has become unreal and give him a kind of proof of existence" (1994: 54). Although he concedes that the media image amplifies a person and, in this amplification, the person finds the proof of his or her own "reality" by virtue of losing the realness, Erzensberger does not hear in this paradox of the "feedback" an echo of the vanishing referent, as The New French Theory would have heard. Instead Erzensberger treats this "feedback" as a pathological case of the twisted sense of the "real" due to the privatized control of the image production and not as the loss of it. The "real" is presented as a fiction in the capitalistic mode of production, while in the socialist mode the "real" becomes transparent to itself. For Erzensberger, the pristine "real," it seems, is identifiable only by means of socialized media, and the perception of the "real" is regulated by the mode of its production. Jean Baudrillard, in contrast, would insist that the above contradiction constitutes not a deviation in the system, but proof of its role.

7. Baudrillard (1988b) writes:

> This is the way the masses escape as reality, in this very mirror, in those simulative devices which are designed to capture them. Or again, the way in which events themselves disappear behind the television screen, or the more general screen of information (for it is true that events have no probable existence except on this deflective screen, which is no longer a mirror) .... This new screen is simply its mode of disappearance ... The object, the individual, is not only condemned to disappearance, but *disappearance is also its strategy*; it is its way of response to this device for capture, for networking, and for forced identification. To this *cathodic* surface of re-

cording, the individual or the mass replay by a *parodic* behavior of disappearance .... They turn themselves into an impenetrable and meaningless
surface, which is a method of disappearing. They eclipse themselves; they
melt into the superficial screen in such a way that their reality and that of
their movement, just like that of particles of matter, may be radically
questioned without making any fundamental change to the probabalistic
analysis of their behavior. (p. 213-13)

8. This seemingly unintelligible phrase is consistent with Baudrillard's claim that
the media are a strategy of the masses to disappear (see the above note, 7).
Reality is always simulacral and the referent always fictive ("as if"); thus the
masses escape the responsibility of the social by simulating it.

9. The media is an evil object for the reason that the masses can find themselves
captured by the media, in the same way that a beam of light captures a deer
on the highway. These are "fatal strategies" (Baudrillard, 1988b: 213) of the
object, a revenge of object against subjects. The "fatal strategies of the object" is one of Baudrillard's favorite theoretical claims, construed on the
premise that the subject/object dichotomy in the time of the electronic media
implode in favor of the image of the object, thus in the favor of object-media.
Simulating the "real," the object-media brings to closure this longstanding
tension between the object and the subject; the object liquidates its opposition,
subjectivity and meaning. Much like Erzensberger, Baudrillard sees the subversive potential of the mass media in reversing the order of power but,
against Erzensberger's commitment to the rational tradition of the Enlightenment, Baudrillard sees the reversion of power coming not from a direct action
by subjects in which everyone acts as a "manipulator" but through the subversion of the "real" by everyone acting as a "simulator." While for
Erzensberger, being a manipulator is subverting media operation for the
emancipation of the masses, for Baudrillard, being an Elvis impersonator is
being more subversive because it is an emancipation from the tyranny of real.
Baudrillard comes to a dramatic anti-semiotic conclusion, whose drama and
radicalness position him apart from the above mentioned theorists, namely,
that the mass media are neither tools for control nor for emancipation, but
rather tools of the subversion of the masses against any structural regimenta-
tion of signification. Prophetically, he states that the mass media are "evil
strategies of the masses" to disappear altogether from the simulacrum of the
social.

10. Virilio (1995) quotes Merleau-Ponty:

> When science has learned to recognize the value of what it initially rejected
> as subjective, this will gradually be reintroduced-through incorporated as
> a specific case in the relationships and objects that define the world as
> science sees it. The world will then close in on itself, and, except for what-
> ever in us thinks and does science, the impartial observer in us thinks and
> does science, the impartial observer that lives inside us, we will have be-
> come a part or a moment in the Great Object. (p. 141)

Although the concept of the "Great Object" was dismissed by Merleau-Ponty
as an illusional perception, Virilio thinks that it becomes the reality of the end
of the millennium.

11. See Balazs, 1970; Deleuze, 1986, vol. 1; Eisenstein, 1968; Jayyusi, 1988; Kuleshov, 1974; Pudovkin, 1970; Reisz, 1967.

12. Balazs (1970), explaining the role of montage in inventing meaning for the shot, writes:

> The meaning of the coloured patch in a painting can be gathered only from the contemplation of the picture as a whole. The meaning of the single note in a tune, the meaning of a single word in a sentence manifests itself only through the whole. The same applies to the position and role of the single shot in the totality of the film ... A smile is a smile, even if seen in an iso-lated shot. But what this smile refers to, what has evoked it, what is its effect and dramatic significance – all those can emerge only from the pre-ceding and following shots ... It is for this reason that montage can not only produce poetry – it can also fake and falsify things more completely than any other human means of expression. (pp. 118-119)

Balazs then gives an example of Eisenstein's *Battleship Potemkin* (1925). The Scandinavian distributors wanted to distribute the movie but were not certain of its commercial success because of the scene in which the sailors shot their officers. Eisenstein agreed to change the meaning but not to take anything out. Eisenstein repositioned the two shots, which changed the meaning of the scene; the officers' shooting was represented as being the result of maggots in the food, rather than revolution. Because changing the position of the two shots produced different meanings, "scissors lie."

13. See Ivo Andric (1977) for an instructive overview of the cultural, historical and ordinary life of Bosnia.

14. Social scientists since Hegel have used the concepts of "reason" and "rational" to totalize the concept of the "real"(see Hegel, 1956). Max Weber (1978: 4) removed the "rational" and "reason" from the domain of objective meaning, relocating it in subjective meaning, whereby social reality is re-constituted as subjective. Alfred Schutz gave the concept of social reality an intersubjective anchorage. For Schutz (1962c), the socially real has no uni-versal meaning structure, but is a contextual category originating in human action for the action. Schutz writes: "'the world of daily life' shall mean the intersubjective world which existed long before our birth, experienced and interpreted by Others, our predecessors, as an organized world. Now it is given to our experience and interpretation. All interpretation of this world is based upon a stock of previous experiences of it, our own experiences and those handed down to us by our parents and teachers, which in the form of "knowledge at hand" function as a scheme of reference" ("On Multiple Realities," p. 208).

Following Schutz's lead, Harold Garfinkel (1984[1967]) refuses to postulate "real" and "rational" meaning beyond members' practices, insisting that they are for ethnomethodologists only topics of the order-related inquiry and not postulated preferences (See "The rational properties of scientific and common sense activities," pp. 262-283). Social reality, Garfinkel asserts, consists only of members' understandings and, on the bases of them, members act and produce social order for themselves and for the social scientists as intelligible structures in a variety of forms and genres of realities. Thus for ethnomethodologists since Edmund Husserl (1970: 41), an "objective reality" is understood to be a methodic operation in and for the constitution of the lifeworld. The "real" as a methodic operation is the member's own accomplishment of various ways of meshing his or her practices reflexively into intersubjective settings and so producing correspondingly various genres of the "real." For ethnomethodologists, the "real" lies at the heart of a member's practices both as "premise" and "outcome". What the "real" means beyond its constituting practices and after its productions is, from the ethnomethodological standpoint, an attempt to create a theory out of one's own analytical ignorance of the criteria of contextual signification. In this sense "rational meaning," "reason," the "real," have in the production of the social world a practical and not theoretical relevance. Acting is in itself already meaningful and real *enough* for the members to act, and, thus, in the intelligibility of their actions they find contextually what is meaningful and rational for them and their occasions. Thus the "real" for ethnomethodologists has no universal presence. It is analytically significant only in terms of the "real"-as-premise and the "real"-as-outcome of a member's practices (Jayyusi, 1991a).

15. At the time I was offered the function of interpreter, my work consisted of various science studies of "instructive respecifications" which required a first-hand account of the practical order of phenomena (Bjelić, 1992, 1995, 1996; Bjelić & Lynch, 1992, 1994). I hoped the same methodological approach of the first-hand account would have been applicable in the studies of media.

16. "Six O'Clock News," Channel 6 (affiliate of NBC), Portland, Maine, September, 1993.

17. In one of his lectures, Sacks, drawing upon developments in literary theory that discount authorship in favor of the reader's grasp of the text (that is, views that discount authoral intentions), laid out what provisionally could have been called a "viewer's maxim of seeing." He used TV advertisements as a case. Anything that the viewer sees in the scene, Sacks claimed, is meant to be there. He contrasted that to the idea that in order to adequately understand the advertisement, one need not do an ethnography that gave the analyst access to the views of the people who produced the tape. (This account is given by Michael Lynch who attended the lecture.)

18. This short analysis on the dogmatic meaning of translation was brought to my attention by David Bogen. See D. Bogen, *Order Without Rules: Critical Theory and the Logic of Conversation* (SUNY Press, forthcoming).

19. Michael Agar, for example, claims: "In my view, ethnography is essentially a decoding operation" (in Emerson, 1988: 68).

Appendix

Transcription Conventions

1. *Numbers in parentheses*, e.g., (0.8), indicate pauses, and silences measured in seconds and tenths of seconds.

2. *A period enclosed in parentheses*, e.g., (.), indicates a "micro-pause," a silence of less than two-tenths of a second.

3. *Letters, words, or phrases in single parentheses*, e.g., (tch) are sounds words or phrases that are indistinct or difficult to make out from the recording.

4. *Double parentheses*, e.g., ((throat clear)), contain transcriber's commentary describing extra-verbal activities which can be seen from the video-tape/film or heard from the recording.

5. *Degree sign*, e.g., °let's see°, indicates noticeably faint sounds or words.

6. *Colons*, e.g., you::, indicate that a prior sound is prolonged; the more colons, the longer the prolongation.

7. *Double slash marks*, e.g., //But we haven't, displays the beginnings of overlapped speech.

8. *Left bracket*, e.g., [But we haven't, displays the beginnings of overlapped speech.

9. *Right bracket*, e.g., //But you put], displays the ending of overlapped speech.

10. *Dash*, e.g., a- a- call, shows a word or sound cut off.

11. *The use of "h"*, e.g., hhhh ah:::, indicated audible breathing. The more h's, the longer the breath. A degree sign (°hhhh) indicates a barely audible inbreath.

12. *Equal sign*, e.g., =That's correct, means a "latching" of utterances; one utterance follows immediately after the one just prior to it.

13. *Italics*, e.g., I *did*, shows voiced stress on a word, phrase or sound.

References

Adorno, T., and Horkheimer, M. (1972). The culture industry: Enlightenment as mass deception. In *The dialectics of enlightenment*. New York, NY: Herder and Herder.

Alexander, J. (1984). Three models of culture and society relations: Toward an analysis of Watergate. *Sociological Theory, 2*: 290-314.

Althusser, L. (1971). Ideology and ideological state apparatus. In *Lenin and philosophy and other essays*. London, UK: New Left Books.

Anderson, D. C., and Sharrock, W. W. (1979). Biasing the news: Technical issues in "media studies." *Sociology, 13*(3): 367-385.

Anderson, R. J., Sharrock, W. W., and Hughes, J. A. (1987, September). *The division of labour*. Paper presented at the Conference on Action Analysis and Conversation Analysis, Paris, France.

Andric, I. (1977). *The bridge on the Drina* (L. F. Edwards, Trans.). Chicago, IL: University of Chicago Press.

Armstrong, S. (Ed.). (1987). *The chronology*. New York, NY: Warner Books.

Asch, P., and Conor, L (1994). Opportunities for "double voicing" in ethnographic film. *Visual Anthropology Review, 10*(2): 14–28.

Atkinson, J. M., and Drew, P. (1979). *Order in court: The organization of verbal interaction in judicial settings*. London, UK: Macmillan.

Atkinson, M. A. (1980). Some practical uses of a "natural lifetime." *Human Studies, 3*(1): 33-46.

Austin, J. L. (1970). A plea for excuses. In J. L. Austin, *Philosophical papers* (J.O. Urmson and G.J. Warnock, Eds.). New York, NY: Galaxy Books.

Ax Fight (1975). Produced by Timothy Asch and Napoleon Chagnon. Distributed by Documentary Educational Resources, Watertown, MA.

Balazs, B. (1970). *Theory of the film: Character and growth of a new art* (E. Bone, Trans.). New York, NY: Dover.

Barnow, E. (1979). *Documentary: A history of the non–fiction film*. London, UK: Oxford University Press.

Barthes, R. (1981). *Camera lucida*. New York, NY: Hill & Wang.

Bateson, G., and Mead, M. (1942). *Balinese character*. New York, NY: Academy of Sciences.

Baudrillard, J. (1983a). In the shadow of the silent majorities or, the end of the social and other essays (P. Foss, J. Johnston and P. Patton, Trans.). *Semiotext(e)*, 1-123.

Baudrillard, J. (1983b). Simulations (P. Foss, P. Patton and P. Beitcham, Trans.). *Semiotext(e)*, 1-159.

Baudrillard, J. (1985). The masses: The implosion of the social in the media (M. Maclean, Trans.). *New Literary History*, *16*(3): 577-89.

Baudrillard, J. (1987). Forget Foucault and forget Baudrillard. *Semiotext(e)*, 9-137.

Baudrillard, J. (1988a). The ecstasy of communication (B. & C. Scutze, Trans.; S. Lotringer, Ed.). *Semiotext(e)*.

Baudrillard, J. (1988b). *Selected writings* (M. Poster, Ed.). Stanford, CA: Stanford University Press.

Baudrillard, J. (1990). Fata strategies. *Semiotext(e)/Pluto*, 7-191.

Baudrillard, J. (1993). *Baudrillard live: Selected interviews* (M. Gane, Ed.). London, UK: Routledge.

Baudrillard, J. (1994). *The illusion of the end* (C. Turner, Trans.). Stanford, CA: Stanford University Press.

Baudrillard, J. (1995a). *The gulf war did not take place* (P. Patton, Trans.). Bloomington: University of Indiana Press.

Baudrillard, J. (1995b). *America* (C. Turner, Trans.). London, UK: Verso.

Baudrillard, J. (1996a). *The perfect crime* (C. Turner, Trans.). London, UK: Verso.

Baudrillard, J. (1996b). *The system of objects* (J. Benedict, Trans.). London, UK: Verso.

Baudrillard, J. (1997). *Simulacra and simulation* (S. F. Glaser, Trans.). Ann Arbor, MI: The University of Michigan Press.

Bellman, B., and Jules-Rosette, B. (1977). *A paradigm for looking: Cross–cultural research with visual media*. Norwood, NJ: Ablex.

Best, J. (Ed.) (1989). *Images of issues: Typifying contemporary social problems*. New York, NY: Aldine de Gruyter. (2nd ed., 1995)

Bible (King James Version). Cleveland, OH: The World Publishing Co.

Bjelić, D. (1992). The praxiological validity of natural scientific practices as a criterion for identifying their unique social-object character: The case of the "authentication" of Goethe's morphological theorem. *Qualitative Sociology*, *15*(3): 221-245.

Bjelić, D. (1994, April). *Lebenswelt structures of Galilean physics: The case of Galileo's pendulum*. Paper presented at the Conference on Inquiries in Social Construction, New England Center, University of New Hampshire, Durham, NH.

Bjelić, D. (1995). An ethnomethodological clarification of Husserl's concepts of "regressive inquiry" and "Galilean physics through discovering praxioms." *Human Studies*, *18*(4): 189-225.

Bjelić, D. (1996). Lebenswelt structures of Galilean physics - The case of Galileo's pendulum. *Human Studies, 19*: 409-478.

Bjelić, D., and Lynch, M. (1992). The work of a [scientific] demonstration: Respecifying Newton's and Goethe's theories of prismatic color. In G. Watson and R. M. Seiler (Eds.), *Text in context: Contributions to ethnomethodology* (pp. 52-78). Newbury Park, CA: Sage.

Bjelić, D., and Lynch, M. (1994). Goethe's "Protestant Reformation" as a textual demonstration: Comment on Jackson. *Social Studies of Science, 24*(4).

Bogen, D. (1989). A reappraisal of Habermas' theory of communicative action in light of a detailed investigation of social *praxis*. *Journal for the Theory of Social Behaviour, 19*(1): 47-77.

Bogen, D. (1992). Organization of talk. *Qualitative Sociology, 15*(3): 273-296.

Bogen, D. (1992, August). *Identity, anonymity, and play in party-line conversation*. Paper presented at the Conference, *Ethnomethodology: Twenty Five Years Later*, Bentley College, Boston, MA.

Bogen, D. (1997, August). *The city from a bus: On the social, temporal and material organization of visually ordered events*. Paper presented at the Annual Convention of the American Sociological Association, Toronto, Canada.

Bogen, D. (forthcoming, 1999). *Order without rules: Critical theory and the logic of conversation*. Albany, NY: SUNY Press.

Bogen, D., and Lynch, M. (1989). Talking account of the hostile native: Plausible deniability and the production of conventional history in the Iran-contra hearings. *Social Problems, 36*: 197-224.

Bourgeois, N. (1995). Sports journalists and their source of information: A conflict of interests and its resolution. *Sociology of Sport Journal, 12*: 195-203.

Box, S. (1981). *Deviance, reality and society* (2nd ed.). London, UK: Holt, Rinehart and Winston.

Brand, S. (1976). For God's sake, Margaret: Conversation with Gregory Bateson and Margaret Mead. *CoEvolution Quarterly*, 32-44.

Bronner, E. (1990, March 9). Poindexter's Iran-contra trial opens. *Boston Globe*, p10.

Burgin, V. (1982). Photographic practice and art theory. In V. Burgin (Ed.), *Thinking photography* (pp. 39-83). London, UK: Macmillan.

Button, G. (Ed.) (1991). *Ethnomethodology and the human sciences: A foundational reconstruction*. Cambridge, UK: Cambridge University Press.

Button, G. (1991). Introduction: Ethnomethodology and the foundational respecification of the human sciences. In G. Button (Ed.), *Ethnomethodology and the human sciences* (pp. 1-9). Cambridge, UK: Cambridge University Press.

Button, G., and Sharrock, W. (1995). The mundane work of writing and reading computer programs. In P. ten Have and G. Psathas (Eds.) *Situated order: Studies in the social organization of talk and embodied activities* (pp. 231-258). Washington, DC: University Press of America and the International Institute for Ethnomethodology and Conversation Analysis.

Caulfield, J. (1992). A framework for a sociology of visual images. *Visual Sociology, 7*(2): 60-71.

Chalfen, R. (1992). Picturing culture through indigenous imagery: A telling story. In P. Crawford and D. Turton (Eds.), *Film as ethnography* (pp. 222-241). Manchester, UK: Manchester University Press.

Chomsky, N. (1969). *American power and the new mandarins*. London, UK: Chatto and Windus.

Clifford, J. (1988). *The predicament of culture*. Cambridge, MA: Harvard University Press.

Cobley, P. (1994). Throwing out the baby: Populism and active audience theory. *Media, Culture and Society, 16*: 677-687.

Corner, J. (1997). Television in theory. *Media, Culture and Society, 19*: 247-262.

Coulter, J. (1979a). Beliefs and practical understanding. In G. Psathas (Ed.) *Everyday language: Studies in ethnomethodology* (pp. 163-186). New York, NY: Irvington Publishers.

Coulter, J. (1979b). *The social construction of mind: Studies in ethnomethodology and linguistic philosophy*. UK: London, UK: Macmillan Press; USA: Totowa, NJ: Rowman and Littlefield.

Coulter, J. (1982). Remarks on the conceptualization of social structure. *Philosophy of the Social Sciences, 12*(1): 33-46.

Coulter, J. (1983). Contingent and *a priori* structures in sequential analysis. *Human Studies, 6*: 361-376.

Coulter, J. (1989). *Mind in action*. Cambridge, UK: Polity Press.

Coulter, J. (1990). Elementary properties of argument sequences. In G. Psathas (Ed.) *Interaction competence* (pp. 181-204). Washington, DC: University Press of America and the International Institute for Ethnomethodology and Conversation Analysis.

Coulter, J. (1994). Is contextualising necessarily interpretive? *Journal of Pragmatics, 21*: 689-698.

Coulter, J., and Parsons, E.D. (1990). The praxiology of perception: Visual orientations and practical action. *Inquiry, 33*(3): 251-272.

Crawford, P. (1992). Film as discourse: The invention of anthropological realities. In P. Crawford and D. Turton (Eds.), *Film as ethnography* (pp. 67-82). Manchester, UK: Manchester University Press.

Cuff, E. C. (1994). *Problems of versions in everyday situations*. Washington, DC: University Press of America and the International Institute for Ethnomethodology and Conversation Analysis.

Cuff, E. C., Francis, D. and Sharrock, W. W. (1990). *Perspectives in sociology* (3rd ed.). London, UK: Routledge.

Czyzewski, M. (1994). Reflexivity of accounts. *Theory, Culture & Society, 11*: 161–168.

Darley, J., and Latané, B. (1968a). *The innocent bystander: Why doesn't he help?* New York, NY: Free Press.

Darley, J., and Latané, B. (1968b). Bystander intervention in emergencies: Diffusion of responsibility. *Journal of Personality and Social Psychology, 8*: 377-383.

de Brigard, E. (1975). The history of ethnographic film. In P. Hockings (Ed.), *Principles of visual anthropology* (pp. 13-44). The Hague, The Netherlands: Mouton.

de Certeau, M. (1984). *The practice of everyday life*. Berkeley, CA: University of California Press.

Deleuze, G. (1986). *Cinema 1: The movement-image* (H. Tomlinson and B. Habberjam, Trans.). Minneapolis, MN: University of Minnesota Press.

Deleuze, G., and Guattari, F. (1983). *Anti-Oedipus, capitalism and schizophrenia* (R. Hurley, M. Seem, and H. R. Lane, Trans.). Minneapolis, MN: University of Minnesota Press.

Der Derian, J. (1989). Arms, hostages, and the importance of shredding in earnest: Reading national security culture (II). *Social Text, 22*: 79-91.

Derrida, J. (1977a). Signature event context (S. Weber and J. Mehlman, Trans.). *Glyph, 1*: 172-197. [reprinted in Derrida, J. (1988). *Limited INC*. Evanston, IL: Northwestern University Press.]

Derrida, J. (1977b). Limited Inc a b c .... *Glyph, 2*: 162-254. [reprinted in Derrida, J. (1988). *Limited INC*. Evanston, IL: Northwestern University Press.]

Devereaux, L. (1995). Experience, re–presentation, and film. In L. Devereaux and R. Hillman (Eds.), *Fields of vision: Essays in film studies, visual anthropology, and photography* (pp. 56-73). Berkeley, CA: University of California Press.

Drew, P. (1978). Accusations: The occasioned use of members' knowledge of "religious geography" in describing events. *Sociology, 12*(1): 1-22.

Durkheim, E. (1982[1895]). *Rules of sociological method*. Chicago, IL: University of Chicago Press.

D'Arcy, E. (1963). *Human acts: An essay in their moral evaluation*. Oxford, UK: Clarendon Press.

Eco, U. (1976). *A theory of semiotics*. Bloomington, IN: Indiana University Press.

Eco, U. (1984). *Semiotics and the philosophy of language*. Bloomington, IN: Indiana University Press.

Eco, U. (1985[1967]). Articulations of the cinematic code. In B. Nichols (Ed.), *Movies and methods* (pp. 590-607). Berkeley, CA: University of California Press.

Eglin, P., and Hester, S. (1992). Category, predicate and task: The pragmatics of practical action. *Semiotica, 88*: 243-68.

Eglin, P., and Hester, S. (1998). "You're all a bunch of feminists": Categorization and the politics of terror. *Human Studies*, Special Issue: Proceedings of the International Conference of the International Institute for Ethnomethodology and Conversation Analysis, *Ethnomethodology and Conversation Analysis: East and West*, Waseda University, Tokyo, Japan (August, 1997).

Eglin, P., and Hester, S. (forthcoming). *The Montreal massacre: Media, moral order and membership categorization*. Waterloo, ON: Wilfrid Laurier University Press.

Eisenstein, S. (1968). *Film forme and the film sense* (L. Leyda, Ed. and Trans.). Cleveland, OH: Meridian Books.

Eldridge, J. (Ed.). (1993). *Getting the message: News, truth and power*. London, UK: Routledge.

Emerson, R. M. (1988). *Contemporary field research: A collection of readings*. Prospect Heights, IL: Waveland Press.

Ericson, R., Baranek, P, and Chan, J. (1989). *Negotiating control: A study of news sources*. Toronto, Canada: University of Toronto Press.

Erzensberger, H. M. (1970). Constituents of a theory of the media. *New Left Review, 64*: 13-36.

Erzensberger, H. M. (1994). *Civil wars: From L.A. to Bosnia*. New York, NY: The New Press.

Fauman, R. (1978). *The socio–technology of knowledge: A case for the use of videotape for ethnography in sociology*. Unpublished manuscript. Department of Sociology. UCLA.

Feitosa, M. (1991). The other's visions: From the ivory tower to the barricade. *Visual Anthropology Review, 7*(2): 48-49.

Feld, S., and Williams, C. (1976). Towards a researchable film language. *Studies in the Anthropology of Visual Communication, 2*: 25-32.

Fish, S. (1989). *Doing what comes naturally*. Chapel Hill, NC: Duke University Press.

Fishman, M. (1980). *Manufacturing the news*. Austin, TX: University of Texas Press.

Fiske, J. (1987). *Television culture*. London, UK: Methuen.

Fiske, J. (1991). Postmodernism and television. In J. Curran and M. Gurevitch (Eds.) *Mass society and society*. London, UK: Edward Arnold.

Flaherty, R. (1924). *My Eskimo friends*. Garden City, NY: Doubleday, Page & Company.

Foucault, M. (1979). *Discipline and punish: The birth of the prison* (A. Sheridan, Trans.). New York, NY: Vintage Books.

Foucault, M. (1991). Introduction. In G. Cangulhem, *On the normal and the pathological*. New York, NY: Zone Books.

Gadamer, H.-G. (1975). *Truth and method*. New York, NY: Seabury Press.

Gallie, W. B. (1955-6). Essentially contested concepts. *Proceedings of the Aristotelian Society, 56*: 167-198.

Gans, H. (1980). *Deciding what's news: A study of CBS Evening News, NBC Nightly News, Newsweek and Time*. New York, NY: Vintage Books.

Garfinkel, H. (1967). *Studies in ethnomethodology*. Englewood Cliffs, NJ: Prentice Hall.

Garfinkel, H. (1974). On the origins of the term "ethnomethodology." In R. Turner (Ed.) *Ethnomethodology* (pp. 15-18). Harmondsworth, UK: Penguin.

Garfinkel, H. (1984[1967]). *Studies in ethnomethodology*. Cambridge, UK: Polity Press.

Garfinkel, H. (Ed.) (1986). *Ethnomethodological studies of work*. London, UK: Routledge.

Garfinkel, H. (1988). Evidence for locally produced, naturally accountable phenomena of order, logic, reason, meaning, method, etc. in and as of the essential quiddity of immortal ordinary society: An announcement of studies. *Sociological Theory, 6*: 103-109.

Garfinkel, H. and Burns, S. (1979). *Lecturing's work of talking introductory sociology*. Unpublished manuscript. Department of Sociology, UCLA.

Garfinkel, H., Livingston, E., and Lynch, M. (1981). The work of a discovering science construed with materials from the optically discovered pulsar. *Philosophy of the Social Sciences, 11*: 131-158.

Garfinkel, H., and Sacks, H. (1970). On formal structures of practical actions. In J. C. McKinney and E. A. Tiryakian (Eds.) *Theoretical sociology* (pp. 337-366). New York, NY: Appleton-Century-Crofts.

Garfinkel, H., and Wieder, D. L. (1991). Two incommensurable, asymmetrically alternate technologies of social analysis. In G. Watson and R. M. Seiler (Eds.), *Text in ontext: Contributions to ethnomethodology* (pp. 175-206). Newbury Park, CA: Sage.

Genosko, G. (1994). *Baudrillard and signs: Signification ablaze*. London, UK: Routledge.

Glasgow Media Group (1976). *Bad news*. London, UK: Routledge and Kegan Paul.

Glasgow Media Group (1980). *More bad news*. London, UK: Routledge and Kegan Paul.

Glasgow Media Group (1985). *War and peace news*. London, UK: Routledge and Kegan Paul.

Goffman, E. (1967). *Interaction ritual*. Garden City, N.Y.: Anchor Books, Doubleday & Company Inc.

Goffman, E. (1971) *Relations in public*. New York, NY: Harper Colophon.

Goodwin, C. (1994). Professional vision. *American Anthropologist, 96*(3): 606-639.

Graddol, D., and Boyd-Barrett, O. (1994). *Media texts, authors and readers*. Clevedon, UK: Multilingual Matters.

Greatbatch, D. (1986). Aspects of topical organization of news interviews: The use of agenda shifting procedures by interviewees. *Media, Culture and Society, 8*: 441-455.

Grusky, O., and Pollner, M. (Eds.). (1981). *Sociology of mental illness: Basic readings*. New York, NY: Holt, Rinehart and Winston.

Habermas, J. (1972). *Knowledge and human interests* (J. J. Shapiro, Trans.). London, UK: Heinemann.

Habermas, J. (1984). *The theory of communicative action: Reason and the rationalization of society* (Vol. 1) (T. McCarthy, Trans.). Boston, MA: Beacon Press.

Hall, S. (1980). Encoding/decoding. In S. Hall, D. Hobson, A. Lowe, and P. Willis (Eds.) *Culture, media, language* (pp. 129-138). London, UK: Hutchinson.

Hastrup, K. (1992). Anthropological visions: Some notes on visual and textual authority. In P. Crawford and D. Turton (Eds.), *Film as ethnography* (pp. 8-25). Manchester, UK: Manchester University Press.

Hegel, G.W.F. (1956). Introduction. In *The philosophy of history*. New York, NY: Dover Publications.

Heider, K. (1976). *Ethnographic film*. Austin, TX: University of Texas Press.

Heritage, J. (1984). *Garfinkel and ethnomethodology*. Cambridge, UK: Polity Press.

Heritage, J., and Watson, D. R. (1979). Formulations as conversational objects. In G. Psathas (Ed.), *Everyday language: Studies in ethnomethodology* (pp. 123-162). New York, NY: Irvington.

Hester, S. (1987, August). *The social organization of contrast and complementarity in assessments.* Paper presented at the International Institute for Ethnomethodology and Conversation Analysis Conference, Boston University, Andover, MA.

Hester, S., and Eglin, P. (1992). *A sociology of crime.* London, UK: Routledge.

Hester, S., and Eglin, P. (Eds.) (1997a). *Culture in action: Studies in membership categorization analysis.* Washington, DC: University Press of America and the International Institute for Ethnomethodology and Conversation Analysis.

Hester, S., and Eglin, P. (1997b). Membership categorization analysis: An introduction. In S. Hester and P. Eglin (Eds.), *Culture in Action: Studies in membership categorization analysis* (pp.1-23). Washington, DC: University Press of America and the International Institute for Ethnomethodology and Conversation Analysis.

Hester, S., and Eglin, P. (1997c). The reflexive constitution of category, predicate and context in two settings. In S. Hester and P. Eglin (Eds.), *Culture in action: Studies in membership categorization analysis* (pp. 25-48). Washington, DC: University Press of America and the International Institute for Ethnomethodology and Conversation Analysis.

Hester, S., and Eglin, P. (1997d). Conclusion: Membership categorization analysis and sociology. In S. Hester and P. Eglin (Eds.), *Culture in action: Studies in membership categorization analysis* (pp.153-163). Washington, DC: University Press of America and the International Institute for Ethnomethodology and Conversation Analysis.

Hill, R. J., and Crittenden, K. S. (1968). *Proceedings of the Purdue Symposium on ethnomethodology* (Institute for the Study of Social Change). Lafayette, IN: Purdue University Press.

Hockings, P. (1975). *Principles of visual anthropology.* The Hague, The Netherlands: Mouton.

Horwitz, J. (1978). *Case studies of the social organization of responses to the camera.* Unpublished manuscript. Department of Anthropology. UCLA.

Husserl, E. (1970). *The crises of western sciences and transcendental phenomenology* (D. Carr, Trans.). Evanston, IL: Northwestern University Press.

Hutchby, I. (1991). The organisation of talk on talk radio. In P. Scannell (Ed.), *Broadcast talk* (pp. 119-137). London,UK: Sage Publications.

Hutchby, I. (1996). *Confrontation talk: Argument, asymmetries and power on talk radio.* Hillsdale, NJ: Lawrence Erlbaum Associates.

Huxley, T. (1917). The struggle for existence in society. In P.A. Kropotkin (Ed.) *Mutual aid: A factor of evolution.* New York, NY: Knopf.

Inouye, D. K., and Hamilton, L. H. (1988). *Report of the congressional committees investigating the Iran-contra affair* (Abridged edition, J. Brinkley and S. Engleberg, Eds.). New York: NY: Times Books.

Jacobs, R. (1996). Producing the news, producing the crisis: Narrativity, television and news work. *Media, Culture and Society, 18*(3): 373-397.

Jalbert, P. L. (1983). Some constructs for analyzing news. In H. Davis and P. Walton (Eds.), *Language, image, media* (pp. 282-299). Oxford, UK: Basil Blackwell.

Jalbert, P. L. (1984a). *Media analysis: On distinguishing a polemic from a critique.* Unpublished manuscript.

Jalbert, P. L. (1984b). "News speak" about the Lebanon War. *Journal of Palestine Studies, 14*(1): 16-35.

Jalbert, P. L. (1984c). *Structures of "News Speak": US Network Television Coverage of the Lebanon Was, Summer 1982.* Doctoral dissertation, Boston University.

Jalbert, P. L. (1989). Categorization and beliefs: New accounts of Haitian and Cuban Refugees. In D. T. Helm, W. T. Anderson, A. J. Meehan, and A. Rawls (Eds), *The interactional order: New directions in the study of social order* (pp. 231-248). New York, NY: Irvington.

Jalbert, P. L. (1994). Structures of the "unsaid." *Theory, Culture and Society, 11*(4): 127-160.

Jayyusi, L. (1984). *Categorization and the moral order.* London, UK and Boston, MA: Routledge and Kegan Paul.

Jayyusi, L. (1988). Toward a socio-logic of the film text. *Semiotica, 68*(3/4): 271-296.

Jayyusi, L. (1991a). The equivocal text and the objective world: An ethnomethodological analysis of a news report. *Continuum: The Australian Journal of Media & Culture, 5*(1). [InterNet]

Jayyusi, L. (1991b). The reflexive nexus: Photo–practice and natural history. *Continuum: The Australian Journal of Media & Culture, 6*(2). [InterNet]

Jensen, K. B., and Jankovski, N. W. (1991). *A handbook for qualitative methodologies for mass communications research.* London, UK: Routledge.

Johnson, J. (1989). Horror stories and the construction of child abuse. In J. Best (Ed.), *Images of issues: Typifying contemporary social problems* (pp. 5-19). New York: Aldine de Gruyter.

Kellner, D. (1989). *Jean Baudrillard: From Marxism to postmodernism and beyond.* Stanford, CA: Stanford University Press.

Kozloff, M. (1979). *Photography and fascination.* Danbury, NH: Addison House.

Kuleshov, L. (1974). *Kuleshov on film* (R. Levaco, Ed. and Trans.). Berkeley, CA: University of California Press.

Law, J. and Lynch, M. (1988). Lists, field guides, and the descriptive organization of seeing: Birdwatching as an exemplary observational activity. *Human Studies, 11*: 271-303.

Lee, J. (1984). Innocent victims and evil-doers. *Women's Studies International Forum, 7*(1): 69-73.

Lee, J., and Watson, D. R. (1993). *Final Report to the Plan Urbain: Public Space as an Interactional Order.* University of Manchester, Department of Sociology.

Leyton, E. (1992). The theater of public crisis. In E. Leyton, W. O'Grady and J. Overton, *Violence and public anxiety: A Canadian case* (pp. 109-191). St. John's, NFLD: Institute of Social and Economic Research.

Livingston, E. (1986) *The ethnomethodological foundations of mathematics.* London, UK: Routledge and Kegan Paul.

Livingston, E. (1987). *Making sense of ethnomethodology.* London, UK: Routledge and Kegan Paul.

Loizos, P. (1992). Admissible evidence? Film in anthropology. In P. Crawford and D. Turton (Eds.), *Film as ethnography* (pp. 50-65). Manchester, UK: Manchester University Press.

Lutkehaus, N. (1994). Interview with Filmmaker Bob Connolly. *Visual Anthropology Review, 10*(2): 71-75.

Lynch, M. (1985) *Art and artifact in laboratory science: A study of shop work and shop talk in a research laboratory.* London, UK: Routledge and Kegan Paul.

Lynch, M. (1991a). Laboratory space and the technological complex: An investigation of topical contextures. *Science in Context, 4*(1): 51-78.

Lynch, M. (1991b). In lecture at Boston University and personal communication.

Lynch, M. (1992). Extending Wittgenstein: The pivotal move from epistemology to the sociology of science. In A. Pickering (Ed.), *Science as practice and culture* (pp. 215-265). Chicago, IL: University of Chicago Press.

Lynch, M. (1993). *Scientific practice and ordinary action.* Cambridge, UK: Cambridge University Press.

Lynch, M. and Edgerton, S. (1988). Aesthetics and digital image processing: Representational craft in contemporary astronomy. In G. Fyfe and J. Law (Eds.), *Picturing power: Visual depiction and social relations* (pp.184-219). London, UK: Routledge.

Lyotard, J. F. (1984). *The postmodern condition: A report on knowledge* (G. Bennington and B. Massumi, Trans.). Minneapolis, MN: University of Minnesota Press.

MacBean, J. R. (1994). Degrees of otherness: A close reading of *First Contact, Joe Leahy's Neighbors,* and *Black Harvest. Visual Anthropology Review, 10*(2): 55-70.

Macbeth, D. (1990) Classroom order as practical action: The making and unmaking of a quiet reproach. *British Journal of the Sociology of Education, 11*(2): 189-214.

Macbeth, D. (1992). Classroom floors. *Qualitative Sociology, 15*(2): 123-150.

MacDougall, D. (1975). Beyond observational cinema. In P. Hockings (Ed.), *Principles of visual anthropology* (pp. 109-124). The Hague, The Netherlands: Mouton.

MacDougall, D. (1985[1969]). Prospects of the ethnographic film. In B. Nichols (Ed.), *Movies and methods* (pp. 135-150). Berkeley, CA: University of California Press.

MacDougall, D. (1992). Complicities of style. In P. Crawford and D. Turton (Eds.), *Film as ethnography* (pp. 90-98). Manchester, UK: Manchester University Press.

MacDougall, D. (1995). The subjective voice in ethnographic film. In L. Devereaux and R. Hillman (Eds.), *Fields of vision: Essays in film studies, visual anthropology, and photography* (pp. 216-255). Berkeley, CA: University of California Press.

Malette, L., and Chalouh, M. (Eds.). (1991). *The Montreal massacre* (M. Wildeman, Trans.). Charlottetown, PEI: Gynergy Books.

Mannheim, K. (1936). *Ideology and utopia*. New York, NY: Harcourt, Brace and World, Inc.

Marshall, J. and de Brigard, E. (1975). Idea and event in urban film. In P. Hockings (Ed.), *Principles of visual anthropology* (pp. 133-145). The Hague, The Netherlands: Mouton.

Martinez, W. (1992). Who constructs anthropological knowledge? Toward a theory of ethnographic film spectatorship. In P. Crawford and D. Turton (Eds.), *Film as ethnography* (pp. 131-161). Manchester, UK: Manchester University Press.

McCarty, M. (1975). McCarty's law and how to break it. In P. Hockings (Ed.), *Principles of visual anthropology* (pp. 45-51). The Hague, The Netherlands: Mouton.

McCarty, M. and Young, C. (1967). *The village* [Film]. Ethnographic Film Program. Department of Anthropology, UCLA.

McCormack, T. (1990). Questions in the aftermath: Engineering feminism. *This Magazine*, *24*(1): 31-32.

McCormick, C. (1995). *The (mis-)representation of crime in the news*. Halifax, NS: Fernwood Publishers.

McLuhan, M. (1964). *Understanding media*. New York, NY: McGraw-Hill.

McLuhan, M., and Fiore, Q. (1968). *War and peace in the global village*. New York, NY: McGraw-Hill.

Mermin, E. (1997). Being where? Experiencing narratives of ethnographic film. *Visual Anthropology Review*, *13*(1): 40-51.

Metz, C. (1974). *Language and cinema*. The Hague, The Netherlands: Mouton.

Metz, C. (1985). On the notion of cinematographic language. In B. Nichols (Ed.), *Movies and methods* (pp. 582-589). Berkeley, CA: University of California Press.

Metz, C. (1992[1968]). Some points in the semiotics of the cinema. In G. Mast, M. Cohen & L. Braudy (Eds.), *Film theory and criticism* (4th ed.) (pp. 168-178). New York: Oxford University Press.

Michaels, E. (1982). How to look at us looking at the Yanomami looking at us. In J. Ruby (Ed.), *A crack in the mirror: Reflexive perspectives in anthropology* (pp. 133-146). Philadelphia, PA: University of Pennsylvania Press.

Molotch, H.L., and Lester, M. (1974). News as purposive behavior: On the strategic use of routine events, accidents and scandals. *American Sociological Review*, *39*: 101-112.

Moore, R. (1994). Marketing alterity. In L. Taylor (Ed.), *Visualizing theory: Selected essays from V.A.R. 1990-1994* (pp. 126-139). New York, NY: Routledge.

Moores, S. (1990). Texts, readers and contexts of reading: Developments in the study of media audiences. *Media, Culture and Society*, *12*: 9-29.

Morley, D. (1980). *The Nationwide audience*. London, UK: British Film Institute.

Morley, D. (1992). *Television, audiences and cultural studies*. London, UK: Routledge.

Muravchik, J. (1983). Misrepresenting Lebanon. *Policy Review*, *23*(Winter): 11-66.

Murdoch, G. (1989). Critical inquiry and audience activity. In D. Dervin, et al. (Eds.) *Rethinking communication* (Vol. 2). Newbury Park, CA: Sage.

Nagel, T. (1986). *The view from nowhere*. Oxford, UK: Oxford University Press.

Nichols, B. (1991). *Representing reality*. Bloomington, IN: Indiana University Press.

Nichols, B. (1994). The ethnographer's tale. In L. Taylor (Ed.), *Visualizing theory: selected essays from V.A.R. 1990-1994* (pp. 60-83). New York: Routledge.

Palmer, R. (1969). *Hermeneutics*. Evanston, IL: Northwestern University Press.

Parkin, F. (1972). *Class, inequality and political order*. London, UK: Paladin.

Primary (1960). Produced by Drew Associates. Distributed by Direct Cinema, Ltd., Santa Monica, CA.

Psathas, G. (1979). Organizational features of direction maps. In G. Psathas (Ed.), *Everyday language: Studies in ethnomethodology* (pp. 203-225). New York, NY: Irvington.

Pudovkin, V. I. (1970). *Film technique and film acting*. New York, NY: Grove Press.

Real, M. (1990). Sport and the spectacle. In J. Downing and A Sreberny-Mohammadi (Eds.) *Questioning the media* (pp. 345-358). Newbury Park, CA: Sage.

Reisz, K. (1967). *The technique of film editing*. New York, NY: Communication Arts Books.

Richardson, K., and Corner, J. (1992). Reading, reception, mediation and transparency in viewers' perceptions of a TV program. In P. Scannell (Eds.) *Culture and power* (pp. 158-181). London, UK: Sage.

Rouch, J. (1975). The camera and man. In P. Hockings (Ed.), *Principles of visual anthropology* (pp. 83-102). The Hague, The Netherlands: Mouton.

Rowe, D. (1992). Modes of sports writing. In P. Dahlgren and C. Sparks (Eds.), *Journalism and popular culture* (pp. 96-112). London, UK: Sage.

Rubington, E., and Weinberg, M. (Eds.) (1987). *Deviance: The interactionist perspective* (5th ed.). New York, NY: Macmillan.

Ruby, J. (1982). Ethnography as trompe l'oeil: Film and anthropology. In J Ruby (Ed.), *A crack in the mirror: Reflexive perspectives in anthropology* (pp. 121-131). Philadelphia, PA: University of Pennsylvania Press.

Sacks, H. (1963). Sociological description. *Berkeley Journal of Sociology 8*(1): 1-16.

Sacks, H. (1967). The search for help: No one to turn to. In E. Shneidman (Ed.), *Essays in self destruction* (pp. 203-223). New York, NY: Science House.

Sacks, H. (1972a). An initial investigation of the usability of conversational data for doing sociology. In D.N. Sudnow (Ed.) *Studies in social interaction* (pp. 31-74). New York, NY: Free Press.

Sacks, H. (1972b). On the analyzability of stories by children. In J.J. Gumperz and D. Hymes (Eds.) *Directions in sociolinguistics: The ethnography of communication* (pp. 329-345). New York, NY: Holt, Reinhart and Winston. [Reprinted in R. Turner (Ed.) (1974). *Ethnomethodology* (pp. 216-232). Harmondsworth, UK: Penguin.]

Sacks, H. (1972c). Notes on police assessment of moral character. In D. Sudnow (Ed.), *Studies in social interaction* (pp. 280-293). New York: Free Press.

Sacks, H. (1974). On the analyzability of stories by children. In R. Turner (Ed.), *Ethnomethodology: Selected readings* (pp. 216-232). Harmondsworth, UK: Penguin Books.

Sacks, H. (1979). Hotrodder: A revolutionary category. In G. Psathas (Ed.) *Everyday language: Studies in ethnomethodology* (pp. 7-14). New York, NY: Irvington.

Sacks, H. (1984). On doing being ordinary. In J. M. Atkinson and J. Heritage (Eds.), *Structures of social action: Studies in conversation analysis* (pp. 413-429). Cambridge: Cambridge University Press.

Sacks, H. (1986). Some considerations of a story told in ordinary conversation. *Poetics, 15*: 127-38.

Sacks, H. (1992a). *Lectures on conversation* (Vol. 1; G. Jefferson, Ed.). Oxford, UK: Basil Blackwell.

Sacks, H. (1992b). *Lectures on conversation* (Vol. 2; G. Jefferson, Ed.). Oxford, UK: Basil Blackwell.

Sacks, H., Schegloff, E., and Jefferson, G. (1974). A simplest systematics for the organization of turn-taking for conversation. *Language, 50*: 697-735. [A "variant" version reprinted in: J. Schenkein (Ed.) (1978). *Studies in the organization of conversational interaction* (pp. 7-55). New York, NY: Academic Press.]

Saussure, F. de. (1966). *Course in general linguistics.* New York, NY: McGraw-Hill.

Saussure, F. de. (1983) *Course in general linguistics* (C. Bally and A. Sechehaye, Eds.; R. Harris, Trans.) London, UK: Duckworth.

Schegloff, E. (1972). Notes on a conversational practice: Formulating place. In D. Sudnow (Ed.) *Studies in social interaction* (pp. 75-119). New York, NY: Free Press.

Schegloff, E. (1979). Identification and recognition in telephone conversation openings. In G. Psathas (Ed.) *Everyday language: Studies in ethnomethodology* (pp. 23-78). New York: Irvington.

Schegloff, E. (1991). Reflections on talk and social structure. In D. Boden and D. Zimmerman (Eds.), *Talk and social structure: Studies in ethnomethodology and conversation analysis* (pp. 44-70). Cambridge, UK: Polity Press.

Schenkein, J. N. (1979). The radio raiders story. In G Psathas (Ed.) *Everyday language: Studies in ethnomethodology* (pp. 187-201). New York, NY: Irvington.

Schudson, M. (1989). The sociology of news production. *Media, Culture and Society, 11*: 263-282.

Schutz, A. (1962a). *Collected papers* (Vol. 1; M. Natanson, Ed.). The Hague, The Netherlands: Martinus Nijhoff.

Schutz, A. (1962b) Commonsense and scientific interpretations of human action. In *Collected Papers* (Vol. 1; M. Natanson, Ed.) (pp. 3-47). The Hague, The Netherlands: Martinus Nijhoff.

Schutz, A. (1962c). The problem of social reality. In *Collected papers* (Vol.1; M. Natanson, Ed.). The Hague, The Netherlands: Martinus Nijhoff.

Scully, D. and, Marolla, J. (1987). Rapists' vocabulary of motives. In D. Kelly (Ed.) *Deviant behavior: A text reader in the sociology of deviance* (pp. 111-131). New York, NY: St. Martin's Press.

Searle, J. (1977). Reiterating the differences: A reply to Derrida. *Glyph, 1*: 198-208.

Shapiro, M. J. (1981). *Language and political understanding: The politics of discursive practices.* New Haven, CT: Yale University Press.

Sharrock, W.W. (1974). On owning knowledge. In R. Turner (Ed.) *Ethnomethodology* (pp. 45-53). Harmondsworth, UK: Penguin.

Sharrock, W. W. (1984). The social realities of crime. In R. J. Anderson and W. W. Sharrock (Eds.), *Applied perspectives in sociology* (pp. 86-105). London, UK: Allen and Unwin.

Sharrock, W.W., and Anderson, R. J. (1982). On the demise of the native: Some observations on and a proposal for ethnography. *Human Studies, 5*(2): 119-135.

Sharrock, W. W., and Button, G. (1991). The social actor: Social action in real time. In G. Button (Ed.), *Ethnomethodology and the human sciences* (pp. 137-175). Cambridge, UK: Cambridge University Press.

Silverman, K. (1983). *The subject of semiotics.* New York, NY: Oxford University Press.

Smith, D. E. (1978). "K is mentally ill": The anatomy of a factual account. *Sociology, 12*: 23-53.

Smith, D. E. (1982, August). *The active text: An approach to analyzing texts as constituents of social relations.* Paper presented to the Annual Convention of the International Sociological Association, Mexico City.

Sorenson, E. R., and Jablonko, A. (1975). Research filming of naturally occurring phenomena: Basic strategies. In P. Hockings (Ed.), *Principles of visual anthropology* (pp.147-162). The Hague, The Netherlands: Mouton.

Spector, M., and Kitsuse, J. I. (1987[1977]). *Constructing social problems.* New York, NY: Aldine de Gruyter.

Stetson, J. (1989, April). *Ethnomethodology and logical analysis.* Paper presented at the Annual Convention of the Midwest Sociological Society, St. Louis, MO.

Stetson, J. (1993). *Constructing victim: Three Case Studies.* Doctoral Dissertation, Boston University.

Stetson, J., and Sato, M. (1996). *Compendium: Sociological essays, notes and transcripts.* Tokyo: Hosei University Press.

Stoller, P. (1994). Artaud, Rouch, and the cinema of cruelty. In L. Taylor (Ed.), *Visualizing theory: Selected essays from V.A.R. 1990-1994* (pp.84-98). New York, NY: Routledge.

Sudnow, D. (1972). Temporal parameters of interpersonal observation. In D. Sudnow (Ed.), *Studies in social interaction* (pp.259-279). New York, NY: Free Press.

Sudnow, D. (1978). *Ways of the hand.* Cambridge, MA: Harvard University Press.

Sudnow, D. (1987). Normal crimes. In E. Rubington and M. Weinberg (Eds.) *Deviance: The interactionist perspective* (pp. 152-160). New York, NY: Macmillan.

Taking the stand: The testimony of Lieutenant Colonel Oliver L. North. (1987). New York, NY: Pocket Books.

Taylor, L. (1994). Forward. In *Visualizing theory: Selected essays from V.A.R. 1990-1994* (pp. xi-xviii). New York, NY: Routledge.

Tomas, D. (1988). Toward an anthropology of sight: Ritual performance and the photographic process. *Semiotica, 68*(3/4): 245-270.

Tower, J., Muskie, E., and Scowcroft, B. (1987). *The Tower commission report.* New York, NY: Times Books.

Truzzi, K. (Ed.) (1974). *Verstehen: Subjective understanding in the social sciences.* Reading, MA: Addison-Wesley.

Tuchman, G. (1978). *Making news: A study in the construction of reality.* New York, NY: Free Press.

Turner, B. (1990). *British cultural studies.* London, UK: Unwin Hyman.

Turner, R. (1969, June). *Occupational routines: Some demand characteristics of police work.* Paper presented to the CSAA Conference, Toronto.

Turner, R. (1971). Words, utterances and activities. In J. D. Douglas (Ed.), *Understanding everyday life* (pp. 169-187). London, UK: Routledge.

Turner, R. (Ed.) (1974a). *Ethnomethodology.* Harmondsworth, UK: Penguin.

Turner, R. (1974b). Words, utterances and activities. In R. Turner (Ed.) *Ethnomethodology* (pp. 197-215). Harmondsworth, UK: Penguin.

Turner, T. (1991). The social dynamics of video media in an indigenous society. *Visual Anthropology Review, 7*(2): 68-76.

Vaughn, D. (1985). The space between shots. In B. Nichols (Ed.), *Movies and methods* (Vol 2) (pp, 703-714). Berkeley, CA: University of California Press.

Vaughn, D. (1992[1979]). The aesthetics of ambiguity. In P. Crawford and D. Turton (Eds.), *Film as ethnography* (pp. 99-115). Manchester, UK: Manchester University Press.

Virilio, P. (1995). *The art of motor* (J. Rose, Trans.). Minneapolis, MN: University of Minnesota Press.

Vološinov, V. N. (1973). *Marxism and the philosophy of language.* New York, NY and London, UK: Seminar Press.

Watson, D.R. (1976). Some conceptual issues in the social identification of victims and offenders. In E.C. Viano (Ed.) *Victims and society* (pp. 60-71). Washington, DC: Visage Press.

Watson, D.R. (1978). Categorization, authorization and blame-negotiation in conversation. *Sociology, 12*(1): 105-113.

Watson, D.R. (1983). The presentation of victim and motive in discourse: The case of police interrogations and interviews. *Victimology: An International Journal, 8*(1-2): 31-52.

Watson, D. R. (1990). Some features of the elicitation of confessions in murder interrogations. In G. Psathas (Ed.), *Interaction competence* (pp. 263-295). Washington, DC: University Press of America and the International Institute for Ethnomethodology and Conversation Analysis.

Weber, M. (1949). *The methodology of the social sciences.* (E. A. Shils and H. A. Finch, Trans. and Eds.). New York, NY: Free Press.

Weber, M. (1978). *Economy and society,* Vol. I. Berkeley, CA: University of California Press.

Weinberger, E. (1994). The camera people. In L. Taylor (Ed.), *Visualizing theory: Selected essays from V.A.R. 1990-1994* (pp. 3-26). New York, NY: Routledge.

Whitehead, A. N. (1925). *Science in the modern world.* New York, NY: Macmillan.

Wieder, L. (1989, August). *The structure and communicative character of practical action: Clues from the study of the performance of magic.* Paper presented at the Annual Convention of the American Sociological Association. San Francisco, CA.

Wittgenstein, L. (1958). *Philosophical investigations.* Oxford, UK: Basil Blackwell.

Wittgenstein, L. (1968). *Philosophical investigations* (G.E.M. Anscombe, Trans.). Oxford, UK: Basil Blackwell; New York, NY: Macmillan.

Wittgenstein, L. (1969). *On certainty.* New York, NY: Harper Torchbooks.

Wollen, P. (1970). *Signs and meaning in the cinema.* Bloomington, IN: Indiana University Press.

Worth, S. (1981). Pictures can't say ain't. In L. Gross (Ed.), *Sol Worth: Studying visual communication* (pp. 162-184). Philedelphia, PA: University of Pennsylvania Press.

Wowk, M. (1984). Blame allocation, sex and gender in a murder interrogation. *Women's Studies International Forum, 7:* 75-82.

Young, C. (1975). Observational cinema. In P. Hockings (Ed.), *Principles of visual anthropology* (pp. 65-80). The Hague, The Netherlands: Mouton.

Zimmerman, D., and Pollner, M. (1970). The everyday world as a phenomenon. In J. Douglas (Ed.), *Understanding everyday life* (pp. 80-103). Chicago, IL: Aldine.

Zimmerman, D., and Pollner, M. (1971). The everyday world as a phenomenon. In J. Douglas (Ed.), *Understanding Everyday Life* (pp. 80-103). London, UK: Routledge and Kegan Paul.

Author Index

Subject Index